MURDER MOST LOCAL

Historic Murders of

SOUTH CORK

PETER O'SHEA

Murder Most Local
Historic Murders of South Cork by Peter O'Shea
ISBN: Soft Cover 978-1-9163796-3-3
ISBN: Hard Cover
Copyright©2021 Peter O'Shea
ALL RIGHTS RESERVED. International copyright secured.
Published by Most Local Press

Printed in Poland by Totem

No part of this publication, including illustrations
or photographs, may be reproduced or transmitted
in any form or by any means, electronic or mechanical,
including photocopy, recording or any
information storage and retrieval system, without
permission in writing from the author.

*To my Uncle John O'Shea,
who encouraged me from the start*

Acknowledgements

First of all, I would like to thank all the people for supporting me and taking such an interest in the darker side of our history. Of course as always when it comes to true crime many do not wish to be mentioned but are more than willing to help. Still, I thank those people who point me in the right direction and decline to be recognised. I also thank those that don't wish to talk for making me want to work harder to get the information.

Thanks so much to Fergal Browne for helping as much as he did and being so kind. His never ending interest in local history is inspiring and his willingness to share his knowledge was gratefully accepted.

I also want to make a special mention of all our retailers this year. We have built up an excellent relationship with the bookshops of Cork over the years. It is always a danger when we take our boys out doing deliveries. They love books and we nearly end up taking more books home than delivering.

I would like to thank Claire O'Donovan for her design work, illustrations and help. Again I can't thank the proofreaders and editors enough. It never gets any easier and we always seem to be in a hurry, thanks to Karen Casey, Kathleen Forrest, Catherine Casey and Janett Murray.

Contents

Introduction 1

Murder Map 2

Lord God Almighty 3
Nohoval 1919

A Costly Tithe 24
Baurleigh Timoleague 1832

The Quandary of the Quarry 31
Carrigaline 1822

A Marriage Settlement 35
Lislevane Courtmacsherry 1904

The Ballineen Four 44
Ballineen 1890

A Shocking Discovery 62
Near Chetwynd Viaduct Rochfordstown 1908

Only A Pawn In Her Game 70
Oldcourt Ballinspittle Kinsale 1821

Wrong Time, Wrong Place 75
Ballinvarosig Carrigaline 1936

A Hatchet Job 100
Clancoolbeg Bandon 1888

A Costly Dowry 104
Barreragh Courtmacsherry 1884

Going Home from the Fair 110
Derrigra West Ballineen 1900

After the Wedding 127
Ballygarvan 1871

Murder at Killeady Hill 136
Killeady Hill Ballinhassig 1826

What Made You Do It 141
Rathnaroughy Innishannon 1882

Jealousy and Revenge 157
Ballymah Waterfall 1851

Plenty More Fish in the Sea 163
Fisher Street Kinsale 1873

An Unlucky Horseshoe 176
Ballynalouhy Ballymartle 1895

A Perilous Profession 183
Passage West 1851

Caught by the Coat 191
Graball Crosshaven 1872

The Cost of Chivalry 203
Passage West 1859

A Day Out Gone Wrong 207
Fountainstown 1884

A Fatal Eviction 219
Knockskagh Clonakilty 1847

Caught in the Crossfire 222
Kilbrittain 1868

Burnt Alive 238
Cappa Bandon 1847

A Brother's Revenge 243
Willowhill Minane Bridge Carrigaline 1843

Get off my Head 245
Lissarourke Newcestown 1916

The Price of Jealousy 262
Horsehead Lodge Passage West 1896

Brien's Betrayal 273
Newcestown 1828

A Brother's Plight 275
Kinsale 1838

Left for Dead 277
Tullyland Bandon 1930

Kiely's Killed 282
Nohoval 1885

The Ballinhassig Massacre 288
Ballinhassig 1845

A Greedy Landlord 306
Barna Innishannon 1838

Do Not Hesitate to Shoot! 311
Timoleague 1889

Murder at the Old Head 325
Ballymackean Old Head of Kinsale 1895

Blueshirts and Beatings 332
Innishannon 1933

Glossary 345

Bibliography 348

Introduction

It doesn't get any easier to write an introduction, especially as this is the fourth book in the Murder Most Local series. I was very pleasantly surprised this time around; someone very kindly contacted me offering help with a story. On reflection, it left me a little amused to think my intentions were so predictable. After covering East, North and West Cork it was obvious that the gap between Clonakilty and Cork would be the next area to be covered.

Please don't anyone be annoyed that I have termed this area South Cork when some of the area covered in the book is actually West Cork. I'm just trying to carve up the county into manageable chunks, keeping the books as much as possible the same size.

What is no surprise though, is that every part of County Cork is dotted with historical murders and South Cork is no different. With motives just as interesting and not always obvious. I continue to seek out the ordinary country murders and the lesser known ones just as much as I have in the series so far. It is by no means a definitive list of these crimes in the area; several have been omitted for various reasons.

Like last year it's been difficult with all the restrictions to get out around the county but we have bided our time and managed it safely.

This year I tried out different methods of getting the stories out there. One was a short film of one of the West Cork murders. For me, it was amazing to see the story translated into the emotions of denial, shock and horror on the actor's faces. It brought it to life in a different way, if only for a glimpse. This year, I have also included some artist impressions of the murder scenes commissioned especially for the book. I hope these give the reader a sense of location.

For me, South Cork is getting closer to home. In Ballycotton, I can easily look out to the southwest and see the coast of Barry's Head, the Sovereigns and on a clear night the Old Head. Next year it will be to the depths of mid West Cork if you can call it that!

Looking forward again to all the lovely feedback we get and I hope people enjoy reading this book as much as I have enjoyed researching and writing.

Murder Map

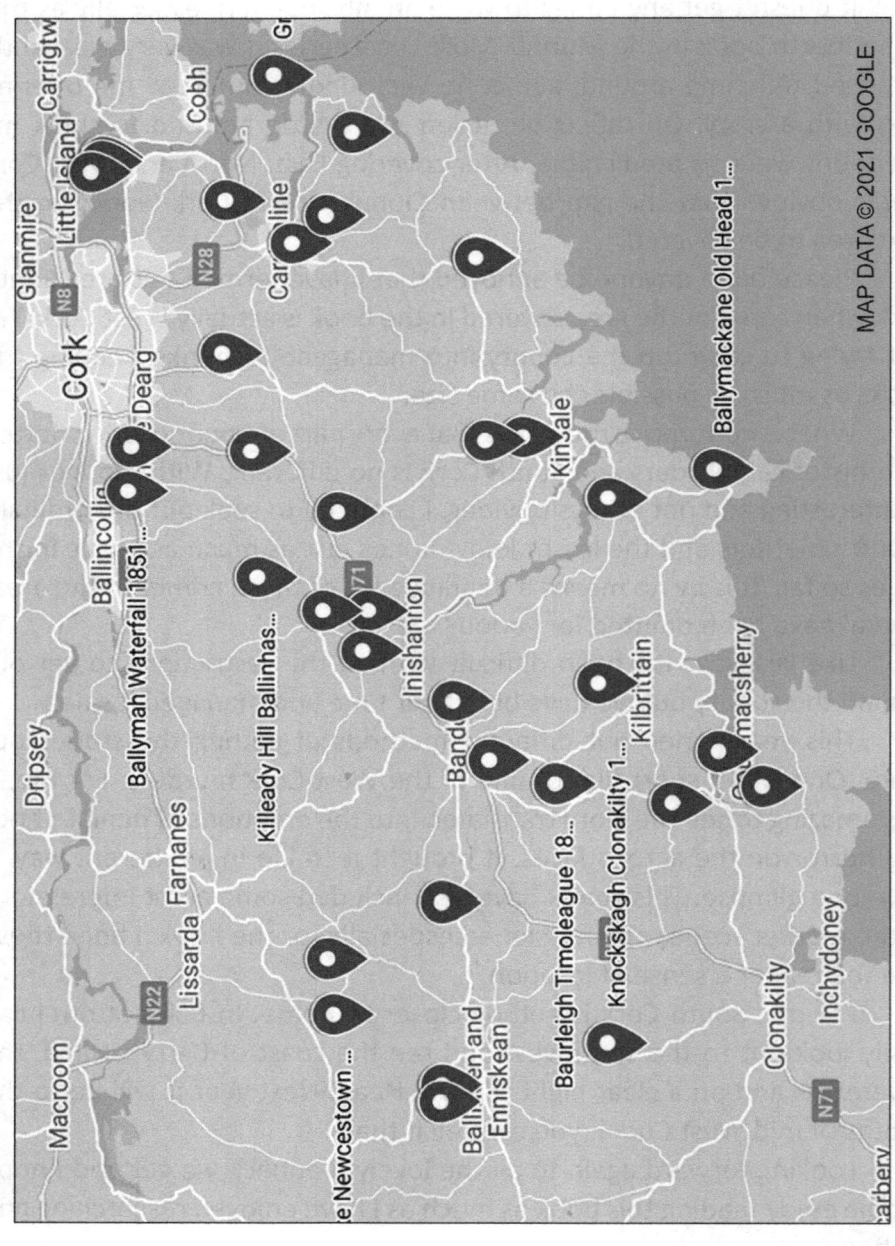

Lord God Almighty
Nohoval 1919

On the morning of the 18th of December, two labourers Patrick O'Hea and Patrick Lyons left for work in the direction of Nohoval. They worked for a Mr Quinn on his farm; Mr Quinn was also the owner of the village pub. It had been bright with a little while when they were coming up to the crossroads at Nohoval on their ponies around 8:30 am. At the crossroads, one road leads East towards Roberts Cove, the other West through the village. One of the men spotted something suspicious near the wall of the St Patrick Catholic Church and decided to take a closer look.

As they approached it became obvious a man was lying near the wall. The labourers went on to Quinn's to put the ponies into the stables there. They returned to the man only to discover he was face down in a pool of blood. It was the local schoolteacher Michael Blanchfield and they now knew he was dead. They noticed a ghastly wound on the side of his head and his coat was all ripped at the back.

One of the men went back to John McCarthy's farm where the teacher had lived for the last number of years. The other went to inform the relieving officer Daniel Cronin as there was no police in the village. It was John McCarthy who sent one of his men to Belgooly to report it to the police there.

Dr J Lane from Belgooly was called to inspect the body. Dr Lane was 26 years old and had only recently qualified from UCC in October. He wasn't yet an experienced doctor and most likely had not encountered such a scene before. None the less he arrived and did what he could. Dr Lane reported that such were the injuries that even if he had been called hours before the teacher would still have died.

Sergeant O'Halloran arrived from Belgooly that morning and examined the scene. Once he was satisfied, he organised for the body to be taken from the street to the dead man's cottage which was only 50 yards away. In the teacher's hand were his hat and keys as if he was approaching his door at the time of his attack.

It soon became clear that Michael Blanchfield had been shot on his way home. Blanchfield had been the local schoolmaster for about twenty years and he had lived in the neighbourhood during that time. He was unmarried and taught in the single roomed Rennies national school with his assistant Miss O'Brien.

The police believed that the gunman laid in wait for him at the crossroads and discharged the first shot from behind. A local woman living near the scene told the police she had been working in Quinn's pub and left for home at twenty to eleven the night before. On her way home, she saw nobody and heard nothing unusual. A while later she heard two shots fired but dared not go out to see what was going on. She had seen the teacher in the pub earlier that evening with a local man named Edward Searles.

The police retraced the last movements of Michael Blanchfield with the hope of uncovering the killer. The teacher had his supper as normal in John McCarthy's Ballyvorane, where he had lived for years. Edward Searles confirmed he had been in Quinn's pub the night before with Michael. They had met at Mrs Haslam's house early in the evening as Mrs Haslam was very ill and dying. After a drink or two in the village, they returned together to the old woman's house and Blanchfield left about eleven while Searles remained in the house.

After questioning the occupants of the village, not many had heard the shots that night and those that did hear them did not venture out. Searles sat beside the old woman only 300 yards from the crossroads and yet he heard nothing. At 3 am he walked home passing the crossroad on his way to the village unaware that the man he had been drinking with earlier lay dead only a few feet away in the darkness.

The first shot fired was from behind and maybe 10 yards or more away. They believed Blanchfield turned around to face the gunman but stooped or fell to the ground. The second shot was fired face on with the head and face being hit badly.

Mr McCarthy his ex-landlord said he "could not understand why anyone could have a grudge against poor Michael. He was never any trouble to anyone but I often spoke to him about carrying that money around with him". McCarthy claimed that the teacher often went about carrying as much as ten, ten pound notes with him. Back then very few possessed a note at all and £100 would be something like a year's wages for a teacher and way more to a labourer. It surely was preposterous that he carried about this much money; McCarthy is the only person who ever mentioned this motive.

Scene of the crime, gunman marked as 1, where Blanchfield was 2, with thanks to Irish Newspaper Archives and the Cork Examiner

After years of lodging with the McCarthy's the teacher had recently bought an uninhabited cottage outside the village. He was in the process of decorating it and had started sleeping there at night. He still continued to go back to McCarthy's house every night for his dinner.

The police questioned many more in the village in a desperate attempt to uncover the killer. Precious little more information was forthcoming as nobody was out in the village that night nor gave their suspicions. The police were slow to reveal any information, most likely as they had little to go on. It was District Inspector Wansbrough from Kinsale who led the investigation. He was a man with decades of experience and coming to the end of his career. Wansbrough had investigated notable cases over the years and was initially confident clues would be found.

The following day at noon which was Friday the 19th of December the inquest was held by coroner John J Horgan in the dead man's cottage. The police were well represented with deputy inspector general Mr Tyacke, County Inspector Clayton and District Inspector Alfred Wansbrough stationed in Kinsale. Solicitor J O'Driscoll from Bandon represented the interest of Blanchfield's next of kin.

A jury of twelve local men was sworn in to decide how the teacher met his death. The jury comprised of farmers Jeremiah McCarthy Ballyhullenkeague, David Drinan Killowen and John Hennerty Springfield. Farm labourers: Edward Long, Daniel McCarthy, and retired Timothy Lyons. Also Patrick Quinn from Nohoval, Michael McDonald, John O'Sullivan, Maurice Ahern, Maurice Kiely, Timothy McCarthy, Douglas Lennon and David B Barry.

The body of Michael Blanchfield was formally identified by his oldest brother Martin. The first witness called was local painter Edward Searles, the last known person to have seen Blanchfield alive.

Coroner Horgan cautioned him that he need not give evidence if he so wished but that it could later be used against him. Searles continued and was questioned by District Inspector Wansbrough. He told how he was a painter by trade and was in the company of the teacher on Wednesday night.

Jurors leaving Blanchfield's cottage after the inquest, with thanks to Irish Newspaper Archives and the Cork Examiner.

What Edward didn't say was that he had lived in Nohoval for fifteen years since he married local woman Hannah Bird. When they married Edward was a sapper with the Royal Engineers stationed at Camden, Crosshaven but was originally from Friar Street Kinsale. Edward came to live with his in-laws in Nohoval and he had since become a painter the same as his father. Hannah's father George Bird had been the postmaster in the village but it was now Hannah who ran the post office and shop.

Wansbrough began by asking him about the events of Wednesday night. Edward recalled meeting Blanchfield in Mrs Haslam's house at half eight that evening which was about 300 yards from the village. Mrs Haslam was very poorly and they believed she was close to dying. He said it was the teacher who suggested going down to the village while Mrs Donovan made up the old woman's bed.

Edward told how they left together heading for the village. First, they went to Searles house where Blanchfield bought a pot of jam from Hannah. Edward said it was a treat for the school children before they finished up for Christmas.

Edward believed it was about nine when they went to Quinn's pub (now the Finder's Inn). They had two quick drinks each and left the pub again at about twenty past nine. Edward had two pints in that time while Blanchfield had two medium glasses of whisky. Edward said they remained at Mrs Haslam's bedside until Blanchfield got up to leave at about eleven. Before he left he told Searles to call him during the night if he needed anything for the old woman. Edward told that he sat by the fire talking to Mrs Donovan until three-thirty in the morning.

It was the Coroner who questioned why he stayed so late and Edward replied: "you never leave a person alone in a house like that. Mrs Donovan had been up a week minding Mrs Haslam and I stayed there to look after things, they are cousins of mine".

Searles went on to say he knew the time as he checked his watch before leaving. He had arranged to call his mother-in-law Ellen Bird when he went home and she would go sit with Mrs Haslam.

He must have passed the body going home and admitted himself that he would have been within a road's width of his friend. Edward saw nothing untoward on his way home saying the night was very dark. His wife was awake when he got home but she hadn't heard any shots fired despite being much closer than he was while at Mrs Haslam's.

Wansbrough then began a line of questioning
"Who else lives in the house? My mother-in-law, I called her to go up to Haslam's when I came home and she went up.
Didn't she hear the shots fired? No sir she is very deaf.
But your wife isn't deaf? No sir.
When did she go to bed that night? I couldn't say.
When does she usually go to bed? About 10 O'clock
Did you see the wounds? No sir.
Were they caused by a gunshot? I couldn't tell you.
You have a gun, haven't you? No sir.
What did you do with it? I never had one except I borrowed it from my brother, we might be out fowling for a day.
Could you give me any idea as to how far you think the shot was fired from? No."

What Edward didn't say was his wife was eight months pregnant and maybe this was why she couldn't sleep, but it didn't explain why she didn't hear the shots.

It was then County Inspector Clayton's turn to interrogate the chief witness. He first asked was Mrs Donovan present in Mrs Haslam's house from eleven to half three. Searles confirmed that she was and had never left that night. Searles went on to say that he knew Blanchfield since August 1905, that was when he married Hannah. They were friends since the teacher often visited their house and he went on to say that Blanchfield visited most houses in the village. He denied that they took drink back to Mrs Haslam's house that night.

The coroner asked did Searles hear anything when he stayed on at Mrs Haslam's that night. This wasn't the first time he was asked. All he had heard was a horse passing about half an hour after Blanchfield had left but couldn't tell which direction it was going.

He answered more questions, yes it was dark when they went to Quinn's but not very dark. As they passed the cross a few men were standing by the church wall near to where the body was found. Searles couldn't identify them though saying it was too dark.

He named the men in the pub that night as Mr O'Neill and Mr Collins but didn't know who was in the taproom saying "I didn't look down". The only person Blanchfield spoke to was in the pub that night was Tim Lyons, they had a joke about killing hares. Searles denied there was any animosity between them saying he believed the teacher was friendly with everyone.

Wansbrough began the questioning again:

"Do you remember when he was assaulted last summer? Yes and we were very surprised at it.

He was not assaulted by a friend, was he? No."

The questions kept coming from the District Inspector and the coroner. Searles said he recalled Blanchfield having a black eye but didn't know who had done it nor had it been discussed with him. Wansbrough said "you are an extraordinary man that you didn't discuss it with your friend" but Searles said he didn't go into other people's affairs.

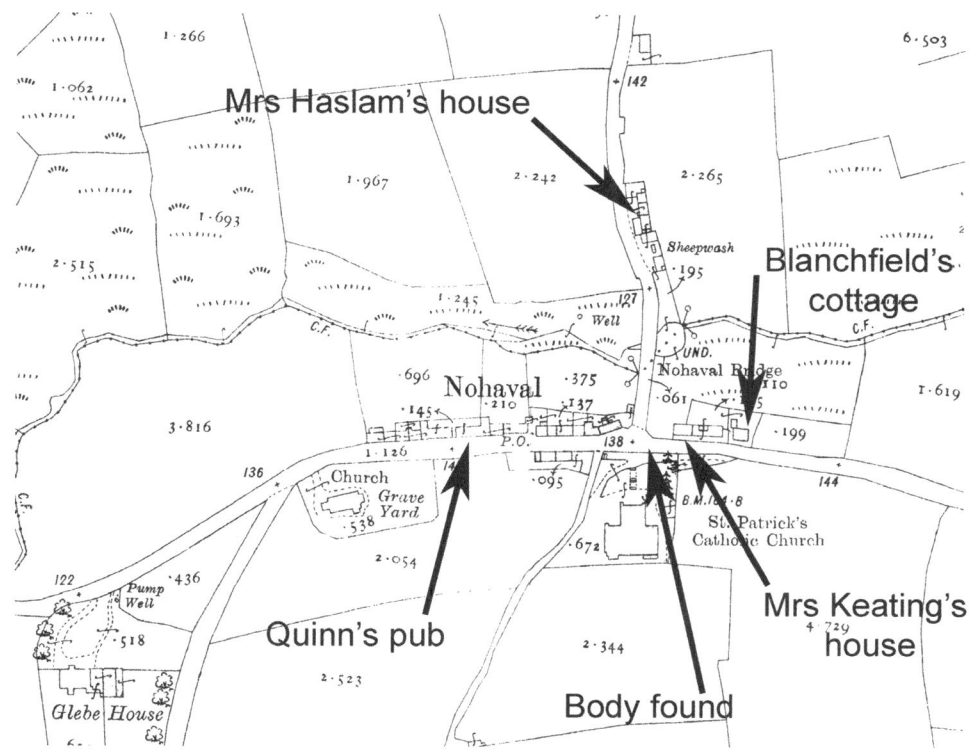

Map of Nohoval at the time with relevant places marked.

When asked was the teacher involved in any dispute either political, personal or to do with coursing, Searles said: "I don't know of any". He said Blanchfield was the secretary of the local coursing club but there was no trouble with it.

Patrick O'Hea told of finding the body with Patrick Lyons when going to work at Quinn's on Thursday morning. At first, they didn't know what was by the chapel wall. When they saw it was a body, they stabled their horses at Quinn's and went back to the scene. Patrick said they found the teacher face down in a lot of blood, he was turned to the wall and his coat torn at the back. The coroner asked did he notice any sign of a struggle but Patrick replied: "no sir, I think he must have fallen and stopped where he was". He also told the coroner that the body was not interfered with, they sent for the relieving officer and also informed John McCarthy.

Mrs Ellen Donovan a widow was called as she had been in Mrs Haslam's house on the night Blanchfield was shot. She confirmed what Searles had said, he arrived with the teacher about half nine. She said Blanchfield left alone at twenty to eleven while Searles remained until three thirty in the morning.

Wansbrough then began a definite line of questions:

"What brought them to the house? I couldn't tell you.

Did they come there together? Yes sir.

Did they bring any drink with them? No sir."

Then the coroner asked:

"Were they sober? Yes sir.

Did you hear any shots fired that night? I didn't.

Did Mr Searles go out of the house between 11 o'clock and 3:30? No.

Were they apparently on good terms? They were sir."

It began to get interesting when O'Driscoll the solicitor who represented the Blanchfield family asked

"Were they in the house before 9:30? No sir.

Did they leave the house from the time they arrived at 9:30 until Blanchfield went away by himself? No sir.

There was nobody else in the house except yourself, Mrs Haslam, Blanchfield and Searles? Mrs Haslam's sister was there."

She then confirmed that when she made up the bed that night no one else was in the house but her and Kate Gribble (Mrs Haslam's sister) who slept by the fire. Driscoll even asked did she see the jam with Blanchfield that night but she had not noticed.

"Did you hear any noise that night? No.

Did you hear a horse passing? I did about 12:30.

Was there a car on the horse? No sir."

From this, it seems that Searles story was the truth. He was at the old woman's all night. But why the discrepancy in the events that night and why had Searles implied Mrs Donovan was alone that night. Surely everyone knew that Kate Gribble had lived with her sister for several years. Why also had he said that he met Blanchfield in the old woman's house and decided to go to the pub to get out of the way while the bed was being made? He even said that Blanchfield suggested it as he had a message to get in the village ie, the jam. Yet the widow Donovan recalled making up the bed and the men only arriving at 9:30. Why Searles would have bothered changing things when he had a sound alibi, was he aware of what was going to happen that night?

Mrs Kate Keating, a widow who lived directly opposite the Chapel was called to tell what she heard on Wednesday night. She had been working in the pub and left for home at twenty to eleven, taking only a minute to get there. She met nobody on the way nor saw anything amiss in the village. It was about fifteen minutes later the widow said she heard a voice say "Lord God Almighty". The coroner asked did she recognise the voice from inside her house. Mrs Keating said:" no sir but it was a man's voice and he had hardly said those words when there was a second shot". The widow then explained how she went upstairs to peer out the window but saw nothing as it was dark. She heard moaning outside from where the shot was fired for about an hour. Mrs Keating didn't dare go outside she said fearing for her own safety.

The questioning continued as they struggled to believe she didn't go out.

Wansbrough: What were you afraid of? I might be shot myself.
Coroner: Did you make any attempt to convey to anyone what you heard? No sir.
Coroner: Are you a Catholic? I am sir.
Coroner: Did you know a man was dying on the road and might want a priest? I didn't know a man was dying on the road and I was alone in the house.
Coroner: Nobody would hurt a woman under those conditions, it shows what the country is coming to.
Wansbrough: Could you see the body from the window? No sir.
Coroner: Did you hear any other voice? No, I didn't

Mrs Keating tried to explain her actions that night saying how her health had recently been poor and she was very nervous. The coroner was wrong though if she ran out that night the gunman would have turned on her to save himself. Having pulled the trigger, the killer would have fled quickly. She could have looked out a while later. Especially when all she heard from outside was the moaning sound.

Another widow Mrs Scully from the other side of the street gave a similar testimony. She also didn't venture out that night or even go close to a window fearing a shot might come through. The widow was going to bed about eleven and upon hearing the shot fired, she quenched her light. She described what she heard as a stifled scream and a moan coming from the other side of the crossroads but not far away. She went upstairs but didn't go to bed for about fifteen minutes. Mrs Scully told the coroner that she knew something had occurred but didn't think a man had been killed. She described the teacher as a quiet inoffensive man. The coroner asked were there any men living in the village, to which the widow answered: "no, no men are living in there".

It was solicitor O'Driscoll who pushed her further asking:
"Did you sleep at all that night? I didn't sleep at all.
You knew somebody was shot? I didn't know.
What caused the screams? I thought he might have got away."
Mrs Scully also heard a horse passing the crossroads later that night as the others had.

Sergeant Daniel O'Halloran stationed at Belgooly described the scene he found by the chapel wall in Nohoval. He said Blanchfield was sort of lying on his side in a pool of blood. In his right hand, Blanchfield was still clutching his hat and keys as he would have been nearing home. The sergeant had measured Mrs Keating's house as 22 yards from the body, Mrs Scully's 23 yards and Blanchfield's cottage 50 yards off. The sergeant claimed Mrs Haslam's house was 500 yards but other sources suggested 300 yards.

The coroner asked him his impression of the crime:
"Do you expect there is anything political about this crime? I am not prepared to say as I don't know the locality; this place is only a recent addition to my district.
Did you know the deceased? I knew him for four or five years he was a quite harmless man."

Sergeant O'Halloran said he had not heard of the assault on the teacher the summer before. What the Sergeant failed to mention was he summoned the teacher to court in April of 1917. O'Halloran was the complainant in a petty case against him where the same 'harmless man' as he since described him, was done for not having a light on his bike. The following year he was done twice more for repeats of the same offences this time by Sergeant O'Leary of Ballyfeard. Also that year O'Leary had done him for having an unlicensed dog in his possession. This was despite the fact that the records show each year Blanchfield had licensed various dogs over several years, collies terriers, greyhounds and setters. Why in these latter years do the police seem to be bothering this "harmless" and "inoffensive" man with such petty crimes? He had lived in Nohoval for decades before without a blemish, were they trying to tell him something.

It was Dr Thomas Bolster Newman from Kinsale who gave the medical evidence and told the inquest how he had carried out the post mortem with Dr Lane. He found the left side of the back of the neck and face covered in small puncture wounds. He said the body's organs were healthy but the left lung was congealed in blood. The lung had been hit and there were several pellets lodged there. The doctor said that the blast was such that the eighth, ninth and eleventh ribs were broken. Inside one of the cracked ribs, a large pellet was found in the tissue. Pellets were also lodged under the scalp but had not gone through the skull.

The doctor couldn't answer how long Blanchfield survived on the roadside. The coroner suggested half an hour but Dr Bolster believed he could not have survived so long. The doctor noted how the shots were fired at close range as the pellets were concentrated and not very scattered. The first shot he said was fired from behind and the second as the teacher was falling to the ground. He concluded the death was a direct result of the blood loss caused by the wounds in the left lung.

Young Dr Lane agreed with his colleague but said Blanchfield was trying to turn around as the second shot was fired.

Dr Lane was also asked how long he thought Blanchfield survived after being shot. He didn't give a definite answer either but thought he must have been unconscious immediately but could have been moaning.

Fr Coveney was not a witness at the inquest but spoke about how shocked he was at the dreadful crime. He was appalled at what had happened so close by, at the chapel wall and intended to denounce it at mass next Sunday. He also intended to appeal to his flock to come forward with any information.

Before hearing the verdict the coroner agreed with what Fr Coveney had said before going on to say "it was one of the most brutal and dastardly crimes that had stained our country for many years".

Horgan regretted terribly that a verdict could not be reached that day against the perpetrator. After all, it was Horgan who held an inquest for the Lusitania in Kinsale and found wilful, wholesale murder against the Kaiser and his government.

The coroner went on saying "so far as I can judge there is no element of politics in the case". Horgan was well able to comment on this as he was quite active in Nationalist politics previously. He, however, was against the violent struggle that had begun earlier that year.

The coroner reminded people again that nobody in the village had gone to the aid of the man despite having heard his moans. There had been a shooting in Kilbrittain just days before and the coroner was glad to hear people suffered life and limb to fetch a priest. Horgan said it was every Christian's duty in such circumstances to risk themselves to get medical and religious assistance for the victim.

He suggested the following verdict "That Michael Blanchfield was wilfully murdered at Nohoval at about 11 pm on the 17th of December by gunshot wounds inflicted by a person or persons unknown, the said wounds causing haemorrhage and shock. We desire to condemn in the most solemn manner this base and brutal crime and to express the hope that every assistance will be given to the authorities, in endeavouring to trace the murderer".

Solicitor O'Driscoll thanked the coroner and the jury for their expression of sympathy towards his clients. He reminded everyone that amongst them in the community was a murderer who must be brought to justice. Driscoll told how he was sure that the perpetrator would be caught saying "murder will out" but that it may take time.

So why was John McCarthy who knew Blanchfield well and had been his landlord for nearly twenty years not interviewed at the inquest? He was quick to suggest a motive of robbery that the press had been keen to believe. The police didn't seem to believe such a motive for this brutal shooting. Their impression was that it was somewhat darker and someone specifically wanted the teacher dead but why?

Depiction of the murder scene by Claire O'Donovan

None of those mentioned as being in the pub were questioned to support Searles story nor was Mrs Searles. If we are to believe Mrs Donovan's version, Blanchfield and Searles arrived together at Mr Haslam's at 9:30. According to Searles, they had come from the pub and Searles shop where he bought the jam. So do we know where they met at all that night or if more events are missing that could be relevant?

Searles' in-laws the Birds had been old friends with the Haslam's for years. George Bird, Hannah's father had been William Haslam's best man when he married fifty years before. So it wasn't that strange that Ellen Bird went round to Mrs Haslam's at three that morning.

After the inquest as was customary, the funeral cortege made its way to Bandon, where Michael Blanchfield was buried in the family plot in the New Cemetery.

The day after the inquest, Saturday the 20th Mrs Haslam passed away. She had been dying for some time. Records show she was 74 years old and had been married to William Haslam but there was no account of him in Nohoval. When they married fifty years before he was the Schoolmaster in Ringabella.

In Bandon, the Board of Guardians condemned the killing of one of their "most highly respected fellow townsman". Mr O'Driscoll suggested the people of Nohoval were "not very Christianised" for leaving the teacher on the roadside for the whole night.

Fr Coveney in Nohoval did what he had promised and denounced the murder from the altar. He defended the people of Nohoval saying the old women were in dread of their own lives that night and never thought a man lay dying so close by. The priest asked of the Bandon Guardians "what would Mr Driscoll have done in similar circumstances?" The priest had a point, nobody knew themselves what they would do until faced with it. It would be over the course of the following year or so that many more would encounter the increase in such activity.

Three days before Blanchfield was murdered, a RIC constable was shot walking to the barracks in Kilbrittain. The killer also laid in wait in the middle of a village under the cover of darkness. The murder weapon was a revolver.

On the 19th of December, the IRA attempted to assassinate the Lord Lieutenant of Ireland but failed leaving one of their volunteers dead. By the end of the year, the death toll was about 17 which was hardly considered a war.

So had these events anything to do with the shooting of Michael Blanchfield? He had no political involvement that we know of, nor were they out to get him. His older brother Patrick was a RIC constable but would anyone in Nohoval have even known this fact.

Michael Blanchfield's name crops up in many lists of civilians killed during the War of Independence but had it anything to do with it at all. The War of Independence began in January of 1919 when Dáil Eireann declared independence. The following day two RIC officers were killed in Soloheadbeg Co Tipperary. That year the War was slow to get going, most of the activity was raids to gather weapons and free those imprisoned.

On St Stephen's day, the police decided to search the area for shotguns that could have been used to kill the teacher. The report detailed four unlicensed guns that were found but no action was taken against the owners. Those found with unlicensed shotguns were all farmers, James Hegarty from Ballyvorane, Patrick O'Neill from Dunbogey and Daniel McCarthy from Ballindeasig. Jeremiah O'Reilly from Farranbrien was also found with a gun but it was not capable of being fired. None of these were seen as serious suspects but the police wanted to be seen to make progress. A rumour spread that a shotgun had been found concealed in a ditch that could have been the murder weapon but it never amounted to anything.

The following year the police investigation didn't reveal any further information nor were any witnesses forthcoming. As the War of independence truly became a war that year the RIC became consumed with it. District Inspector Wanbrough retired from the service only weeks later in February of 1920, while the going was good. He was then sixty three years old and had a substantial pension of £433 annually to retire on.

Also in February of 1920, Patrick Blanchfield was involved in an ambush in Aghern near Conna. Two constables and a sergeant were on patrol when they were surprised by a band of masked volunteers. They left the three RIC men tied up unharmed at the side of the road without their weapons.

Michael Blanchfield, with thanks to Irish Newspaper Archives and the Cork Examiner.

Michael Blanchfield had come to Nohoval as the teacher in Rennies School in 1899. When he arrived at Rennies School that year he was only twenty five years old. He was not a popular man by any means but may have been unaware of that fact. As a teacher, he had that air of importance and was said to be a strong willed man who made his presence known. He grew up in Bandon, the son of a stonemason who became a prosperous merchant. Without this success behind him, it would have been difficult to receive an education to become a teacher. In the little village of Nohoval, Blanchfield saw himself as someone important. Someone who should be listened to and not just by the children. While he would not have been as revered as the priest he wasn't a man to be told.

His father Michael Blanchfield Senior originally came from Kilkenny, where the name is still prevalent. He arrived in West Cork during the building of the West Cork Railway. He was a stonemason by trade and is said to have built many of the railway stations. It was during this time he met the Coakley's of Manch as the line passed that way. He married Maryanne Coakley in Bandon in 1865 when she was just eighteen and they settled in the town. The following year Martin was born, the first of eleven children. Michael Blanchfield was the fourth eldest born in 1874; he had seven brothers and three sisters.

Michael Blanchfield's will was left to his younger brother Edward who was a press correspondent in the Cork Examiner. He died in 1924 aged only 35 from Tuberculosis. His youngest brother Mortimer then became a reporter for the Examiner.

Martin the eldest in the family also died later in 1924 aged 56 of heart failure. He had been living in Courtmacsherry for the last number of years after selling the Blanchfield Hotel in Bandon. John, the second eldest, was also a teacher but immigrated to America and settled in Detroit. He died in 1927 aged only fifty nine.

In July of 1896, Michael Blanchfield came first in an examination having gained experience with Mr Quinlan at the Shannon Street National School in Bandon. He was then sent off to the De La Salle training school in Waterford to complete his education.

It was when schoolmaster Thomas Desmond died of cancer in 1899 aged only 41, that Michael Blanchfield got the job in Rennies National School.

In 1910 Blanchfield applied to become a rate collector in the Bandon area. It was such a sought after position that the six candidates were examined in several subjects in which Blanchfield came third. He told a white lie and gave his address of his father at South Main Street Bandon. One of the conditions was that the rate collector must live in the district and have no other employment. This ruled out several of the candidates including Blanchfield but they had solicitors on hand to swear otherwise. What was revealed was Blanchfield was at the time earning £100 annually as the schoolmaster in Rennies School. This further shows John McCarthy's suggestion of robbery as unlikely, no teacher would casually carry about a year's wages.

He was over six feet tall and powerfully built and maybe that was why the killer chose a gun as the murder weapon. They definitely didn't want Blanchfield surviving to tell the tale. He had been assaulted sometime before and had been seen with a black eye.

In all the years of teaching in Nohoval, Blanchfield had lodged with McCarthy's in Ballyvorane until he purchased a cottage close to where he died. At the time he was in the process of renovating the cottage but was still taking his meals in McCarthy's. It was only two weeks before that he had started sleeping in his cottage.

It has been mentioned that Blanchfield was killed over a woman and this makes some sense. If he had got the black eye from a jealous husband he would be reluctant to tell who the attacker was. If it was an attempted robbery it would surely have been reported to the police and an arrest made.

The police report referred to the teacher as a "Sinn Feiner" and could see no political motive in killing him. The police made no reference at all to the suggestion of robbery and most likely didn't even consider it. Their hunch was that more personal matters were at the root of it. There were mentions of Blanchfield's involvement with his teaching assistant Miss O'Brien and it was alleged that he treated her badly. They had information that he had been courting Miss O'Brien the previous summer when he acquired the black eye. The report concluded with the statement "it is believed that a woman is at the bottom of the murder".

Many believed Blanchfield was a protestant, just because of his name, but that was not true at all. He could not have been teaching in the local school unless he was a Catholic. His father Michael Blanchfield

Senior who died in 1914 was a known Nationalist and supporter of John Redmond. It was the teacher's friend Edward Searles that was Church of Ireland, not that it mattered, but in 1919 things were different.

Was there a conspiracy against Blanchfield the blow in teacher or did the killer act alone? In all the time he had spent in Nohoval, only the McCarthy's were really on good terms with him. Some may have chosen to associate themselves with the teacher for appearances sake.

Outside of Nohoval alternative versions and motives existed. Some of those believed that Michael had overheard a conversation in the pub that night. It was reputed he heard some ex-pupils planning to kill a friend of his and the would be killers knew he would tell. They claimed this was the reason he was shot as it was the only way to silence him. We know from the inquest that Blanchfield joked with Tim Lyons about killing hares in Quinn's Pub that night. Surely Searles a friend of the teacher would have also picked up on it and mentioned it at the inquest. The quiet village of Nohoval was far from the type of place where one expected to overhear such things, yet a murder did take place. At the time there was not even an active company of volunteers in the village.

The scene of the crime from Blanchfield's cottage.

It's an unlikely story as who would plan a shooting in a pub with several ears listening. Especially not in front of the school teacher who was friendly with their target.

Much more likely was the local rumour of involvement with a local woman, maybe a married woman. He had been assaulted the summer before and reluctant to tell who had struck him. Robbery was briefly suggested and dismissed, no matter how much money he had would someone tackle a big man like Blanchfield. So if it was a jealous desperate husband, every married man in the area who could get his hands on a shotgun, could be a suspect.

Did someone with a grudge against Blanchfield grab the opportunity after the shooting in Kilbrittain, in the hope it would be seen as a political killing by the authorities? Constable Bolger's killing in Kilbrittain was not the norm at the time as most engagements were attempts to gather weapons. Not everyone had access to a revolver; a shotgun was much more readily available in the countryside. Bolger seems to have been active in arresting local IRA volunteers and stood witness against them in November. Days before the shooting several of the volunteers had been released.

John McCarthy seems to have had some suspicions and suggested robbery in the hope of maintaining his ex-tenants good name. The robbery theory worked at first as the papers ran with it but soon wore thin. Firing a shotgun from that range and then firing again could only be an act of revenge and hatred.

The silence of the village suggests people certainly had more than an inkling of the motive but couldn't or wouldn't say anything. In Kilbrittain a gunfight broke out when the other constables heard the shots, Bolger's daughter ran to the barrack door asking for her father. Yet in Nohoval only two shots were fired and it seems nobody dared venture out until morning. It was also left to two labourers to raise the alarm, those that heard the shots made no attempt at all.

An ad in the Cork Examiner almost exactly a year before suggests another motive. A reward of £5 was offered for information leading to persons found laying snares or hunting with dogs on lands preserved by the Nohoval Coursing Club. We know that Michael Blanchfield was the secretary of the Club and was heavily involved. Was this the sign of a clash between him and a local landowner over hares or land? We know the teacher was not a man to back down easily and exerted his will on those that disagreed with him. The Nohoval Coursing Club met at Hurley's forge the Sunday before he was killed. During the conversation in the pub the night of the murder, with Timothy Lyons, the teacher had "joked" about killing hares. It was no joke when the club was willing to offer a substantial sum of £5 reward. The club was often looking to purchase between fifty and one hundred hares, such was the demand for the sport at the time.

In the Irish countryside when such dreadful things happened it was often claimed it had never happened before. Nohoval though was like any other village, in the Irish countryside one is never far from murder. The story of Michael Blanchfield failed to go away, the killer was never found and rumours continued. So much so that in November 1921, Bartholomew Collins a farmer from Dunbogey summoned Daniel McCarthy from Ballindeasig to court. The charge against McCarthy was slander with damages claimed at £100.

In court McCarthy, who had been caught with an unlicensed shotgun handed in a statement: "I hereby withdraw the remarks I made about Batty Collins and regret having used them, and I freely and voluntarily acknowledge that I have no reason to think that he had any connection with the murder of Michael Blanchfield". There was then applause in court.

In the area at the time were two Bartholomew Collins both very close in age, one was the unmarried farmer from Dunbogey, the other married from Ballindeasig. Was it because of the court case that the name Bartholomew Collins lived on being connected with the killing of Michael Blanchfield despite no obvious evidence? Searles had named a Mr Collins in the pub that night, was this Batty Collins and Mr O'Neill his neighbour? Of course, this is merely circumstantial and proves nothing at all.

But now over a hundred years after the murder, the perpetrator is well dead, without ever making a confession. There were various reasons why someone could have wanted Michael Blanchfield dead and we will never know for sure.

South Main Street Bandon, where Michael Blanchfield had grown up, image courtesy of the National Library of Ireland.

A Costly Tithe
Baurleigh Timoleague 1832

Rev Charles Ferguson Rector of Timoleague was travelling from Timoleague to Bandon with Mr Hewson Sweete. He was on his way to Dublin, an arduous journey back then and made even worse by Ferguson's unpopularity. He was so hated that an armed escort of five soldiers had left Timoleague with him that morning. Outside the village, Ferguson insisted they return and was confident of his safety. The night before he had been warned not to undertake such a journey and that his life could be in danger.

In the townland of Baurleigh on the "high road" to Bandon, the horse slowed going uphill and refused to go on. At this point, the pair were approaching where the Baurleigh School has since been built. When Ferguson noticed a mob of men approaching quickly in a field he realised he had made a grave error.

With no hope of coaxing the horse on Ferguson and his companion abandoned the horse and fled through the fields with several men in hot pursuit. Ferguson was said to have abandoned his overcoat in the hope of getting away faster. Behind him he could hear them chanting "stop him, stop him, knock him down, knock him down". They headed for Baurleigh House which was a few hundred yards to the East. It was near a small stone bridge that Ferguson's progress was hampered by another group of men and he knew he was done for. He was armed with a pistol and dagger but for some reason made no attempt to defend himself, maybe it all happened so quickly he never got the chance.

It was in the field near the bridge that the mob took the law into their own hands. Ferguson's head and face were beaten in with a big stone and when they were finished with him he was barely recognisable. Somehow Hewson Sweete managed to make it to Baurleigh House where he was taken in.

It was said to be passing policemen that came upon the beaten body of Charles Ferguson shortly afterwards. There was still a large mob in the area so they were forced to continue on their way to Bandon to raise the alarm.

Ferguson's body was brought back to the Glebe in Timoleague for the inquest which was held the following day, Sunday the 16th of December. At the inquest, Mr Sweete gave evidence of seeing Ferguson being pursued across the field but didn't actually see the men who killed him. The other evidence was the same; many had seen it happen but from a distance and all failed to identify the killers.

Dr Hayes described the terrible head injuries Rev Ferguson had sustained and the horrific death he had suffered. With no suspect, the jury could do little but return an open verdict in accordance with the medical evidence - "that some persons unknown did with stones feloniously and wilfully make an assault upon Charles Ferguson and by striking the said Charles Ferguson on the head with stones, mortal wounds were inflicted and of said wounds, Charles Ferguson died."

On Wednesday the 19th the funeral cortege left Timoleague for Lisslee Graveyard, south of Courtmacsherry. All the great and good in the area turned out to mourn the loss and pay their respects. Such was their fear of violence breaking out again that a large posse of military escorted the cortege to the graveyard.

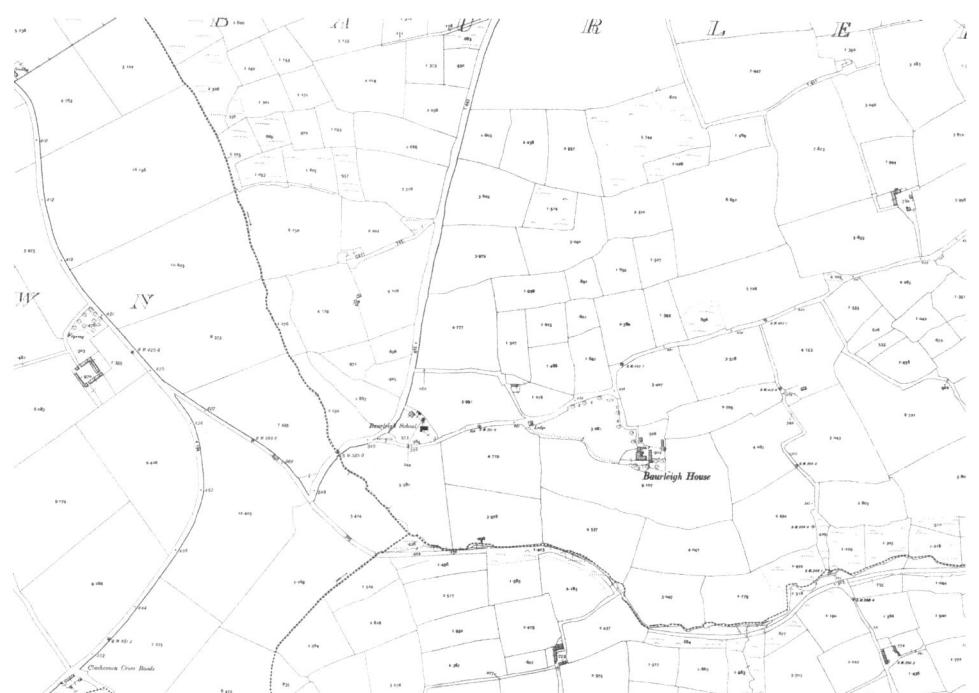

Map showing Baurleigh House and School

Reports described Ferguson as a respectable gentleman, and I'm sure he was to his own kind but not to the poor. Once the news got out it sent shockwaves through a certain class, the wealthy who felt they might be next.

By early January a reward of £400 was offered by the Lord Lieutenant for information leading to apprehending the murderer. Another £900 reward was raised by individuals. The Earl of Shannon, Lord Bandon and Lord Carbery all gave £50 each.

Rev Charles Ferguson was only thirty five years of age when he was killed and had been in Timoleague for about six years. Coming from the privileged place in society that he did, Charles went to Trinity College and graduated with a master's degree. While at the time the poor only received a very rudimentary education before going off to work in the fields. Back then many such young gentlemen chose religion as it elevated their position in society and came with many perks. Charles was the son of James Ferguson and his brother Rev Samuel had recently been promoted. Samuel Ferguson had a tithe income of some £600 annually in Thurles.

Within a few years, Charles found himself living in a fine Rectory house in Timoleague and automatically entitled to a Tithe income of £400 a year taken from the poor. It seems this didn't bother Charles at all, quite the opposite; he was active in pursuing those that owed him. But no matter how much he tried the poor resisted and refused to pay what they believed was wrong. Some Rectors chose not to stir trouble and left the arrears to build up. Half of the clergy claiming tithes did not live in the areas at all. Some chose to sell their tithe income to someone better able to collect it. Charles was one of those that seemed to feel a sense of entitlement to what was theirs and took steps to get payment. He took an active part, even going around to farms with the tithe valuators checking what each farmer possessed.

By 1832 the Tithe War was well underway, forced payment of tithes and resisting payment caused 242 killings throughout the country. The tithes in the Timoleague district had been in arrears for three years and nobody would pay. Charles did everything he could legally to try to get the money and wrote to the Chief Secretary of Ireland in Dublin Castle numerous times. He asked the Chief Secretary how far could he go to get what was rightfully his, it was hopeless though as they wouldn't pay.

Image showing the road up past Baurleigh School and the scene of the crime.

Tithes in Timoleague had been in dispute for much longer, in 1827 tenants appealed against the tithes in Timoleague being too high and it was reduced to the sum of £370 annually. It went as far as a court case heard by Baron Pennefather at the Cork Assizes. Daniel O'Connell came and argued the case for the parishioners in Timoleague against Rev Ferguson. Before that tithes had been set at £413 a year for the parish of Timoleague, a good income and many times greater than the average farmer let alone labourer.

Despite such a generous reward, a pardon was also offered to any who witnessed the crime and took a lesser part if they gave information. Information was slow; initially the authorities believed a reward would entice someone desperate enough to talk.

Eventually, someone did talk, the informer was said to be Michael Sullivan.

One Sunday in January four men from the Timoleague Kilbrittain area were arrested. Three of the four men were James Mahony aged 34, James Hurley 26 and Patrick Desmond 25 it was Sullivan who had given them up. It took a large posse of both infantry and Calvary to escort the men to Bandon, fearing the country people would attempt to free them.

In Bandon a large mob surrounded the military, a riot almost broke out and several stones were thrown. Captain Vignoles had prepared for this and ordered the cavalry to hold back the mob on the bridge. Otherwise, they would never have managed to get the four prisoners into the Bandon Bridewell.

A few days later the four men were transferred to the country gaol to prevent any further riot in Bandon. The informer Michael Sullivan was also kept in custody for his own safety as the whole countryside would turn against him. No matter how desperate the police were to get the killers they still didn't seem to believe the informer. No other witnesses were found to back up Sullivan's statement. The four were to be tried at the upcoming Spring Assizes but the crown prosecution knew they didn't have enough evidence to convict and the case against them failed.

In the following months, another man was arrested but again released due to lack of evidence.

In early February the Rev Thomas Waggett was transferred to Timoleague. It was a promotion for him as he had been a curate in St Pauls in the city. At the same time, the Freeman's Journal sarcastically ran an article titled "the starving clergy". It had actually been The Herald that had originally printed the article which claimed the clergy of the established church were in need. It claimed their incomes had drastically been cut and many had only managed to collect six months worth in the last three years. The Freeman's Journal reply to the article had no sympathy with the established church at all saying the church themselves should help out their own.

Not only did the protestant clergy feel entitled to be granted such cushy numbers and demand a portion of the poor people's income. But they did not want to claim they were close to starving. What they meant by starving though, was not the same as the poor. They still had fine big rectory houses, servants and other sources of income. They didn't give a damn that much of the country had to starve to give them a better lifestyle.

So it's no surprise the poor came to resent them so much, paying one tenth of everything they earned each year to a "chosen" member of another religion.

It was two years later before the Tithe War in Ireland came to a head. In Gortroe near Rathcormac Arch Deacon Ryder used the military to force payment on outstanding Tithes from a widow amounting to forty shillings. The locals resisted and twelve men were gunned down. For more information read 'Murder Most Local, Historic Murders of East Cork'. Afterwards, the use of the military to collect tithes was no longer allowed and the system fell apart when many refused to pay. Eventually, the tithe was incorporated into the rent and collected by the landlord which in effect increased rents.

In 1843 the murder of Charles Ferguson came up again when Patrick O'Leary admitted being the killer. O'Leary was at the time serving as a private in the 69th Regiment of Foot in New Brunswick Canada. He was in custody for deserting the army for the third time when he decided to mention the murder from eleven years before.

When the news reached Cork it caused quite a fuss, would O'Leary when he was brought back be forced to give up the names of those involved. Why had he chosen now to break his silence when he was thousands of miles from the scene of the crime?

It was early July when Patrick O'Leary arrived in Liverpool aboard the ship Normanton in the custody of Canadian officers. He was held in custody in Liverpool at first then escorted to Dublin and on to Cork to await his trial at an upcoming Assizes. Straight away cracks began to appear in O'Leary's story. When questioned he told of being from St Finbarr's in the city. His father, a tailor was still there and also his sister a dressmaker. Why would O'Leary have been involved in a country murder with an agrarian motive so far from the city?

When O'Leary arrived in the County Gaol in Cork he changed his story entirely. He denied any involvement claiming he learned of the murder from another soldier in custody called Duncan. From this story, he concocted his confession all in the hope of getting back to Ireland and away from the dreadful conditions in the army prison. It turned out Patrick O'Leary was only in his mid twenties and had hardly committed such a murder when he was fourteen or fifteen.

So was it now suspected that it was Duncan who was involved in the brutal murder of Rev Ferguson eleven years before? It was all too late though as when O'Leary first made the statement he knew that Duncan had died in custody. It makes sense though that Duncan was involved for why else would he still be talking about the murder eleven years afterwards.

Nobody ever came forward for the killing of Rev Charles Ferguson and why would they. While murder can never be condoned, those that did it must have felt driven to drastic actions by a hatred of a privileged man. The poor had very little but a subsistence living, while Ferguson had not just the law but the whole system on his side.

Many chose to just not pay the Tithe and failed to understand why a stranger who had done nothing for it was entitled to ten per cent of theirs.

The Quandary of the Quarry
Carrigaline 1822

On Friday morning the 24th of May, Patrick Linehan went to work as normal in a quarry on the outskirts of Carrigaline. His wife Eleanor went looking for him when he didn't come home from work that night. She was told that a sheep of his had been stolen and he had gone in pursuit of it. Eleanor returned home thinking if her husband didn't turn up soon, he would probably have gone to Cork and be back in the morning.

On Saturday morning a young servant of Patrick Linehan's emerged from the house and went to local farmer Denis Twomey. The boy had been hiding in the house all night in dread of his life as intruders had broken in the night before.

Twomey along with several others armed themselves believing the intruders were still there. Cautiously they went round to Linehan's house ready for trouble. They discovered the house had been ransacked and anything of value had been taken even the bed. Amid the chaos was the body of Eleanor Linehan lying on the floor in a pool of blood.

This had to be far more than just robbery, her head had been smashed to pieces and her brains were said to have spilled onto the floor. She was heavily pregnant at the time of the brutal attack.

Magistrate William Henry Worth Newenham of Coolmore House was informed and he set out for the quarry to find Patrick Linehan. Traces of blood were found which led them to another nearby quarry. Linehan's body was found under a heap of stones. Patrick suffered a similar death to that of his wife; he had suffered serious head injuries inflicted by a heavy instrument.

Nobody had seen Linehan alive since he went to work twenty four hours before. Michael Cahill who worked with Patrick was not to be found, he was either also dead or knew something about the crimes and was in hiding. Newenham quickly grew suspicious when he heard of an earlier disagreement between Linehan and Cahill. Patrick had gone to the quarry owner Mr Hewitt and complained about Cahill's work. Then when Cahill went to be paid he only received 2/6 which enraged him.

The magistrate issued a warrant for the arrest of Cahill and dispatched Constable Godfrey to the city where Cahill's brother resided. Patrick's father John Cahill, an old man, was located in Carrigaline and brought to Coolmore House to be questioned by Newenham.

Patrick Linehan had been a farmer but lost possession of the land yet he remained living in the same house near Carrigaline Castle to the east of the village. With his sudden change of circumstances, he was forced to resort to working as a labourer. A deal was struck with Henry Hewitt who owned a nearby quarry and Michael Cahill was also involved. Soon after the agreement about the quarry turned sour between the men but nobody expected it to end so badly.

That Saturday an inquest was quickly arranged with a jury of local men. Newenham having taken an interest in the terrible tragedy also acted as the foreman of the inquest. Over twenty witnesses were produced at the inquest over several days but most of the evidence was circumstantial in nature.

While the inquest sat that Sunday news arrived that Michael Cahill had been arrested. The constable found Michael Cahill in his brother's house in Globe Lane of Frenchs Quay in the city. He had signs of blood on his shirt especially the sleeves which he could not explain. Cahill was duly arrested by the magistrate and questioned by the Lord Mayor in Cork. He was arrested close to Elizabeth Fort and the convict depot, where female prisoners awaited their transportation.

Newenham sent word back that Cahill should be produced before the inquest where the bodies were. It was unusual but given the brutality of the crimes the magistrate most likely wanted to provoke a response or a confession from Cahill. If Cahill was cold enough to smash in two skulls in quick succession over a disagreement he was hardly going to crack so easily.

It was Wednesday the 29th of May before a verdict was reached normally an inquest only took a few hours. Details of the inquest were not recorded but the verdict was "that Patrick Linehan came to his death in a certain quarry on the morning of Friday the 24th May on the lands of Carrigaline, in consequence of various deep wounds which he received on parts of his head, by which the skull was considerably fractured, inflicted by Michael Cahill of Carrigaline, a labourer with some blunt instrument such as a crowbar or sledge and further that the said Michael Cahill was aided, abetted and assisted in doing so by his father John Cahill of Carrigaline aforesaid, labourer".

Not only did they implicate Michael Cahill in one murder but the jury also found:

"That Eleanor Linehan came to her death on the night of Friday the 24th of May in her dwelling house at Carrigaline in consequence of a severe fracture of the skull which was broken in pieces and part of the brain protruding, willfully, maliciously and feloniously inflicted by Michael Cahill labourer with such weapons as a spade and that she received various wounds on her left arm inflicted by said Michael Cahill at the same time and place with some sharp pointed instrument such as a bayonet".

This alone was enough to keep Michael Cahill in police custody but now a coroner's warrant could be issued to detain his father also on a capital charge. There is no record of a magisterial inquiry into the murder but if there was the verdict would have been swayed by that on the inquest.

After months in jail, the father and son must have understood that they were doomed when it came to a trial before a jury at the Assizes. Judge Baron Pennefather was well known for handing out the death sentence without hesitating. Execution was never more prevalent than in the 1820s and by the end of 1822 nineteen would be hanged in Cork alone. At the Summer Assizes, that year before Cahill's case, several men had been sentenced to death for far lesser crimes. One for stealing 46 sheep and another man for stealing a horse.

It was Thursday 29th of August when father and son were called before the Summer Assizes with the infamous Baron Pennefather. If he had his way both men would be hung by Saturday. At the time the 1752 Murder Act was still in place, its objective was to deter serious crime. Those found guilty of murder had to be executed within two days of being sentenced. Executed murderers were denied a Christian burial and bodies were generally sent for dissection or hung in gibbets.

In the court that day, it was heard that the police searched Cahill's house after he had been arrested. There several items were found with bloodstains. Attempts had been made to clean some of them. It was also proved that Michael Cahill had given Linehan's graffaun to his sister-in-law to sell. She had done as asked and gave the money to Cahill.

Chief witness Judith Duggan said she was passing the quarry that Friday when she saw a man on the ground lying on his face. There was a man standing over him beating him to death with a graffaun. As he laid into the defenceless man he called out to his father. Judith couldn't identify either the man on the ground or the killer saying she cleared so fast. She did however recognise John Cahill saying he was the man who was called "father". She swore that there were only three men in the quarry that day.

It was four in the afternoon when Baron Pennefather summed up the case and charged the jury. The judge's address took over an hour and a half, the jury returned with the verdict of guilty against both men.

On Saturday morning appeals were made to Baron Pennefather for a reprieve of the death sentence against John Cahill. He was an old man and had maintained his innocence in the crimes. Pennefather gave in and decided to save the old man from the hangman by giving a reprieve but he would end his days in jail.

Michael Cahill had also insisted that his father had taken no part in the crime. He had asked his father to help conceal the body in the quarry but he said the old man had refused to help.

Father and son were still at the jail that morning when they heard the news. The men hugged before being separated forever. By now the terrible rage that Michael must have had was gone and was replaced with regret. Before leaving the jail that morning Michael confessed to his terrible crimes and admitted that he deserved the death sentence which he was about to face. As the executioner secured his hands for the march to the gallows Cahill said his crimes were so bad he deserved to be dragged by the neck to his place of execution.

On the scaffold at Gallow's Green Cahill again confessed at the last minute and admitted how sorry he was for what he had done. He also apologised for accusations and lies he had told about respectable neighbours of his. He left the world knowing at least that his father was not to suffer the same fate as he was. A great crowd had gathered before the gallows that day to see the spectacle. Often angry mobs gathered in protest to an unjust sentence but all agreed that day that Cahill deserved his lot. In his last moments, Michael begged God for forgiveness and then the hangman pulled the bolt and he hung there for all to see. Execution despite being common back then was not as refined as it became decades later. The hangman didn't calculate the drop and until the 1850s the short drop was used. This avoided decapitation but often left them hanging there for minutes for all to see before dying of strangulation.

Cahill was left hanging for some time and then cut down and his body was taken to the county infirmary for dissection.

A Marriage Settlement
Lislevane Courtmacsherry 1904

Long ago in Ireland, one of the most popular times to get married was shrovetime. Marriage was not allowed during lent so anyone who couldn't or didn't want to wait forty days had to get married beforehand. Shrove Tuesday was the most common of these days and any couple that didn't manage to get married by Shrove Tuesday could be subject to mocking and jeering.

One couple that managed to marry on Shrove Tuesday was Jeremiah O'Connor and Ellen O'Leary. Ellen was a twenty three year old seamstress that lived with her parents in Lislevane near Courtmacsherry. Her father Bartholomew or Batt as he was known was the local blacksmith in the village. Batt had married Ellen Donovan back in 1870 and their daughter Ellen was their only surviving child.

Jeremiah came to Lislevane working as a journeyman the April before. Batt was getting old and needed help in the forge so Jeremiah stayed with the O'Leary's and worked with Batt as a blacksmith for three months. Jeremiah then only twenty three worked hard, was sober and got on well with everyone. He left the area briefly and worked in Bandon for a few months. He must have grown fond of young Ellen in his time with the O'Leary's and when he returned there was talk of marriage.

Back then almost all marriages were some sort of bargain. In this case, Jeremiah was coming to live with the O'Leary's and would take over the business. What they agreed was that the house and business would be given over to Jeremiah and he would become the man of the house. The old couple were to continue living in the house and be maintained from the business with a payment of £6 a year.

It seemed like an ideal arrangement, their daughter was married, the old man could retire and the business would be taken care of. Better still the forge would remain in the family except they all had to live under one roof.

About the same time in Lislevane tenants were given the opportunity to purchase their holding from the landlord the Earl of Shannon. The terms were very high, he wanted all arrears settled and twenty four years rent.

This was the beginning of the dissolution of the big estates and a chance for the ordinary man to own their plot outright.

Back in the village forge, the argument of ownership was not with the landlord but between themselves. Not long after the young couple were married the old man was moaning that Jeremiah wasn't keeping his part of the bargain. Within weeks the men in the house were not speaking to each other and the women most likely tried to keep the peace.

Jeremiah took over the forge and the old man now had nothing to occupy him except dwell on the disagreement with his son-in-law. To make matters worse the young man was doing well in the forge and was popular with his customers. Maybe Batt who needed help in recent years now couldn't bear to see someone else take over and found himself pushed aside.

As this is a book of true crime murders; someone must die in each story. One could easily imagine it would be Batt O'Leary in this case but it wasn't. On the 2nd of August 1904, there was a funeral in the village of Lislevane, by the end of the day Jeremiah O'Connor lay dead in the forge. The peace & quiet of the rural village was broken and it had been a spectacle for all to see. Nobody was in any doubt at all as to what had occurred as it was done most likely out of passion and spite in broad daylight. Many people said such a thing had never occurred in the area before, well not for about twenty years at least.

The news spread quickly and soon everyone in the area knew what had happened. The following day Jeremiah's father Timothy, mother and brother arrived in Lislevane. It must have been horrendous for them to see Jeremiah still lying there in the forge waiting for the inquest.

It was Thursday the 4th of August when coroner Neville arrived in Lislevane to hold the inquest. The body of Jeremiah O'Connor still lay covered in the forge where he had drawn his last breath. The police had kept a close eye on it and the body was not moved until the coroner arrived. The inquest was held in Barrett's public house.

A jury of fourteen local respectable men were to decide what caused the death of the young blacksmith. The jury was made up of Thomas Brophy, Jeremiah Keohane, Patrick Holland and Timothy Holland all farmers from Lislevane. Also farmers Cornelius O'Leary from Currahevern West, John O'Hea Tirrycremmin and James Hurley Ballinluhig. From Tirnaneam were Timothy Holland Carpenter and farmer, John Coleman a Mason. The remainder was John Brickley fisherman Lehenagh, Patrick Murphy, John Holland, Denis and John Donovan. District inspector Walsh from Clonakilty was there keeping an eye on the proceedings for the prosecution.

The first witness called that day was Ellen O'Connor who had been married to Jeremiah for less than six months. She formally identified the remains of her husband when he was lying in the forge. Ellen told how she had lived with Jeremiah and her parents since their wedding. She laid out the bickering and rows between the men that had led to the recent events.

Ellen recalled seeing her father take a knife from the dresser and go outside sharpening it. She demanded that he put the knife back but he refused and left the house. She watched her father leave and head towards Jeremiah Keohane's house. Her father had been at a funeral in the village that day and had some drink taken.

The next time she looked her father was standing outside Mrs Minihane's door across the street. She saw her husband cross the street and punch her father so hard he was knocked into Mrs Minihane's doorway. Ellen said it was then she ran across the street and heard her father say "you will be summoned next court day" as he regained his feet. She hit her father, warned him to keep quiet and not be saying things to her husband.

At the same time, Jeremiah tried again to hit her father but she intervened. Now it was the old man who lashed out instead. He pulled out the knife and plunged it into Jeremiah's chest. He didn't stop there and made another swing at him striking his shoulder this time.

Ellen saw blood and ran to Keohane's to send for a doctor. Meanwhile, her husband was struggling to stay on his feet and staggered back across the street. He managed to make it as far as the forge door where he fell for the last time. He never spoke another word and died a few minutes later. Answering the coroner Ellen thought this all happened about six in the evening and her husband was stabbed just inside Mrs Minihane's door.

A few minutes after her husband had died, her father came to the door of the forge and asked was he dead. Then Batt went into the house and just sat there until he was arrested. There was no sign of the murder weapon at all nor was it ever found.

Mrs Ellen Minihane was next examined and told how she heard Batt O'Leary speaking badly of Jeremiah's father that evening. Jeremiah who was still working in the forge right across the road heard it as he was meant to. He left work and came to her door saying "Batt you son of a bitch, what are you saying to my father, he is as good a man as you. I would break your face". With that, he struck Batt knocking him in her door.

Ellen described being outside when the whole thing unfolded and how she got an awful fright. She saw Batt making for Jeremiah but didn't see him being stabbed. What she did see was Jeremiah's chest covered in blood as he left and heard his wife cry out that he had been stabbed. From her door, she saw Jeremiah cross the street and fall into the forge. She turned to Batt and said "you have the man killed" but he couldn't manage a reply to her.

Dr Patrick O'Driscoll of Timoleague gave the medical evidence. He had carried out the post mortem examination with Dr Cleary from Clonakilty. The doctor described the chest wound as one inch from the breast bone, puncturing the left ventricle of the heart and the lung. The wound had bled profusely and he also found considerable internal haemorrhaging. Otherwise, he found the body to be that of a healthy man in his twenties. The second wound was in the shoulder and much smaller.

The doctor believed that a table knife with a sharp point could inflict the wound as it was over two inches deep and could not have been done with a penknife.

The coroner asked that the jury only refer to the cause of death, not who, how or whether it was wilful. Yet the foreman then remarked it was a wound in the heart.

A juror named Holland said it was wilful and the foreman again interjected with "caused by Batt Leary". After some debate, the verdict was read out "That the deceased died on the 2nd of August 1904 from a wound of the heart caused by having been stabbed by his father-in-law Bartholomew O'Leary".

With this verdict, the prosecution was now confident they would secure a conviction of wilful murder against Batt O'Leary. The murder weapon was an ordinary table knife that he had only minutes before sharpened. He was also heard provoking his son-in-law to give him an opportunity to use the knife. It would be argued that this clearly showed it was wilful premeditated murder.

The quiet village of Lislevane in more recent times.

Batt O'Leary had been in police custody since shortly after the stabbing and had not even attempted to flee before being arrested. He was brought before Justice of the Peace O'Hea and remanded to Cork Gaol.

The day after the inquest the O'Connor family took Jeremiah's remains back to Bantry for the funeral and Lislevane went back to the quiet little village it had been. For Ellen and her mother, it would never be the same again. There was now no man living in the house. It was highly unlikely Batt would be back in Lislevane any time soon. The forge next door to their house was silent for the first time.

On the 17th of August, the case came before the Petty session's court in Timoleague. There was a fair in the village that day so it was busy and crowds gathered at the train station to catch a glimpse of Batt O'Leary as he arrived on the train from Cork. He was escorted by a heavy guard of police the short distance to the courthouse. The escort was needed as the mob became angry outside the courthouse.

When the old man entered the court he was handcuffed by the police and he seemed at first unperturbed by his predicament. He was described in court as "a big, burly, muscular man" but respectable looking.

It wasn't until he saw his daughter across the room that he gave away his emotions. When Ellen first saw her father that day she cried out for all to hear and the old man couldn't bear it. Each time she cried out in court that day, he too was reduced to tears knowing the hurt he had caused.

Batt was charged that day that he did with malice aforethought unlawfully kill and slay one Jeremiah O'Connor by stabbing him.

District Inspector Walsh led the case for the prosecution while O'Leary was represented by Clonakilty Solicitor Patrick O'Donovan. Walsh gave the details of the case and then asked that the magistrates send O'Leary for trial at the Assizes once they had heard the evidence against him.

As before at the inquest, Ellen O'Connor, Mrs Minihane, doctors O'Driscoll and Cleary told the same account. Also questioned that day were carpenters Daniel and Denis O'Sullivan. They were working across the road from Mrs Minihane's that evening and had seen the scuffle between the two men. However, neither of them saw Jeremiah being stabbed that day as Ellen was in the way trying to stop the pair.

Sergeant Patrick O'Rourke told the court he first heard of the occurrence at half six that evening. He immediately proceeded to Lislevane and saw the body of Jeremiah O'Connor lying in the forge. Next door in O'Leary's house he found Batt sitting there. Without delay, he charged Batt with wilful murder giving the normal legal caution. The old man muttered something like "this is manslaughter, not murder, I suppose the place will be mine now". He thought that Batt had some drink taken; he was not drunk but quite sober.

The sergeant admitted to knowing about the trouble in the O'Leary household before that day. The March before he was called there, because Batt complained they would not give him food. O'Rourke didn't believe the complaint at the time but had to go to Lislevane to keep the peace.

The sergeant then produced the bloodstained clothes Jeremiah wore the day he was killed. Seeing this it was Ellen's mother who couldn't take any more and called out "Oh may God forgive you".

Constable Hogan then testified of also being present when Batt was arrested and told how later that evening he took charge of the prisoner in Courtmacsherry. It was then the prisoner voluntarily made a statement to him which he related to the court.

"He ran over to Nellie Sexton's threw me down and kicked me on the ground and called me a blackguard. He kicked me out of the forge on the 10th of last May. He never gave me a farthing out of the little pension he promised me. He struck me in bed on the 9th of July. Of course, I will be tried for it. A bigger blackguard never entered my house. Is he dead? I tell you I am shamed but I am not one bit sorry for it. I suppose I will be tried before a barrister. Now, will this place be mine after all this is over? I would rather be shot. It is not murder only manslaughter. Only for shame sake, I would not be one bit sorry for it. He promised me six pounds a year but never gave me threepence. They cannot hang me for it. I suppose I will suffer for it. I would confess to my God and priest my guilt and who knows it was I killed him at all. Of course, I will suffer. All they can do is hang me. There was better men than me hanged".

When the prosecution concluded Batt O'Leary was asked had he any statement to make but it was his solicitor O'Donovan who replied for him saying he refused to say anything.

O'Donovan addressed the court and made a speech on behalf of his client. He had no witnesses to call, nor evidence to produce but applied that O'Leary be allowed out on bail while waiting for the trial. The magistrates in court that day all decided that bail be refused and Batt O'Leary was sent for trial at the next Assizes. Without delay, he was escorted from the court and taken back to Cork Gaol on the 4 pm train from Timoleague.

It must have been playing on Batt's mind for the next few months waiting for the trial in jail. He knew well that the charge of murder could be proved against him and he might meet a hangman before Christmas.

On Wednesday the 7th of December at the Munster Winter Assizes in Limerick, Batt O'Leary would finally hear his fate. The case was presided over by Justice Kenny with Mr Moriarty leading the prosecution and Mr Cullinane the defence.

When called that day Batt O'Leary pleaded not guilty of wilfully killing his son-in-law on the 2nd of August. Moriarty opened the case for the prosecution by asking the jury to look beyond the accused mans advanced years. It was a case of wilful murder he said and the evidence would prove it. He suggested Batt left the house armed that day and set out to provoke his son-in-law. The old man intended to use the knife against Jeremiah and regain ownership of his house. Moriarty strongly suggested that the charge could not be reduced to manslaughter.

The evidence produced that day was a repeat of that which had been heard already. As murder cases went it was straightforward, Batt O'Leary had a motive, was seen pulling out the knife and plunging it into his son-in-law.

As Cullinane cross examined the witnesses he tried to show that it was not premeditated. Ellen admitted her father often left the house with a knife, but why then did she seem worried and try to get it from him. It was also heard that Jeremiah had assaulted Batt once before.

When the prosecution rested their case, Cullinane gave a speech to save Batt's life. He completely disagreed with Moriarty's opening speech saying there was no evidence to show Batt intended to kill just because he carried a knife. He tried to get the jury to see it from the other side. He suggested Batt had been assaulted that day by his son-in-law and then his daughter. It was only when faced with another attack from a younger stronger man that he pulled the knife. The aggressors that day were Ellen and Jeremiah according to the defence. He went further saying if Batt O'Leary was defending himself he should be acquitted of all charges.

Justice Kenny summed up for the jury and went through the circumstances for both murder and manslaughter. He made it clear if they found him guilty of murder he would be bound by law to sentence the old man to death. Kenny did concede that he believed there was no premeditation but maybe he didn't want to condemn the old man to death. He left it to the conscience of the jury to decide for themselves whether it was manslaughter or murder.

It took only twenty minutes for the jury to decide and return with their verdict guilty of manslaughter. Justice Kenny then sentenced O'Leary to four years of hard labour in prison.

Had Jeremiah stabbed his father-in-law would the jury have been so lenient? There seemed to be a reluctance to find him guilty of murder on account of his age.

After the conviction at the Winter Assizes, Batt was transferred to what was then known as Maryborough prison (now called Portlaoise prison). His four years were to start from his date of arrest in August. He was an old man to be spending time in jail and it would be hard for him to face his family on his release. Having worked hard all his life, his health failed in prison and Batt O'Leary died in the prison hospital on the 27th of

December 1906. He was buried on the grounds of the prison and in some ways was saved from the dilemma on his release.

Ellen may not have known the day she saw her husband stabbed by her father that she was about five weeks pregnant and by the time her father was convicted at the Assizes, she was five months pregnant.

Her son Jeremiah Patrick was born in March the following year and sometime later in his life, he would come to know the sad story of his male descendants. Ellen became the main breadwinner for the family and set herself up as a dressmaker to make ends meet. Her mother Ellen Senior died in March of 1911 aged seventy seven. By that time her daughter had not remarried and her son Jeremiah Patrick was six years old.

The Ballineen Four
Ballineen 1890

Cornelius Crowley a local labourer was found dead in the yard of Donovan's public house in the village of Ballineen. He was a young man and the circumstances around his death were certainly suspicious. An inquest was called to hear the evidence and decide how they believed he met his death.

When the inquest sat on the 15th of November the objective was to get the facts and find out how Cornelius Crowley came to be lying dead in the yard of the pub. The publican and the doctor's evidence were heard first. Dr Neville believed that Crowley had died as a result of direct violence.

The coroner wrote out the verdict he believed the jury should find but they refused. They were having none of it and said more evidence should be heard. Inquests at the time certainly seemed rushed as they usually found the verdict the day after death but this time the jury were not prepared to take the direction of the coroner at all.

The police district inspector stated that hearing further evidence would interfere with the police investigation. The coroner was satisfied that whatever it was would be heard later at the magisterial investigation. It wasn't just the jury though that were not satisfied with the inquest, several others present were also not happy. Coroner Dr James Somerville was put out saying he had never heard of this happening before, he must have believed the jury was there to merely agree with him. Sommerville said there was no evidence heard to incriminate anyone and so they must proceed with finding a verdict.

Eventually, the jury were encouraged to agree to an open verdict. Death was recorded as found dead, congestion of lung and clot of blood in the left ventricle of the heart from external violence. What was the secrecy behind the death of Cornelius Crowley, a twenty-five-year-old labourer?

It was the suspects! Four men had been arrested but they didn't fit the bill of your normal bar brawlers.

On Thursday the 13th of November Cornelius Crowley arrived into Patrick Donovan's public house drunk. His employer Thomas Tanner was in the pub and Crowley demanded a shilling from him. Tanner refused, asking him what he wanted the money for as if he needed to ask. Crowley persisted saying "I'm in your employment and you should give it to me". Tanner who was drinking with a few friends finally gave in and handed him two shillings. Cornelius left but returned shortly afterwards and an argument broke out between him and the Railway Station Master William Follis. Both men ended up on the ground during some kind of fracas and later Crowley was found dead in the yard of the pub.

The local police were then informed and District Inspector Roberts took over the investigation. He informed the coroner and arranged for the inquest but no arrests were made by the police.

Rumours must have spread throughout the area about what had gone on in the pub. It's hard to believe that the police couldn't get more information regarding the suspicious death but they seemed to wait for the inquest to decide how to proceed.

On Saturday morning at ten the coroner Dr Somerville opened the inquest. A jury of thirteen local respectable men were sworn in to do their duty. It was made up of foreman John Hannigan, shoemaker and shopkeeper Enniskeane, from Ballineen merchants John Hosford and Patrick Fehily, William Canty Shoemaker. From Enniskeane was publican Timothy O'Driscoll, shopkeeper George Eedy and William Hosford. More from Ballineen were: Harness maker Patrick Donovan and shopkeeper David Coakley. Also on the jury was Edwards Woods, John Canty, Patrick Peyton and J Kearney a farmer from Shanaway.

District Inspector Roberts was present for the prosecution. The first witness was Patrick Donovan the publican in whose premises Crowley had died. Donovan recalled that Thursday afternoon saying Crowley seemed very much under the influence of drink when he entered the pub. He saw Thomas Tanner giving him two shillings and then he left with William Shorten.

It was about fifteen minutes later that Crowley returned and soon he and Mr Follis had a hold of each other in an argument. The publican seemed reluctant to give details but thought both fell twice against a table.

The publican claimed that John Shorten and Jonathan Tanner tried to separate the men and all four ended up on the floor. He said Crowley got up and headed out the back to the yard and Thomas Tanner followed him. That was all the publican revealed and Crowley was found dead out the back shortly afterwards.

At this point, the inquest adjourned for a while as the doctors had not carried out a post mortem. It must have been tense that day waiting for the doctors to see would their evidence agree with the publican. It didn't though for if it had, we would not be writing about it.

Eventually, the doctors returned and were questioned. Dr Neville began by describing the injuries he found, a bruise over the left eye, a cut on the left ear and also the jaw. They had not opened the scalp as there were no signs of a serious head injury.

Neville also found wounds and bruising on the 2nd, 3rd 4th and 5th ribs, other marks on the 8th, 9th and 10th ribs. The coroner asked directly "what then was the cause of death?" The doctor reckoned direct violence. The coroner asked would a fall like the publican said, do it? Doctor Neville said it would have needed considerable force.

Doctor Purcell was of the same opinion. The coroner told the jury there was no evidence incriminating anyone and asked would they find the verdict according to the medical evidence. But first, for some reason, he asked Dr Purcell could the injury be consistent with Crowley being kicked. Dr Purcell didn't think so but Dr Neville at this point disagreed with him. Neville believed that if a person was kicked when lying on the ground, it would create such injuries. A juror asked could a violent fall have done it, and Neville said, it could, only to leave everyone even more confused. Dr Neville had examined the yard where Crowley was found and said there was nothing that he could have fallen against.

The publican was recalled as he had found Cornelius Crowley in the yard. He said that Crowley seemed dead to him and his head rested against the wheel of a sidecar.

With this the coroner tried to wrap it all up, saying "well Gentlemen, I suppose you will all agree to this verdict: that the said deceased was on the evening of the 13th found dead in the backyard of Patrick Donovan's public house and that his death was caused by direct violence." It was Patrick Fehily, juror, who objected first, saying he was here under oath to do his duty. He had no intention of agreeing on a verdict until more was heard. Fehily asked why the others present in the pub that evening were not being examined. He seemed to have a consensus with the other jurors.

The coroner replied for the District Inspector and the Resident Magistrate Captain Welsh by saying that a criminal court must investigate the matter further. Still, Fehily was having none of it, saying, inquests should go fully into the evidence before finding a verdict and he was right. Often back then the inquest would find a verdict against a particular person and they could be arrested with a coroner's warrant alone.

District Inspector Roberts assured him that the Crown would investigate it fully. Fehily was still not convinced and objected entirely saying that he would leave the inquest. When he got up to go the coroner said: "policeman stop that gentleman". A constable did what he was told and stopped Fehily from leaving. At this point, the juror was completely done with it and said he would only stay if physically forced to, which he was.

The coroner tried again asking "gentlemen, the cause of death has been shown to you by the doctors, what more do you require?" Now several of the jurors waded in and wanted to hear from the other witnesses.

Resident Magistrate Captain Welsh asked the coroner to remind the jury of a recent murder case in Macroom. On that occasion, evidence was available but wasn't gone into at the inquest. Another juror John Canty said, "we want to know why Crowley came by his death, we have only been told how". The coroner contradicting his own opinion replied "we don't know at present how death was caused" but he didn't want to hear more.

Mr Fehily who was now there against his will said he had been given a list of witnesses and only the publican had been called. They were completed divided, the jurors wanted more but the District Inspector said it would prejudice his case. Fehily asked again what of the other witnesses. The more it went on, the more it seemed like a cover up.

The coroner just wanted a verdict but the jury would not oblige. Again Fehily had enough and got up to leave for a second time, but was prevented again by the policeman. Another juror suggested adjourning until Monday but it was not accepted. The coroner threatened he was leaving at 5 that evening, either way. It was then 2 pm. He said he would leave and return at 4 and hope the verdict was agreed but he ended up never leaving the room. The District Inspector and Captain Welsh were whispering in a corner, while the jurors all agreed amongst themselves that they would not find a verdict.

Eventually, the District Inspector made an announcement saying "Mr Foreman, I wish to inform you that Mr Thomas Tanner, the clerk of the petty sessions has been arrested in connection with the case".

The coroner seemed surprised saying "he was to be a witness" yet he had no intention of calling him. Patrick Fehily was even more surprised as being local he would have known Tanner and he asked how could Tanner be arrested, saying he didn't understand it at all. Again the coroner tried to reach a verdict with "Mr Foreman do you all agree to this verdict" but the foreman refused. He then tried the opposite tack with "do you all disagree" but didn't get a consensus either.

Fehily then changed tack also and suggested signing the verdict although it was most likely sarcastic. He asked again why Tanner had been arrested with "I think it was wrong to arrest Thomas Tanner, there is no evidence against him". The district inspector put his foot in it with his reply "oh but we have evidence against him though". Patrick Fehily admitted he didn't know much about the law but still felt the evidence should be heard at the inquest before anyone was arrested.

The coroner tried, at last, to explain the function of an inquest without going into too much legal jargon. He said the inquest's duty was to find how the deceased came by his death and by what cause but didn't need to know by whom. But then he admitted that the inquest had failed to find how Crowley had met his death.

He said a coroner couldn't examine an accused person at the inquest except with permission from the Queen's Bench. Maybe he was trying to say that all those present in the pub that day were suspects and would become the accused.

The local clergy then waded in saying that people had little confidence that justice would be served. He said this explained why the jury wished to hear all the evidence.

The coroner tried one last time to obtain a verdict with "if you don't reach a verdict our business is finished if you bring in an open verdict such as I read for you, you commit yourselves to nothing, the crown will be sure to investigate fully".

It was Fehily again intervened asking why Tom Tanner had been arrested saying "there is no evidence against Tom Tanner beyond that he went into the yard where Crowley was found". He asked why others had not been arrested.

In what seemed to be a distraction the District Inspector suddenly let on he would allow more witnesses to be examined asking for a list. The coroner didn't know where it was going to go at all and seemed exasperated "in all my life I have never seen such a thing". It went on like this for a while before finally the jury gave in and signed the verdict the coroner had earlier suggested.

Once the inquest was over there was a special sitting of the petty sessions by Captain Welsh, the Resident Magistrate. Thomas Tanner was charged in the very court he was normally the clerk of. The police were sent out to arrest the other suspects, William Follis the railway station master, farmer Jonathan Tanner and John Shorten harness maker. They were all produced before Captain Welsh and all four were charged.

The prosecution called Robert Driscoll a labourer who happened to be passing Donovan's pub the night in question when he heard some noise from the kitchen. He went into the yard and saw Crowley, Thomas Tanner, Jonathan Tanner and John Shorten. Crowley was saying something to Thomas Tanner. Next, he witnessed Thomas Tanner catch Crowley with one hand and make a go for him with the other but missed. A second blow struck Crowley who fell against the cartwheel. Tanner told Driscoll to close the gate, which he said he pulled out and left.

Driscoll said he didn't stay away from the yard long returning about fifteen minutes later to find people standing over Crowley saying he was dead. It struck Driscoll that Crowley was in a different position than when he left. When he pulled out the gate Crowley's legs pointed towards the pub door but on returning Crowley's legs were towards the gate.

As the four accused had not yet employed legal representation it was up to themselves to cross examine. All four declined to examine Driscoll which was telling in itself. Thomas Tanner was well aware of the normal goings on in court and that when the accused questioned a witness they often fell into the trap of incriminating themselves further.

That night all four were remanded into custody and taken to Cork Gaol until the following Thursday when they would appear before the Ballineen Petty sessions. It must have been strange for Follis to pass through Ballineen Station that evening as a prisoner rather than the stationmaster.

The inquest was badly managed at best and left nobody with any clue of what had actually happened. After all the drama of the inquest, the courtroom in Ballineen was packed on Thursday 20th November, as people wanted to finally hear the details.

That day the 4 suspects were brought back to Ballineen by train. Everyone strained to catch a glimpse of them now that they were prisoners. Before Resident Magistrate Captain Welsh and Achilles Daunt all 4 were charged with the murder of Cornelius Crowley on the 13th. Thomas Tanner knew well what to expect in court, being the clerk of the petty sessions. He was really in a predicament as the deceased was also his employee.

District Inspector Roberts was there to fulfil the promise he made at the inquest to investigate the matter fully. Jonathan Tanner and John Shorten were represented by solicitor P McCarthy from Bandon, William Follis also had a Bandon solicitor, Mr Levis and Thomas Tanner employed Dunmanway solicitor, Mr F Fitzmaurice.

It was Dr Morgan O'Brien Neville from Warrensbrook that was first called. He said about 5 pm on the 13th he got a report of a man "dead drunk" in Donovan's public house. The doctor arrived to find Cornelius Crowley stretched before the kitchen fire dead. In the doctor's initial examination, he found cuts and bruises on the face. He examined the pub and went to the yard where there was a sidecar, the shafts of which pointed to the street and on one of the spokes of a wheel he found a spot of fresh blood.

He told how he found more wounds during the post mortem; one cut was inside the upper lobe of the left ear. This was where he believed the blood on the wheel spoke had come from. He described the cuts and wounds on the chest and over the ribs. The left lung was congested while the other was normal. The right ventricle of the heart was also heavily congested with blood which led him to believe death was due to shock as a result of direct violence. He thought the wound over the left eyebrow could not have been done with a punch, but something narrow and sharp. However, he thought the blow on the jaw was the result of a fist. The doctor couldn't see how Crowley would have walked any distance after sustaining such injuries.

Cross examined by Levis he was asked how long could Crowley have lived after the injury to the heart, the doctor replied only 10 or 12 seconds. The real question was how did he get to the yard, but Levis asked was he beaten in the yard. The doctor couldn't say. Each of the defence solicitors tried to question the doctor but little more was revealed. Dr Neville was inclined to say a fall couldn't have done it but he couldn't completely rule it out either.

Fitzmaurice asked would a fall against the table or other furniture in the kitchen have done it. The doctor seemed reluctant but admitted a fall on the corner of a chair might have. The defence was grasping for excuses but the magistrate stood up for the doctor.

Dr George Purcell, as before, concurred with his colleague on the cause of death. He believed that Crowley had suffered two distinct injuries with some time between, but he couldn't say how long. He said that Crowley received the injury to the lung first as that did not kill him. As for the injury to the heart, however, he agreed with Dr Neville that Crowley couldn't have survived more than ten seconds afterwards.

It must have been hoped that day that if anyone could clear up the matter it would be the publican as he was present after all. Patrick Donovan was sworn in and began by saying that Cornelius Crowley came to his pub at about 4 pm on the 13th. He went out to the yard and tackled a pony for a Mr Cotter who then bought him a drink. He said Crowley was under the influence of drink but could walk about and talk.

He named those present on the premises at the time as Thomas Tanner, Jonathan Tanner, John Shorten, James Shorten a shopkeeper in the village, Bessie Connell an aunt of the publican and Michael Donovan the publican's brother. When Mr Cotter left with the pony Crowley entered the pub again and went into the kitchen where Thomas Tanner was. He heard Crowley demanding money from Tanner who said: "I don't see that you want it at the present time". Crowley persisted demanding "why not you give it to me, haven't I earned it from you". Donovan saw Tanner hand over a shilling and then another when Crowley asked again. With that Crowley went to the bar offering to treat James Shorten but was refused by the publican's brother. Donovan said he was then asked to serve but he also refused Crowley saying he had enough and was not fit company for those present.

Donovan was then asked by the magistrate "did you refuse him because he had too much drink taken or because you wanted to get rid of him?" The publican said it was for both reasons, explaining that Crowley could be rough with drink taken and he was nervous. Crowley then left for another pub with William Shorten but returned not long afterwards on his own. He said Crowley went into the kitchen again where William Follis the stationmaster was standing at the fireplace.

The publican believed he heard Crowley calling Follis the Stationmaster names and then caught him by the collar of his coat. Follis did likewise to Crowley and they shook each other about roughly but no blows were exchanged. They pulled each other around for a few minutes and both fell against the table and ended up on the floor. When they got up both men insulted each other again before resuming the struggle.

The publican said they caught hold of each other once more and this time fell even harder against the table. It was then that Jonathan Tanner and John Shorten stepped in.

Daunt asked did Crowley appear weaker after falling against the table for a second time but Donovan was not sure.

He said when Tanner and Shorten got involved all four fell on the ground roughly, on top of each other. He recalled Crowley was on the bottom with Jonathan Tanner on top of him.

Daunt asked the publican did it seem like all the others had turned on Crowley. The publican didn't think so, saying Tanner and Shorten initially tried to make the peace. When they got up he said Crowley grabbed a saucepan from under the table and he thought he made a go for Jonathan Tanner. The publican said he was standing in the door between the pub and the kitchen and had a clear view of everything. It was his brother Michael who took the saucepan from Crowley who he said appeared exhausted from it all.

It was John Shorten who caught hold of Crowley around the waist and flung him down between the tables. In his efforts, John also fell and while on the ground struck Crowley with a punch to the head or face. John Shorten got up unaided but the publican couldn't say the same with any certainty for Crowley. He saw Jonathan Tanner make a kick at Crowley but wasn't sure if he actually hit him. At this point, the publican admitted being confused with the whole thing as there was so much going on. He described it as a lot of pulling and hauling and he didn't know it was serious until Crowley was thrown down.

After Tanner tried to kick Crowley, Donovan said not much more happened. Crowley went out to the yard, Thomas Tanner having gone out before him. John Shorten went to the yard also. Donovan recalled it being noisy but he still heard Crowley say something to Tanner. The publican could no longer see what was going on but Daunt asked if had any idea what was happening based on what he heard. He couldn't be sure but thought Crowley seemed weak when he said to Tanner "You're as bad as another to me to allow the other parties to beat me". Tanner did not reply. The publican knew this as he was now looking in the yard and saw Crowley pointing at Tanner.

Next, he saw Crowley make a go for Thomas Tanner, who pushed him away. Crowley fell against a cartwheel, but Donovan didn't know if he banged his head against it or not. That was it according to the publican and then he heard Tanner say "I think the man is dead or nearly dead". Donovan ran out, stood over Crowley and found the same. The publican said he was out of his mind about it, but arranged for him to be brought into the kitchen and the doctor sent for.

Each of the defence solicitors then got their chance to question the key witness and attempt to make it look better for their respective clients. Levis who represented Follis asked, "was it your duty to turn Crowley out being under the influence of drink?" Donovan suggested he could also have turned Follis out too for he was also under the influence. He denied Levis' suggestion that Follis had only come to tell him a case of soda water was at the train station for him. The publican said Follis and Crowley were equally as rough in the struggle which lasted a few minutes. The publican made out it was all Crowley's fault saying only for him there would have been no argument. He believed Crowley was an alcoholic and was troublesome after drink. He said Crowley brought it on himself; Follis only did what he did to defend himself.

Solicitor McCarthy who represented Jonathan Tanner and John Shorten was next to question the publican who admitted that Jonathan Tanner said nothing while Crowley and Follis struggled. He said John Shorten was the first to intervene but failed and Jonathan Tanner then helped him separate them. With McCarthy's encouragement, the publican said that during the struggle Jonathan Tanner did nothing but attempt to kick Crowley.

Donovan was aware that Crowley and John Shorten were friendly but had heard Crowley insulting him that day. He now revealed that Jonathan Tanner and John Shorten shoved Crowley towards the door when Thomas was already in the yard.

When questioned by Fitzmaurice who represented Thomas Tanner, the publican said he never knew Tanner to be in trouble before and he had known him for 17 years. When the tussle went on in the kitchen that day Thomas Tanner never got involved. In the yard, he raised his hand to prevent Crowley from hitting him but it would not have knocked a sober man he thought. He also believed Tanner only gave Crowley money that day for the sake of getting some peace from him.

The District Inspector then asked how Crowley appeared to be after being flung down by Shorten. Donovan admitted he seemed injured by it. One of the magistrates then asked the publican to clarify the state of the accused men that night. He said Thomas Tanner appeared sober, Jonathan Tanner had some drink, John Shorten was slightly under the influence and Follis, who he earlier said was as bad as Crowley, he said had some drink taken.

There was no more evidence heard that day but instead of a lengthy remand, the proceedings were only adjourned till the following morning when the publican's brother was called and his version of events was much shorter than Patrick's. He saw Follis attacked by Crowley and the whole lot of them fell to the ground. He thought at the time it was funny when they fell in the kitchen and didn't think the argument was serious. Michael also saw John Shorten strike Crowley a blow to the head with his fist while on the ground.

The next witness was John Shorten but not the accused, another one. In all of the publican's testimony, it had not been made clear that there were, in fact, two John Shorten's in the pub that day. This John Shorten was a cattle dealer from Kilnacranagh West, while the accused was a harness maker. He saw his namesake strike Crowley a blow to the head with his fist but from there, his version was different to that of the publican. He said Crowley never got up again, while John Shorten got up of his own accord. What he said next was even more shocking, Jonathan Tanner and John Shorten dragged Crowley out of the kitchen. A minute or two later he heard Crowley was dead in the yard.

The magistrate summed up what he had heard that day and quickly returned all four for trial at the next assizes. After all the drama at the inquest the magisterial investigation ended quickly but who was telling the truth? Only for what John Shorten, the cattle dealer had said there was no hope of it being returned for trial. It was strange that the doctors gave the medical evidence first and the witnesses were allowed to hear it. Patrick Donovan's version seemed concocted to fit in with what the doctors had said. It is easy to see they all wanted to be rid of Crowley from the pub that day as he was annoying at best when drunk. All those present thought they were a class above him but now they had to answer to the law.

One can't help feeling that if it was Thomas Tanner for instance that lay dead in the yard that the inquest and investigation would have been far different. If the cattle dealer was telling the truth it seems they dragged Crowley out after beating him, only to drag him back into the kitchen again when they realised it was serious. Now it was all up to a jury in December as to whether the four, so called respectable gentlemen, would be found guilty of such a serious charge.

William Follis who struggled with Crowley was the Station Master of Ballineen railway station. At sixty three years old he was a retired RIC head constable who had been stationed in Cahersiveen and Dunmanway for many years. In his time in the RIC he would have encountered many such situations. He had only been widowed the year before.

Thirty five year old Thomas Tanner was well known in Ballineen being the clerk of the petty sessions and living in Ballineen House at the west end of the village.

Jonathan Tanner was a twenty eight year old farmer from Caher, a townland to the west of Ballineen. He had married Mary Daunt only a year or so before and she was pregnant with their first child. Jonathan had also been in the police a few years previous. John Shorten was a harness maker; he was about forty years old and unmarried.

Ballineen House outside the village where Thomas Tanner lived at the time.

On Tuesday the 9th of December the Munster Winter Assizes were held in Nenagh. For the Ballineen four, it was the first time the legal proceedings were held away from the village. Up until then everyone involved from the inquest jurors to the magistrates would have known them well. Now they were just four ordinary suspects the same as everyone else when called before Justice O'Brien.

For the four the charge had been reduced to manslaughter by the crown, so the threat to their own lives no longer existed. Still, it was a very serious charge against them, all pleaded not guilty.

The sheer amount of legal representation was confusing, to say the least. Now the crown prosecution was carried out by Mr Stephen Ronan Queens Counsel, Mr J.B Sandford and Mr H.T Wright Crown Solicitor. Dr Falconer with Bandon solicitor Mr Levis represented William Follis. John Shorten and Jonathan Tanner had Mr Powell and Mr P O'Sullivan also a Bandon solicitor. Finally, Thomas Tanner had employed Redmond Barry as well as Dunmanway solicitor Mr Fitzmaurice.

It was Mr Ronan who opened the case for the crown by first speaking about the four accused men. He said they appeared to be four respectable men to him in court and their records also proved this. All 4 were friends in a pub, more or less under the influence. Ronan painted the scene in the pub, enter the lowly figure of Cornelius Crowley, a servant boy. He said Crowley was a younger more vigorous man, and he was disrespectful to his social superiors. He was later found dead outside, his body bruised and injured.

He didn't make out that the 4 intended to harm Crowley to such an extent but said the violence was inflicted by them. It led to the young man's death and now the jury had to decide was it lawful or unlawful? In other words, could they prove self defence; otherwise Ronan said they were guilty of manslaughter.

The first witness was Patrick Donovan, the publican, who gave a similar account as before. Now though we know his testimony was at serious odds with John Shorten, the cattle dealer. Donovan ran into trouble in his account when he said his brother took the saucepan from the deceased who didn't appear exhausted. The judge pulled him on that saying he previously stated the opposite. Ronan asked did he give a statement to Mr Wright only 2 days previous saying Crowley was exhausted. Now though the publican said "he appeared to be pretty strong at the time". The judge then asked the jury to ignore the last statement from the witness.

The prosecution now had the publican conflicting his own story never mind that of anybody else. He had just made the case for the prosecution by proving he could not be trusted. The examination of Donovan then went on to the kick Jonathan Tanner made at Crowley. The publican still refused to say Tanner kicked his head despite it being proved Crowley's head was closest to Tanner. Donovan did reveal though that Crowley had complained that Tanner had kicked him at the time.

He still maintained Crowley went to the yard of his own accord after Thomas. He thought Jonathan Tanner and John Shorten were close to Crowley and maybe shoved him out.

Ronan was clever not to question the publican on the cattle dealer's version; instead he left the publican to prove nothing. Ronan then recalled an earlier statement of the publicans saying "listen to this; Crowley appeared to have no strength from the time he fell until the time he went into the yard". The publican now refuted this with ambiguity, saying Crowley had some strength.

When Ronan had proved his point, it was Dr Falconer, one of the defence who stood. The judge stopped him, saying he could see no case against Mr Follis. Instead, Mr Powell rose for John Shorten and Jonathan Tanner and tried to clear his clients. It went on picking over small points as Donovan was inclined to be unclear. At one point a juror intervened asking the publican, did he not try to stop it and make peace? It was Justice O'Brien who quickly replied with "he tried to make money". With this, it was shown to the jury that the publican's interest was in the 4 well off friends, not the poor labourer. Michael Donovan, his aunt Bessie Connell, and all generally backed up the publican.

But it was the cattle dealer John Shorten who did not, he told the court that when he first saw Crowley carried out of the pub, he thought it was to give him air after the effects of drink. The remainder heard that day was merely a repeat of before. Dr Neville concluded by saying Crowley died from shock, caused by extreme violence but the prosecution did not call Dr Purcell who was present.

When the prosecution rested, the defence called Dr Purcell, who now claimed the death happened quickly, the result in his opinion, of a fall.

The defence called Daniel Connor, a justice of the peace from Manch. He gave a good character reference for Thomas Tanner. Redmond Barry, representing Thomas Tanner called Sergeant McAllister who was at the magisterial investigation. He swore to hearing Thomas Tanner say "I admit I gave him a shove but the shove I gave him would not hurt a fly". He also heard Shorten say "This is a nice way we are treated when we were only acting as peacemakers".

Dr Falconer made the case for his client Mr Follis who he said was an old man. He maintained that Follis only did what he did in self defence and when Crowley was on the ground outside Follis went to his aid. The solicitor also drew the jury's attention to William Follis' long career as a head constable and his good conduct.

Mr Powell argued for Jonathan Tanner that he only separated Crowley and Follis to keep the peace. Of the alleged kick Powell said even if he had done it, Dr Purcell said Crowley died of a fall.

Redmond Barry claimed that his client Thomas Tanner took no part in the violence in the kitchen. He quoted Crowley's statement "you are as bad as the others, you let them beat me" saying this proved it. Barry made out that Tanner's action in the yard was merely self defence. He then pleaded with the jury to acquit Thomas Tanner saying he had nine children and if convicted would lose his job.

The proceedings went on late into the night in an attempt to complete the case in one day. Justice O'Brien went over all the evidence heard that day for the jury. He couldn't see how Follis' actions led to the death of Crowley. The judge seemed convinced though that Crowley got a beating which resulted in his death. It was up to the jury to decide did the men act in self defence or did they inflict more force than was necessary.

The jury took over two hours to reach a verdict. They found John Shorten and Jonathan Tanner guilty of manslaughter; the others were to be acquitted. Justice O'Brien was confused and asked the clerk did they find Thomas Tanner not guilty. Still not satisfied with the reply he asked for the slip of paper the clerk had gotten from the foreman and read it himself. Still, after reading it he asked again "do you say Thomas Tanner is not guilty?" It took the foreman to confirm this time that they had. The judge asked again as if there was confusion between the two Tanners "you mean the man who was outside in the yard". When he was told again that Thomas Tanner was to be acquitted he asked on what grounds had they reached this decision. The foreman said, "because we believe that if Crowley was not nearly dead at the time of the light shove he received from Thomas Tanner it would not have injured him". Eventually, the judge seemed satisfied saying "very well" and moved on addressing the guilty men.

Justice O'Brien made it very clear he believed that the court had not heard the real cause of death. He said Crowley's behaviour in the bar that day did not remove any responsibility from any of them. He claimed that Crowley was dragged from the pub in a dying state.

Crowley had been struck by John Shorten and then Jonathan Tanner attempted and possibly succeeded in kicking Crowley as he lay there on the ground. He was not impressed at all with the evidence of the publican Patrick Donovan claiming he had been dishonest. Justice O'Brien was sure that Crowley had suffered a much more severe beating than had been told to the court but couldn't prove it now. Finally, before handing out the sentence he reminded the pair that it would be much more severe except for these extenuating circumstances. Both John Shorten and Jonathan Tanner were given six months of hard labour dated from their first day of imprisonment in November.

Thomas Tanner maintained his job as clerk of the petty sessions and his place in society as did Mr Follis. For the other two, six months hard labour must have come as a shock, but it wasn't long considering Cornelius Crowley had lost his life. One can't help think that if it was Thomas Tanner that had been kicked, dragged about and died those responsible would have suffered much longer sentences. At the end of it all, it was not murder and there was no deadly assassin lying in wait for the victim. It was a few minutes of a bar brawl gone wrong. It highlights the stark social hierarchy that existed at the time, even the prosecution referred to the four men as Crowley's "social superiors". Back then the law believed that a brutal crime like this was an act of the lower classes not respectable gentlemen, but that wasn't always the case.

The following year a civil case was taken by Mary Crowley the elderly mother of Cornelius. It was alleged that the old woman was completely dependent on her son and now had no means to live on. She sued Jonathan and Thomas Tanner for £500 damages resulting in the death of her son.

Donovan's pub in Ballineen depicted by Claire O'Donovan

The case was defended and argued that Cornelius Crowley was prone to drink and had not contributed much to his mother. It was proven that he had been sacked about twelve times by Thomas Tanner in six years.

Thomas Tanner's solicitor argued his client had only put up his hand to protect himself against Crowley. Jonathan Shorten's legal counsel made a similar argument.

Then some people were surprised in March when a petition was asking for signatures in Ballineen. It was to be sent to the Lord Lieutenant asking for the release of Jonathan Tanner. No such petition was set up for John Shorten nor was he even mentioned. Some suggested this was because Tanner was a well off protestant while Shorten was a Catholic. Dr Joseph Kenny who was an MP for South Cork was to bring the matter up in the House of Commons.

The damages case rumbled on without a decision and was heard by arbitrators later in March. Mr Powell representing the old woman said the case was one of damages and just to agree on an amount. He suggested it should be based on the expected life of the deceased who was only twenty six.

When Mary Crowley was questioned she said her son was healthy and paid her rent as well as giving her 6 shillings a week. Dr Neville was also called and proved that Crowley was medically healthy before he died.

Thomas Tanner however told that he only paid Crowley £6 annually and reckoned Crowley would spend half on drink alone. Powell jokingly suggested that £3 would not cover what he drank himself in a year and maybe £10 might not also.

Bandon solicitor Mr McCarthy for Jonathan Tanner conceded a little, instead of arguing against compensation he argued it should be based upon the life expectancy of the old woman and not the deceased. No decision was made on the case that day.

The following month some settlement was made out of court to Mary Crowley.

Then later in April Jonathan Tanner was released from prison five weeks before his sentence was finished, but Shorten was not. This divided opinion of the people in the area who felt Jonathan Tanner was getting preferential treatment.

It was Dr Tanner a controversial Home Rule MP for Mid Cork that brought up the matter in the House of Commons. He asked Arthur Balfour the Chief Secretary for Ireland why was Jonathan Tanner released early and Shorten remained in prison. Balfour referred to the petition for Tanner's release and how it had been signed by the Protestant Rector and the Parish Priest. He said the Lord Lieutenant had ordered Tanner's release because of the petition and that the civil case had been agreed upon. Dr Tanner suggested it was because Jonathan Tanner was a wealthy protestant, while Shorten was an ordinary Catholic but Balfour would not be drawn on the issue. It was a few weeks later when Jonathan Shorten was released.

A Shocking Discovery
Near Chetwynd Viaduct Rochfordstown 1908

On the evening of Sunday the 28th of June, John Murphy was walking along the road by the Chetwynd Viaduct with his brother. He left the road going towards a fox cover. Here he noticed a patch of grass below him on the bank of a stream had been flattened by recent activity. Looking a little closer he noticed two little feet sticking out of the ground.

One of the men went off to Victoria Barracks and soon Sergeant Kinahan was on the scene investigating. He found a baby only a few weeks old crudely buried headfirst in a shallow grave. Kinahan began by questioning the locals had they seen anything suspicious in the area in the last few days. One young girl had spoken to a woman with a baby who was looking for the way to Kinsale. The baby was crying at the time and the woman was feeding it milk from a lemonade bottle.

The next day coroner Horgan held an inquest to enquire into the circumstances surrounding the death of the baby. All that was heard was the evidence of finding the body near the stream and a few locals who had seen a woman nearby. Dr Keating proved that the baby had died from suffocation from drowning in the stream only a few yards away.

All the inquest could do was to find that the baby died from drowning but they had no information to identify it or the mother at that point.

The hunt began to find this woman who it seemed had been walking about the roads with a newborn baby. More investigation led the Sergeant to a house in the city and Mrs Ahern there admitted a young woman with a baby had been staying with her but left on the 26th when the baby would not stop crying. Mrs Ahern identified the baby's body and now the search began for the mother Julia, who was alone and believed to be vulnerable.

Following her likely path to Kinsale amounted to nothing and there was no trace of her there. What they did find out was that the baby had been born in Dunmanway a few weeks before and the woman told people she had walked to Cork. The baby's father was a merchant seaman and Julia was heading to meet him when his ship landed there.

It was a few days later though before there was a breakthrough in the case. On Saturday evening the 5th of July just after eight in the evening

Julia Kingston was arrested in Cockpit Lane off the Coal Quay by Sergeant Bryan of the nearby Bridewell.

Mrs Finn who had helped Julia near Waterfall was then brought to the barracks to identify her. Seeing the woman who had helped her out Julia broke down saying "I was in your house, I will tell the truth".

From the birth records, the baby was recorded as Thomas Kingston born in Dunmanway Workhouse Hospital on the third of June. The father was stated as Thomas Kingston sailor of no fixed abode. Julia gave her maiden name as Connolly but no record of the marriage to Thomas in the preceding years has been found. Aside from the fact, the father was away at sea, Julia gave away no other details of their domestic arrangement at the time. It's possible they were not married at all and this could be why she did not seem to have the support of any family.

From the Police enquiries at the Workhouse hospital, they discovered Julia had spent some time there under the care of District Nurse Mary Agnes Coffey. She had left Dunmanway on the 17th of June and the nurse told them the baby was healthy then. She had also told the staff of the Hospital that her husband was in the merchant navy and her maiden name was Connolly.

Julia was then brought before justice of the peace Dr Magner and remanded to custody for eight days in the Cork City prison. A few days later at the Douglas Petty sessions, Julia was charged with the murder of her own baby. The medical evidence was heard of how the baby had been drowned and then buried nearby the stream.

Sergeant Bryan gave evidence of arresting Julia in Cockpit Lane in the city. He told the court that when he cautioned her she said "My god Sergeant who said that? I admit that I gave birth to a child about a month ago. It is not a month ago altogether. Who is going to swear against me? Will I get twelve months for it? I suppose I will. What ought I do Sergeant? Don't be hard on me. I gave the child to a woman in Douglas Street. I cannot tell you her name, I gave her 35s to mind it for me and she said she would send it to the workhouse when I would be away. I was out the road near Waterfall; I called into a house and was speaking to a woman. Wasn't I a fool to come back here at all".

It was also heard in court that Julia had told the story that she had given birth to a baby a few weeks before but claimed to have handed it over to a woman in Douglas who she had also given 35 shillings.

The judge decided that from what he had heard a prima facie case existed and Julia was sent for trial at the upcoming Assizes.

By modern standards, the justice system back then could be very swift as less than a month after the killing Julia Kingston was at the Cork Assizes before Justice Fitzgibbon charged with the dreadful act. The indictment read out to her was that on the 26th of June she killed and murdered her child aged three weeks and three days named Thomas Kingston.

Mr McElligott representing the accused asked for a jury to be empanelled to enquire into whether Julia was fit to plead or not. Justice Fitzgibbon agreed with him asking had he the evidence to produce.

Dr James Cashman one of the medical officers at the Lunatic Asylum was called. The doctor had examined her only that morning and described her as "I think she is of low mental calibre, low intellect but at the same time I am of the opinion that she is not insane and can understand the gravity of the charge made against her". He then went on to say she was "neurotic and of hysterical temper". He believed she would have enough understanding to follow the case in court but would not be able to challenge a juror.

The doctor was then asked:
In the course of your investigation into this case did you discover that after the confinement the milk function of one of the breasts ceased? Yes.
Is it evidence of insanity? It is a premonitory symptom.

Justice Fitzgibbon then suggested that this might also be applied to the question of her sanity at the time of the killing. The judge said that the evidence also pointed towards Julia not being fit to plead. The doctor was asked again and he still believed she was fit to plead and understand the legal procedure.

So the case went on and Mr Moriarty opened the case by describing in detail Julia Kingston's movements and how the child came to be found. He outlined for the jury the different options before them. They might decide it was an accidental death and she would be acquitted. If they believed she had been involved in the death he said the verdict must be guilty of murder and her life would be forfeited. Or they could reach the decision that Julia Kingston was suffering from insanity at the time and not responsible for her actions.

The prosecution then called several witnesses to prove Julia was seen near the Viaduct with a baby. Mrs Margaret Finn who lived near Waterfall identified the accused saying she had called to her house on the 24th of June. Julia had a baby with her and told her she had walked from Innishannon. She also mentioned how she was going to Cork to meet her brother who lived there.

Another woman from Waterfall that gave evidence was Julia O'Keeffe. On the 24th of June about half six her dog was barking and she went out to find Julia Kingston on the road. Mrs O'Keeffe said she was feeding the baby who she called Tommy and described him as "a fine fair child". They spent about ten minutes talking on the road and Julia told her she was weak after walking from Innishannon. This time she said she was going to Cork to meet her husband a merchant sailor.

The scene at Chetwynd Viaduct depicted by Claire O'Donovan

However, it was Mrs Anne Ahern of Grattan street Cork who was called. At about ten o clock on the night of the 24th of June Julia came to her house. Anne told the court she had known Julia before that night but didn't explain how. It must have been a while since they met as when Julia came into her house that night she said "look Mrs Ahern what I have for you" showing her the baby. Anne then warmed some milk for the baby and Julia fed the child.

Julia told her she had come from the Dunmanway Workhouse and had nowhere to go. Anne offered her a place to stay and she did for two days but left on Friday with the baby. Before Julia left she gave her a lemonade bottle full of milk, Anne now identified the bottle found at the scene as being the same. She had also bought clothes for the baby when Julia was staying with her and identified these when produced in court.

When Julia left that Friday she told the Ahern's she was going to Douglas Street where she had found a nurse to look after the child. Anne warned her to make sure nothing happened to the baby and it was looked after, Julia said "indeed no mam, I would not do anything like that". The baby had been crying that morning and Julia left saying she did want it bothering Mrs Ahern's husband.

Anne then told the court she went out the following morning and met Julia by the chapel close to her house. Anne asked where she spent the night but Julia told her she had been up all night as Tommy was cross. She also mentioned the woman in Douglas Street and that she was kind to the baby. Later that day Julia returned asking for a change meaning nappy for the baby.

It was a week later on the evening of Saturday the 4th of July before Anne met Julia again. Anne told the court how she asked about the baby and Julia said it was grand. Julia then said her husband was joining the army and asked would she take in the baby, to which Anne agreed. Julia mentioned she had left Douglas Street and was now on the Ballinlough road and even told her to come to see the baby there. The defence declined to cross examine Mrs Ahern that day.

Sergeant Kinahan told the court how he went to the scene near the viaduct of the 28th and described retrieving the baby's body. Later he went back to the scene and found a lemonade bottle thirteen feet away from where the body was found.

The sergeant had conveyed Julia from the Bridewell to Douglas court and there she made a statement to him. McElligott objected to this statement being entered as evidence saying that the accused was of a weak mind, otherwise he would not object. Justice Fitzgibbon though allowed it and the Sergeant went on telling Julia had asked him "what will I do Sergeant? Will I tell the truth?" Returning from the court she asked

"When will I be brought up again? I suppose I will go up for two years? I will tell the truth. The father of the child is a merchant sailor; he is the mate of the vessel. He wrote me a letter he was coming to Cork. They will bury me in the gaol. I can't stick it. Then going to the Bridewell for a second time she once more opened up to him saying "What will I do? I am ashamed. It will kill me. I know the two women that were against me the last day. I could chalk a line from their house. Sergeant if I got a chance I could go into a convent."

Despite his objections, McElligott cross examined the witness and the sergeant admitted that Julia was highly excited when she had spoken to him. A juror then asked about the hole the baby was found in and Sergeant Kinahan said he believed the hole had been dug by hand.

A young girl was then called in court, Hannah Mary Cronin a ten year old that lived near the Viaduct. On the evening of the 26th of June, she was going to the well for water when she met the accused with a baby, who asked for a drink of water. She then saw her feeding the baby from a bottle and asked how far it was to Kinsale. As she left the woman was heading towards the viaduct trying to put the baby to sleep.

Dr Keating from Ballinhassig when questioned by Sergeant Moriarty gave the medical evidence. He had at first carried out a superficial examination and only found a small circular mark on the nose that corresponded to a hole in the baby's clothing which had been wrapped around the head.

During the post mortem when he was assisted by Dr O'Flynn water came from the nose and mouth, the lungs were filled with water. In the stomach, he found a milky fluid that appeared to be watered down. When asked by Moriarty, the doctor concluded that death was by suffocation from being submerged in water. The Sergeant asked again to clarify "you mean it was drowned while alive?" Yes.

McElligott cross examined asking about the baby and the doctor told him it appeared to have been well developed, healthy and well nourished.

One of the jury then asked, "would you infer the body was completely submerged?" The doctor replied, "I would not say completely submerged but it would require the head to be submerged to fill the lungs".

At this point, Sergeant Kinahan was called to give further information on where the baby was found. He described a pool of water a foot deep that was only six yards from where the body was found. He also told that the stream nearby did not run dry.

The prosecution then rested their case against Julia Kingston and McElligott made the case for the defence. He called Dr Cashman again hoping to prove Julia's mental state. He asked Dr Cashman "have you arrived at any conclusion as to her mental condition on the 26th of June". Strangely the doctor replied, "oh no I am only concerned with her mental condition at the present time." The doctor did say he had no reason to believe her mental state had changed since the 26th of June. Dr Cashman reiterated his earlier opinion that Julia was able to understand the seriousness of what she was being accused of, she was hysterical and neurotic but not insane.

The judge probed further about her likely mental state after childbirth. Dr Cashman told the court he was experienced in dealing with women suffering from mental issues after childbirth. He believed that the evidence that one of Julia's breasts stopped lactating could be an indication she was suffering from puerperal mania.

In summing up for the jury Justice Fitzgibbon laid out the options and the different possibilities of a verdict the jury may reach. He asked to consider all the facts saying he found it a most peculiar case. Infanticide he believed was common at the time but remarked it was normally unmarried mothers calling them children of shame. The judge had no reason to believe that Julia was not married as she had given the same story on so many different occasions. If it was a delusion though he did think it might reveal the woman's mental state even more.

He asked the jury to consider Julia's wandering since leaving the workhouse, the affection she had shown for the baby; really he was asking them to take some pity on the woman and her awful predicament. On the subject of motive he made no suggestion then Fitzgibbon posed several questions to the jury:

1. Did the prisoner commit the act charged of killing the child, Thomas Kingston as alleged?
2. If so, was the prisoner at the time of the doing of the act insane, so as not to be responsible according to the law?
3. If so responsible was the act wilful and of malice aforethought?
4. Was the act unlawful but without malice?
5. Was the act involuntary and without culpable neglect of duty?

The jury were only gone for twenty minutes when the foreman returned and handed a slip of paper to the clerk. They found that Julia had committed the killing as accused but without intent as she was insane at the time and not responsible for her actions. It was announced she was guilty of manslaughter but not responsible due to her mental state at the time. Justice Fitzgibbon then sentenced her to be held in custody at the will and pleasure of the Lord Lieutenant.

On the 25th of July, she was transferred to the Dundrum Central Mental Hospital. The judge had seemed convinced that Julia was telling the truth about being married but when she was held in custody records show that the next of kin was left blank. She told so many different stories, meeting her husband in Cork and also her brother. Yet she told Anne Ahern who she knew well enough to stay with that she had nowhere to go. Julia even went so far as to tell Anne the baby was fine and asked her to look after it when the baby was dead for over a week. We do know Julia had come from Drimoleague originally so why had she not gone there when she left the workhouse. It does seem like she was trying to hide something and the immense pressure she was under not only exacerbated her mental state but was probably the cause of it. In the history of this country, how many more women were left helpless when society and their families turned their backs on them in similar circumstances?

Only A Pawn In Her Game
Oldcourt Ballinspittle Kinsale 1821

On Monday the 5th November Mary Stanley reported that her husband was missing since the evening before. She said a posse of men came looking for him the previous night and lured him from the safety of his house. Some time afterwards a shot was heard outside and Mary had not seen her husband since. This all occurred in a quiet rural townland called Oldcourt, between Kinsale and the Old Head.

On Tuesday her husband's body was found in the ruins of a house not that far away. Mary still maintained he had been coaxed from the house by an armed gang on Sunday evening. The only people in the house that night were David and Mary Stanley and a servant of theirs William Leary. David Stanley was described as a substantial farmer. He had married his wife Mary almost ten years before but they had no children.

An inquest was held in Kinsale by coroner John Isaac Heard who was the Sovereign of Kinsale that year. He was assisted by several other magistrates and a jury of respectable men. Locals were shocked at the occurrence and came forward as witnesses at the inquest.

Suspicion centred on Mary Stanley and the servant William Leary who couldn't give a credible story. Mary said she was in bed that night but didn't explain why she didn't go looking for her husband. There had also been rumours that Mary Stanley was having an affair with the servant Leary and wanted rid of her husband.

The verdict of the inquest was that David Stanley died of a gunshot wound inflicted by both William Leary and Mary Stanley. Right after hearing the verdict the suspects were arrested and taken into custody.

Mary then confessed in an attempt to save herself. She said it was William who shot her husband but denied knowing about it before. This was an admission that she aided and abetted William in the killing of her husband. It was a desperate attempt to save her life. Leary though maintained that Mary was present when Stanley was killed.

When the pair appeared before the Cork Spring Assizes on Tuesday the 9th of April, Mary Stanley must have realised how grim her prospects were. Back then murder cases didn't go on for weeks, they would be over in a few hours. A guilty verdict would see them dead before the weekend. No time for an appeal or no chance to argue their case.

It was Counsellor Connell the Recorder of Kinsale who opened the case for the crown prosecution. He merely stated the facts of the case. He described David Stanley as a respectable and hardworking farmer, living reasonably comfortable. The direct evidence against the suspects was somewhat lacking but the prosecution tried to build the case against them.

He told how there was no one else in the house but the three connected to the case. A female servant had been dismissed by Mary and a replacement told not to come for a few days. David's dog that was normally free to roam the farm had been tied up. Mary Stanley was seen close to where the body was found on Monday.

The witnesses were almost all circumstantial in nature. A servant Joan Donovan had been hired by the Stanley's and said she went there that Sunday. Mary sent her away saying to come back again the following day but Joan never did go back. She heard David Stanley was missing on Monday and realised he was dead on Tuesday morning.

Another witness called was Mary Dempsey, who ceased working for Stanley's several weeks before David was shot. She told how David would sometimes leave on a Sunday to visit his relations and often didn't return until Tuesday. During this time she never saw her mistress keeping company with the servants in her bedroom or anywhere else.

However another employee told a different story, Jeremiah Collins looked after the place while David was away. He was coaxed to speak in English for the court but refused saying he couldn't. Jeremiah recalled an occasion when he found Mary Stanley in bed with William Leary, with their clothes on, in March of that year.

Under cross examination, Collins said he had no animosity towards William Leary until he threatened to kill him. He didn't explain why he had never told David Stanley about his wife. Collins made out he had never been in trouble but when pressed, he admitted running off with a man's daughter.

Surgeon Daniel Kelly gave the medical evidence as he had examined the body. He described the injuries as consistent with a gunshot. The entry wound was between the shoulder blades and it exited at the collar bone which was fractured. Death was a result of the blood loss as the bullet passed through several blood vessels. All the surgeon could conclude was that Stanley was shot from behind and the gun had been pointed upwards.

So far they had no evidence at all to prove who had shot David Stanley; all they had was circumstances that connected them.

It was John Isaac Heard the Sovereign of Kinsale who could change that. He had also been the coroner of the inquest. He recalled going to Stanley's house on the 6th of November when the body was found. He saw David Stanley face down in the ruins of an old house. He described a stream of blood from there back to Stanley's farmhouse. Very near the body, a large footprint matched that of William Leary's boots. They also found a gun in the loft of Stanley's house near where Mary slept. John said it appeared to have been recently fired, slugs and gun powder were found hidden in the thatch.

He then moved on to tell of a sort of confession Leary had given in Kinsale Gaol a few days after being arrested. Heard told how Leary had talked of his own accord without any questions put to him, pen and paper were got and what he said then was written down and Leary swore to it. It all hung now, pardon the pun, on whether the judge would rule this confession admissible or not. Legal counsel for Mary Stanley objected to the statement being allowed as evidence.

The judge however quickly ruled that what Leary had said before it was written down could be allowed. John Heard recalled what Leary told him; Leary confessed to being in a terrible predicament and regretted ever going to work at Stanley's. He admitted that he was involved in the murder but at the repeated insistence of Mary Stanley.

He mentioned how Mary had made a confession on the Thursday after the Inquest but he was not present at the time. Another witness Mr John Good was called and had heard what Mary said that day. He admitted there was some inducement in getting Mary to talk and the judge ruled that it could not be heard.

The jury took an hour and a half to decide that day; this was bound to be due to the circumstantial nature of the evidence. The jury returned the verdict of not guilty for Mary Stanley. It was not without the remark that they were convinced of her guilt but couldn't prove it sufficiently. Mary must not have understood what the judge had said and turned to the person beside her desperately asking was she to die. Once Mary knew she was safe she let out "Oh thank God" for all to hear. The crowd in court were shocked by the verdict and quickly showed their disapproval. Mary was described in court as a good looking woman but with a stern appearance and in her mid forties.

William Leary was found guilty on the charge of wilful murder. Baron Pennefather who was no stranger to the black cap said: "I perfectly concur gentlemen in your verdict and your reasons for it". Many judges dreaded a death sentence but not the Baron and he went straight into it. He reminded William Leary that he had taken away a man's life and now his own must also end. Pennefather said he knew Mary Stanley was guiltier than him but there was nothing he could do about that now. William Leary was reminded that he must pay the penalty for the crime and his life must be taken the following Thursday.

Leary reacted violently to the sentence against him but Pennefather had heard it all before. William cursed in court that he wished God would give him the power to pass sentence on the judge someday, but it was all meaningless now.

Under the law of the time, William Leary could have been tried for the more serious crime of Petty Treason. This was the murder of one's superior and the punishment could be far more brutal. Mary could have also have been tried for Petty Treason as back then her husband was seen as her superior.

On the 11th of April William Leary was taken from the county gaol and marched with a heavy escort to the place of execution at Gallow's Green. The execution was held for all to see and crowds would have gathered in anticipation.

In his last days William seemed to change his ways and now regretted the way he behaved at the court. In the final few moments while the hangman made everything ready Rev England made a statement that Leary had asked him to say.

In it, William Leary made a full confession that he alone was the killer of his master David Stanley. He said it was not done out of malice or hatred towards Stanley who had always been kind to him. It was carried out at the insistence and encouragement of Mary Stanley. He admitted that he had been involved with her for a very long time and that it was wrong. She had made several suggestions on how it should be done, slit his throat with a razor or poison him.

Leary also said that he had not told the truth to Heard in Kinsale, Mary was not present when he shot David; she had gone to bed before. The gun he used had belonged to the victim himself.

In his last few moments, William Leary prayed and appeared repentant for his dreadful crime. Once hung Leary was left hanging there for some time to ensure he was dead. Then he was cut down and taken to the county infirmary where his body was to be dissected.

It was the 15th of April when Mary appeared before Baron Pennefather again. Now she was said to appear even more composed than at the trial, safe in the knowledge her life was to be spared. Before she could be charged a proclamation had to be read out asking was there any offence she could be charged with. If there was any other way the judge would have done something as he was convinced of her guilt. When the court finished that day Mary Stanley was discharged from custody and free to leave. The angry mob outside the court was such that it was said she would have been safer going back to jail than walking onto the street.

What became of Mary Stanley now that both her husband and lover were dead? Could she possibly have remained on the farm after all that had gone on? Often in such cases, the family would try to remove the woman from the farm, but Mary was closely related to David before marriage. It turns out that David Stanley was a first cousin to his wife; she was also Mary Stanley before marriage. It was probably more common back then, for families with land it was a way of keeping it in the family and preventing disputes about dividing farms.

David Stanley's father James Stanley was still living about two miles west of Bandon. Now his niece had done away with his son and gotten away with it.

There was no chance at all that Mary would remarry as everyone knew it was she who was behind the death of her husband. Even William Leary had admitted his master deserved better and wasn't a bad man. Mary Stanley just wanted more and got it into her head to get rid of him at all cost. William Leary was just a pawn used by her to get her wicked way.

Wrong Time, Wrong Place
Ballinvarosig Carrigaline 1936

Just after nine on the morning of Wednesday the 25th November 1936, Daniel O'Mahony, a farm labourer driving out the cows made a grim discovery in a field about a mile and a half south of Carrigaline. He had passed by earlier in the morning taking the cows to be milked but it was dark then and he noticed nothing amiss. The labourer quickly ran to the nearest farm and his discovery was reported to the local Garda barracks.

The Gardaí arrived from both Carrigaline and Ballyfeard Garda Barracks to realise little could be done but report to headquarters in Union Quay Cork. Soon the field swarmed with Garda activity led by Chief Superintendent Hannigan. It didn't need any detective skills to realise that foul play had been involved. The body of a man in his forties lay near a ditch about 200 yards from the public road. A flow of blood from the left ear was the only sign of injury; his tie had been used against him.

This led the Guards to believe strangulation was the cause of death and that he had been brought to the spot before being murdered. There were no trace of the body being dragged there nor tyres marks nearby. No signs of a struggle in the field suggested to the guards the victim went there voluntarily. In a second field further from the road, about 15 yards from the body more items were found including a cap and belt.

Initially that morning the body was not identified, as he was not known by any of the locals. The motive also wasn't known but soon the pieces would fall into place. An abandoned Ford car outside Douglas was a start. Locals confirmed a similar car was seen parked near to where the body had been found earlier that morning and the night before.

It was much easier back then to identify a car as the number of cars on the road was far less than today. An abandoned car in the 1930s must also have been a rare sight as cars were driven by doctors, priests and such. The Ford car left in Douglas was a taxi, its registration LG 1531 was registered to Thomas Vickers living on Glasheen Road. When it was realised Vickers had not been home on Tuesday night the guards felt they were getting somewhere.

The motive seemed to point towards robbery, take a taxi to a deserted spot then turn on the driver and get his cash. Maybe the robbery went wrong and the taxi driver became the victim. The taxi was taken away for analysis and checked for fingerprints. Inside a spanner was found in a toolbox placed on top of the Evening Echo from the day before. Was this instrument somehow connected to the crime?

Initial enquiries at the taxi rank on Patrick Street had shown that Vickers was last seen there when he picked up a tall man. Before the guards could even piece together the last movements of the taxi, locals near Ballinvarosig told what they knew.

About half eleven the night before there was a knock at the back door of Thomas Foley's house. The man outside was not let in but asked could he explain something. A Ford taxi was parked outside and he walked around the house for some time before leaving in the car. Foley said he stayed up all night with his gun for safety. In the morning, he saw the same car back again near his house but this time the man didn't approach his door. The most significant piece of information Thomas Foley could reveal was he knew the man driving the car as he had employed him some two weeks before. The man was James Tierney who was in his twenties. Tierney had been painting Foley's house that month but left before the work was completed. Previous to that, Tierney had worked as a farm labourer for Mrs Farrissey of the same townland.

Finally, the guards had a description of the man who acted suspiciously in the area and was seen driving the dead man's taxi. It was this information they acted on and put out a nationwide search to find Tierney. Other than the fact that Tierney had worked in Ballinvarosig that year not much else was known about him in the area.

Despite the revelations, the Garda presence in the area intensified further. A murder investigation in rural Ireland was rare enough at that time. The scene was closed off that day to await official photographers and State Pathologist Dr McGrath to arrive. All through Wednesday night, two Gardaí stood guard over the covered body in the field.

As the news broke that Wednesday people in the locality were truly shocked with what had occurred so close by. In Cork, Thomas Vickers wife was informed of the terrible news and was said to be devastated. At their house on 2 Clashduv Place, Glasheen Road, the garage door was still open from the night before but Thomas never came back. Thomas Vickers had been married to Monica Keating for 23 years, they had no children. They had married in England in 1913 when Thomas was a soldier in the British

Army. Monica was also originally from Cork. Thomas served in WW1 as did his brother and all his brothers-in-law and they returned home after the war. Most likely it was around then he took on taxi driving, following his father James who had been a soldier and then a coachman.

*Scene of the crime,
with thanks to Irish Newspaper Archives and the Evening Echo.*

That Wednesday Garda Stations all over Ireland received a description of Tierney who was on the run or possibly hiding out somewhere. He could not have got too far as he had been seen driving the taxi just that morning and they assumed it was he that abandoned it near Douglas.

In Edward Street, Limerick, Garda Brosnan and Butler, listened carefully to the description before setting out on the beat that night. Between them, they must have thought about how a man on the run would travel and what he would do. The train and bus station seemed the obvious place such a man would need to pass through and it wasn't far away. Across the street, they searched in several of the lodging houses and asked around. One lodging house said a man fitting the description had checked in for the night but left again. The guards laid in wait and later that night about eleven, Brosnan and Butler spotted a man fitting the description going back to the lodging house on Davis Street, directly opposite the Train Station. Having watched him for a while they were confident enough it was their man on the run and swooped in to make the arrest. The man confirmed to the guards he had travelled from Cork but could give no reason for being in Limerick except that he was a mechanic who travelled for work. He told the guards he arrived by bus but had told the woman in the lodging house his car had broken down.

Chief Superintendent Hannigan in Cork who was leading the investigation was informed and left immediately for Limerick.

Where the body was found from another angle, with thanks to Irish Newspaper Archives and the Cork Examiner.

Back in Cork on Thursday morning, the State Pathologist arrived on the scene to begin his examination of the body. When finished with the scene the body was removed to an outhouse of the nearest farm. Once he had completed the post mortem the inquest was opened by Coroner John Horgan. All that was to happen that day was merely identification and medical evidence. By the 1930s inquests in such cases had become a mere formality and the proceedings were to be adjourned indefinitely to await the Garda investigation and trial. Decades before under the English system the jury would have found a verdict that very day or maybe over two days. Back then the verdict could identify the suspect and therefore affect the police investigation. The coroner even had the power to issue a warrant for the arrest of a suspect based on the findings. Now though in the Free State the system seems to protect the details of the Garda investigation.

That Thursday it was Monica Vickers' brother-in-law Richard Heffernan who identified the body. Heffernan stated how he had last seen

Vickers alive on Sunday evening, when he was his usual self and in good health.

State Pathologist Dr McGrath gave the medical details of the post mortem. He concluded that "death was caused by asphyxia brought about by ligature tied around the neck". McGrath replied to the Coroner that he was quite sure how the deceased had met his death and Dr Hurley from Carrigaline who assisted with the post mortem concurred with this.

Directly after the inquest was adjourned a special court was held in the barracks in Carrigaline. There James Edward Tierney was charged before local peace commissioner H.W Roberts with killing Thomas Vickers. Superintendent Doyle from Bandon gave evidence of arrest and State Solicitor D Casey applied for a remand. Tierney was described as being dressed shabbily that day but clean shaven. He was said to be a powerful looking man at six foot two inches tall and in his mid twenties.

Dr. McGrath State Pathologist with Supt Murphy, with thanks to Irish Newspaper Archives and the Cork Examiner.

When asked did he have anything to say concerning the charge against him Tierney replied "no sir". His address was given as Carbery Hotel, Oliver Plunkett Street as he had been staying there for two weeks before.

Not a lot was known about James Edward Tierney as he was not from Cork and had only been working in the area in recent months. He was born in Dublin but spent many years living in England. He was said to have spent several years working for the Palestine Police before returning to Ireland.

Gardaí began to interview witnesses who had met Tierney in the weeks before. He had told people while he was in the Palestinian police force he was sending money to a girl in Dublin. When he left the force Tierney came to Dublin to find her but she was not to be found. He heard she was in West Cork and this is how he ended up in Cork. By now he was almost penniless except for some odd jobs he could find. Those that met Tierney in November all recalled how every day he said he was returning to England but didn't have the price of the ticket for the boat.

On Saturday the 28th James Tierney was brought before Justice Padraig Ua Súilleabháin at the District Court. Tierney had no legal representation despite the serious charges against him and again declined to say anything. The proceedings were over in a matter of minutes and he was remanded to Cork Jail for a further fourteen days.

The investigation continued and the guards asked for anyone who lived near the scene or had met Thomas Vickers that Tuesday to come forward. They needed to track both men's exact movements to discover what exactly had happened and the motive behind it.

After several remands, evidence began to be heard at the Cork Courthouse on the 12th of December. Tierney was represented by a solicitor Neville while Kevin Haugh and state solicitor D Casey led the case for the prosecution. Appearing in court Tierney was described as a tall handsome man of powerful looking physique and smartly dressed.

It was Haugh who opened the case by stating the facts which the prosecution could prove. He said Vickers met his death by strangulation and with the state pathologists evidence, this could not be doubted. He said Tierney was living in the Carbery Hotel in Oliver Plunkett Street and was trying to gather money to return to England.

The prosecution also connected Tierney to the scene by the fact he had previously worked for Thomas Foley. Haugh told how several witnesses saw Tierney driving the taxi of the deceased even up to the time the body had been found. They also suggested the motive of robbery saying Vickers had been robbed of about 18 shillings and just a single farthing was found on the body. Yet Tierney, when arrested in Limerick, had 3s 6 ½ d on him and it would have cost him a few shillings to get to Limerick. With all this evidence the prosecution was right to be confident a magistrate would return the case for trial before the Central Criminal Court.

It was also heard that 72 witnesses were to be called in total by the prosecution and the proceedings would last for several days. From all the witnesses though there was no direct evidence against Tierney as nobody had actually seen what had occurred.

What the testimony of several witnesses shows was Tierney was a desperate man. He had been sacked from at least one job and left others unfinished. He was described by many as a "down and out" and would have been homeless but for the generosity of those, he met in the city. Much of his time spent in the Carbery Hotel had not been paid for and many felt had he come into money he would have bought a ticket to England. The most recent job Tierney had was driving a truck for a Mrs Perry from Kyrl's Street in the city but got sacked for some reason.

The Gardaí had traced every movement of Tierney on the 24th and 25th of November and now it was all to be heard in court. Evidence was heard of several identity parades that had proved Tierney was driving the Ford Taxi. He had been returning to the Carbery Hotel on Tuesday night leaving the Ford Taxi parked nearby. The following morning he left early and several witnesses told how they saw him near what was to become the crime scene.

A bus conductor told how Tierney purchased a ticket from Douglas to the City Centre jumping on the bus at sixteen minutes to nine. He purchased a single fare for 2½d while a few miles out the road Thomas Vickers lay yet undiscovered. The conductor recalled how the man's trousers seemed muddy and he appeared to not have slept much the night before.

Next Tierney was seen in a restaurant in Paul Street where he had a breakfast of eggs and bacon. Timothy O'Flynn recalled Tierney asking for more tea and bread and paid 1s 1d for his meal. After two in the afternoon, Tierney turned up outside Frank Daly's office. He had also called earlier in the week asking for a ticket to England. This time he said "a ticket to Fishguard will do me now" but Daly sent him packing with a shilling. Later in the afternoon with hopes of getting to England dashed, he left for Limerick on the 3:45 bus.

Superintendent Murphy described an identity parade that had been held in the prison on the 9th of December. He said Tierney was instructed to pick any place in the line but objected saying "I have agreed I was there and everything, I don't know what it is for really". He told that Tierney had been recognised by eleven people at the parade.

Ellen O'Regan who managed the Carbery Hotel for her daughter gave interesting evidence of Tierney's stay in the hotel. He arrived on a Wednesday evening, exactly two weeks before he left, and paid 1/6 for his food and lodging. That she said was the only money he paid and every day Tierney said he was leaving for England. Normally she would charge £1 a week for food and lodging.

Other witnesses from the Carbery Hotel mentioned a collection that was held for him with several residents giving 6s each. They seemed to feel sorry for him and Tierney kept promising he would pay them back and how he had a job lined up. Tierney even produced a letter signed by Frank Daly from the Butter Market saying he had a job for Tierney and all his bills would be paid. Tierney told everyone the job was driving a solicitor earning him £2 10s a week. He claimed to be getting measured for a suit on Tuesday and would start his new job that Wednesday but instead he disappeared from the hotel. Tierney never returned to the hotel that Wednesday after leaving in the taxi that morning and had no luggage to collect.

Frank Daly was called to court and confirmed that James Tierney had called to see him on Monday the 23rd. Tierney asked for a ticket to England but was refused. Daly confirmed he did not offer Tierney any employment. Tierney returned the Wednesday afterwards again asking for help to get back to England. Daly said he again refused to help telling Tierney he should ask the Lord Mayor but gave him a shilling for his trouble. In fact, Tierney had been back to Daly's on two occasions, also on Tuesday the 24th that Frank might not have been aware of. He spent two and a half hours waiting in the afternoon after being refused the day before. He spent between six and seven that night at Daly's before going back to the Carbery Hotel.

Detective Superintendent told the court he was present with Chief Superintendent Hannigan in Limerick when Tierney was arrested and brought to Cork. He produced in court a union key that Tierney was found to be in possession of when arrested. O'Driscoll recalled asking Tierney what the key was for and was told it was from a boarding house in which he had stayed in London. The detective superintendent then informed the court that the union key Tierney had, fitted the front door of Vickers house. A former tenant of the same house and a locksmith were produced to back up this evidence.

The best evidence that placed Tierney near the scene was that of Thomas Foley who lived a few hundred yards from where the body was found. Foley had married two years before and was related to Mrs Farrissey who owned the surrounding farmland.

He told of first meeting Tierney in July or August that year when he worked for Mrs Farrissey for several weeks. He said he employed Tierney to do some interior painting between the 9th and 11th of October. They agreed that it should take two days but Tierney left without completing the job. He promised to return but never did and was not paid for it. Foley said it was only afterwards when Tierney failed to come back that he noticed a £1 note missing from a drawer that had £5 10s in notes.

Then at about half eleven on the night of Tuesday, the 24th Tierney came to Foley's bedroom window just as he was about to go to bed. Thomas Foley said it was his wife that spoke to Tierney; he never knocked at the door. Thomas went to the kitchen and stood there silently for a few minutes. When he lifted the blind of the back door James Tierney was standing there. Despite Tierney's insistence he refused to let him into the house saying it was too late. James told him he wouldn't be long as he had a car waiting and wanted to explain why he never finished the painting. When not allowed in Tierney bid him goodnight but didn't leave. Foley recalled him looking in the windows and heard footsteps outside for another hour afterwards. Thomas Foley said he didn't sleep at all that night and sat with his gun fearing Tierney would return.

The following morning at about half seven Foley saw a Ford car on the road near his house. He believed it was Tierney back again and heard sounds like he was fixing something in the car. Finishing his testimony that day in court, Foley said he heard nothing unusual that night apart from Tierney walking about the house.

Evidence of finding the body was given by James Murphy who lived on his sister's farm, her name was Mrs Farrissey. Just after nine on the morning of the 24th one of the labourers, Daniel O'Mahony came to him in a state saying he found a body in the second field from the farmhouse. Murphy assured the court that the body was not interfered with in any way but recalled how the man's tie appeared to be pulled very tight.

James Murphy, who had been one of the first on the scene, with thanks to Irish Newspaper Archives and the Cork Examiner.

When asked about the accused, Murphy said James Tierney came to work for his sister on the 26th of August to help at harvest time. He was paid 10s weekly and also got his food and lodging there. While working there they had no issues with him at all. He said Tierney left on the 19th of September saying he had got a job in Dunlops. Tierney had told him a little of his past and how he had spent time abroad with his father in the police. He also said he was a good mechanic and could drive any class of car.

Murphy reckoned it was the 5th of November when he saw Tierney again. On that occasion, Tierney said he was driving a lorry and delivering furniture to a house nearby. He handed Murphy Mrs Perry's business card saying if he needed a truck, to call and he would do him a good turn.

When asked about the night before the body was found, Murphy said he stayed up until twenty past one reading in his bedroom. He heard nothing unusual outside that night.

Medical evidence was given by State pathologist Dr McGrath who had carried out the post mortem with Dr Herlihy from Carrigaline. McGrath described the scene where he found Vickers body, in a field 3ft from a gate to another field. He said the body was face up stretched out with feet apart and fully clothed. He found the tie around Vickers's neck was tight but not extremely so as he could get his finger inside it. The tie though was tied using a granny knot rather than the usual Windsor knot. The face and head were red from an accumulation of blood due to the ligature on the neck. He saw no evidence or marks on Vickers's neck to show he was choked using hands. McGrath described in detail the scene and the clothes saying there was very little sign of a struggle. Two bruises were found one on the chin and the other at the back of the head.

During the post mortem, he discovered the windpipe and lungs were congested in blood, as was the brain. McGrath described in detail removing the organs stomach, intestines, spleen, kidneys and brain and placing them in jars which were then sealed. He sent these to Mr Kearns for analysis but had not yet received a report.

The State pathologist concluded that "death was due to asphyxia and congestion of the brain and that these were brought about by a ligature tied around the neck. The tie as found on the neck would be sufficient to produce these results. Besides the strangulation, there was evidence of two blows which produced bruising, both of which therefore were inflicted before death." Dr Herlihy gave evidence of assisting the State Pathologist and agreed with what he had said.

Witness Henry Hitchmough an accountant living in Ravenswood recalled driving home on the 24th on the Ballea Road. He encountered a car stopped with its parking lights on. Henry slowed down and recognised the LG number plate as a taxi driven by a man who lived in the city. He even knew the previous owner of the car Mr Sinnott from Douglas Road.

Henry said it was only about ten past nine, he passed the taxi and he didn't recognise the driver who was alone. He noticed that the sole occupant seem to be trying to read something like a map. On his way to work the following morning, Henry again passed the car but now it was abandoned close to Douglas.

The guards had tracked down another boarding house that Tierney had called to on Washington Street. Mrs Eileen Mahomet took the stand and said on Tuesday the 24th James Tierney called to her looking for a room for the night. Eileen was reluctant to take him in and told him she normally only took boarders on a recommendation. She said James insisted saying it was only for the one night and he would be gone the following day. She agreed but reminded him that she locked up at eleven and he would need to be in before that.

Tierney told her that he had to go out on a job between nine and eleven that night and should be back a few minutes after eleven. He promised to pay the 5s for his board when he returned. He even told her he had a job lined up at Dunlop's and would be starting the following day.

Eileen said she prepared the bed for Tierney and worked until eleven before locking up as normal. She stayed up until half eleven but he never returned nor did she hear anyone knocking during the night.

Tierney went back to the Carbery Hotel that night and several Gardaí recalled seeing the Ford taxi parked nearby. Patrick McCabe told the court how he let Tierney into the Hotel that morning at 2:15 am. He commented to Tierney about the late hour but all Tierney said was time slipped away on him and he didn't realise how late it was. Patrick felt at the time that Tierney seemed to be excited at that hour in the morning. Despite the late hour Tierney was up early and left in the car again in the morning. Another lodger who shared a room with Tierney noted how he was not normally an early riser and he thought it strange that Tierney was up before him. He quizzed Tierney about why he was up so early and was told he had to deliver a car to a Mr Daly before eight. Tierney was probably so excited that he didn't sleep a wink that night and neither did Thomas Foley who was expecting his return.

All this went nowhere towards proving James Tierney had killed Thomas Vickers but it did demonstrate the web of lies Tierney was weaving everywhere he went. He seemed willing to say anything to get by without thinking it would all catch up on him. Why did Tierney suddenly decide to leave the Carbery Hotel where people had been good to him and then change his mind? He certainly set out on the night of the 24th to get money by some means. Was he thinking of robbing Mrs Farrissey or Foley, guessing there would still be a few pounds in the drawer. It is likely Vickers the honest hardworking taxi man got wind of Tierney's plans and intervened, not knowing just how desperate Tierney was.

It took several sessions in court that December before all the witnesses were heard. The last day in court was the 22nd of December when Chief Superintendent James Hannigan again took the stand. He gave evidence of going to Limerick when Tierney had been arrested. Hannigan told how on two occasions in Edwards Street Garda Station he cautioned Tierney but each time Tierney volunteered a statement. Those statements had been committed to writing and the suspect signed them. Those documents were then produced in court but Mr Haugh intervened saying he did not want the statements read out at this stage. He said Mr Neville for the defence had been given a copy of the statements already. Instead, the documents were handed to the judge who looked over them before continuing to examine the Chief Super.

That last afternoon in court the proceedings were held in secret and the press and public were asked to leave. The statements Tierney had given were then read out, but from the public's point of view saved for the trial. With what had been heard both publically and privately District Justice Ua Súilleabháin had no option but to send Tierney for trial at the Central Criminal court the following year. There was no question of bail on a capital charge but even more so in this case as there was no reason for Tierney to stay in the country.

In the months he languished in jail waiting for the trial did he understand the peril his life was in? With the evidence against him, there was a good chance he could be sentenced to death. It had been nearly three years since the last execution in Ireland when John Fleming was hung for murdering his wife. The last Cork case was when David O'Shea was executed for the rape and murder of a young woman near the Kerry border. (*see Murder Most Local, Historic Murders of North Cork*) The evidence against O'Shea was much more circumstantial than in this case yet he got no reprieve. It is doubtful Tierney knew these facts let alone grasped his own predicament. This was much more serious than the scrapes he had gotten himself into before.

As time went on the guards discovered more about Tierney's chequered past. He wasn't James Edward Tierney at all but had been born James Edward O'Neill in Dublin in 1909. His father Michael was at the time employed in the Dublin Metropolitan Police but left to become the chief inspector of the Straits Settlements Police now known as Malaysia. James spent several years in the Far East with his father, mother and sister until Michael retired and moved to Eastleigh near Southampton in 1921. So James Edward O'Neill spent his formative years in England. According to himself, he had served his time as a motor mechanic. This must have been in the mid 1920s. It was when he was about eighteen that strange things begin to occur.

In 1927 James was mysteriously found unconscious in the middle of the road about 100 yards from where he lived. He had fallen from his motorbike without explanation and was out cold for about two hours. His father believed it was just a common motorbike accident and allowed him to continue using it.

Thomas Vickers, with thanks to Irish Newspaper Archives and the Cork Examiner

August of the following year James was again found unconscious in the same place. As before he had fallen from the motorbike but this time he was taken to Hampshire hospital where he was treated for concussion for five days. Three months later when working in a convent, James was again found unconscious but this time it was not from a motorbike accident. He had just fallen without any explanation at all and couldn't say it was the motorbike this time. As before James spent another five days in hospital before returning home.

Sometime in 1930 O'Neill joined the 1st Regiment Grenadier Guards despite what we would now call a medical condition. Maybe it was his father's connections that got him enlisted into the service. Over the next few years, O'Neill saw action in Egypt during riots there.

In 1934 when stationed at Aldershot, O'Neill absconded from the army and there was no trace of him in England. He left with a £10 cheque belonging to the Brigadier of the regiment.

His father had by then moved back to Ireland and was living in Castledermot, Co Kildare and that is where James headed for, staying there on and off until April.

On the 11th of April that year James was found lying unconscious on the Naas Road, Dublin and was admitted to Stephen's Hospital. He spent almost a month in hospital and it must have been then that the English authorities caught up with him.

Once he got out of hospital James was arrested and quickly found himself back in England before a military court in Aldershot. He was charged with several petty crimes of taking money belonging to the King and the £10 cheque of his superior. James couldn't explain his actions at all but said he intended to go back and own up to it. His best excuse was having been in hospital but he had three months to return before that. He was sentenced to six months in jail and his military career was over.

It would seem his father had had enough of James as this time he didn't return to Ireland. He wasn't one to learn from his mistakes and again in 1935 spent three months in jail. This time it was for the robbery of 14s and a gold watch from a signalman. James almost seemed to believe the excuses he made claiming he was sorry and intended to repay. His reasons for doing it were being depressed and unable to get work.

He then got a job working in Alderwood house near Newbury; it was described as a guest house for abnormal people. By May of 1936, James was in trouble again for taking a car from one of the guests and disappearing for several days. He was assigned a probation officer and strangely was taken back on at Alderwood house.

In July he left for Ireland and at the end of the month he was found unconscious on the streets of Limerick. After spending several days in Barrington's Hospital he was released on August 6th and headed for Cork. He stayed, in the Salvation Army Hostel before going to work for Mrs Farrissey.

In early April 1937, the trial began in the Central Criminal Court in Dublin before Justice O'Byrne. When charged he was still to be known as James Edward Tierney despite the fact by now everyone knew his real name was O'Neill. The prosecution was led by Martin Maguire with Kevin Haugh and the chief state solicitor. While the defence was represented by P.J Roe, Vaughan Buckley and solicitor Neville.

Mr Maguire said that the prosecution had no responsibility to show a motive. He suggested it could have been a robbery or maybe Vickers was concerned Tierney couldn't pay and pursued him into the field. Did Tierney react violently to this and then do the terrible deed?

Monica Vickers who was seated in the front row of the court was seen crying when evidence of finding her husband's body was heard.

Maguire entered Tierney's statements into evidence whereas, before the District Justice, they were kept secret. Tierney admitted hiring Thomas Vickers taxi on Patrick Street to take him to Mrs Farrissey's farm. When they pulled in he said the driver asked how long would he be and he replied about three quarters of an hour. Tierney claimed the driver asked would he mind if he went with him rather than wait in the car and he said: "not at all".

Both men then walked across the fields to get to the farmhouse. When they went through the gate into the second field Tierney said he felt movement behind him, it was the driver's hand above his head. It was then Tierney said he turned about suddenly and struck the driver with a right hander so hard he knocked him to the ground. Both men were dragged down and in the struggle; Tierney said he got his hand to the driver's throat. He said the struggle turned into silence but he didn't realise he had done anything so serious. Without explanation, he pulled the man's tie tighter and then dragged him into the other field closer to the road.

He admitted being terrified and not knowing what he should do next but went back to the car. He sat in the car for what could have been two hours before going up to Foley's house, which was the reason he came there in the first place. We already know what happened when he went there. Tierney said he was worried about the £1 he had taken and wanted to explain himself.

The statement also told how he returned to the area the following morning, to see if the driver was still there. When he got there though, he found himself unable to go back to the scene of the struggle so he returned to Cork. The statement ended with "I had no intention of killing the man. I had no idea of the strength I could put behind myself. I am sorry for what I have done".

There was some truth in the statement. He had hired the taxi, killed Thomas Vickers and returned to Cork. When it came to the details though, nothing could be believed from James Tierney, not even his name. Would a man like Tierney with no money afford to leave a taxi driver waiting three quarters of an hour while he explained himself to Thomas Foley? Even more preposterous was the claim he still went to Foley's to explain himself while nearby a man lay dead.

Michael O'Neill father of the accused leaving the court in Dublin, with thanks to Irish Newspaper Archives and the Irish Independent.

Had Tierney not gone round to Foley's that night he might just have gotten away with it as there would have been nothing to connect him to the scene. The only thing that makes sense is that he didn't get enough money on Vickers so he went round to Foley's knowing there might be a few pound in the drawer.

From an evidence point of view in court, it placed him at the scene and committing the act. For the defence, it left a tough job and only one option to argue that it was not murder and try to get a reduced sentence for their client.

Despite months having passed, the evidence for the prosecution was much the same as what had been heard at the District Court. The state obviously felt that now especially with the statement from the accused they had a good case for the capital charge.

A prison guard named Joseph Walsh was called as James gave him a statement when he was when admitted to jail. Walsh told the court how he asked the prisoner "were you convicted or on remand". The answer James gave indicates that he didn't fully understand it "I am on the capital charge. It was self defence. He drew a spanner at me. I managed to duck and got him first. I don't know what happened after that. This happened while crossing the field. I don't know what happened after that".

For the defence, Mr Roe argued why the jury could not find a verdict of murder against Tierney. He would call evidence to show that Tierney suffered from acromegaly which explained the fits and bouts of unconsciousness. He said this could be proved with an x-ray, showing a gland in Tierney's brain was enlarged. He also pointed out another symptom was his enlarged lower jaw. He said epilepsy was connected to this and explained why he was found unconscious so often. This resulted in his client being prone to bursts of violence which he may not recall afterwards. In short Mr Roe and the defence team were attempting to prove insanity. He also argued against the motive being robbery and suggested self defence. Why he asked had the two men crossed the field in the darkness before the struggle took place. He also claimed that Vickers had at least £1 9s 2d on him at the time, while Tierney had 3s 6d when arrested and spent 19s 2d that day. This didn't add up but Tierney could easily have gotten rid of a few shillings more that day. What the defence couldn't account for was where did Tierney get that money if he didn't rob Vickers? Up until then he couldn't pay his bills and left Cork still owing people. Roe explained away the fact Tierney had the dead man's house key by saying it was with the car key and he must have pocketed it while driving the car. What he didn't explain was how Tierney had got his hands on the car keys in the first place.

The first witness called for the defence was the accused himself, who gave his career to date and how he ended up in Cork. Obviously enough the version he gave left out much of the trouble he had gotten himself into.

When it came to the events of the 24th of November he gave a very similar account to the statement he had given previously but he couldn't recall anything after the struggle. It was the judge who intervened and asked why he moved the body. Tierney replied, "I lifted him and carried him in my arms. I was afraid the cattle would wake on him". Justice O'Byrne pushed him further suggesting he knew what he had done by asking "you knew he would not get up from the ground". Tierney was hesitant in replying "I did not know whether he would or not".

Cross examined by Martin Maguire he was asked what the purpose of going to Carrigaline that night was. Tierney still said it was to explain the missing £1 in Foley's which he never managed to do. When asked what he did until going back to the hotel that night, Tierney admitted he may have unconsciously gone back to the scene of the crime. He was adamant though that he had not taken anything from Vickers pockets at all. The prosecution pushed him that in his earlier statement he admitted he pulled Vickers tie tighter when he fell silent. Now Tierney couldn't recall ever saying that but said he may have pulled the tie during the struggle.

Tierney could not explain why he went back to Carrigaline the following morning but didn't think he went near the body then. He also couldn't explain his actions that day saying he just stopped the car and caught a bus to the city. On why he went to Limerick, Tierney claimed he saw the bus and got on it without thinking. Maguire asked had he thought about leaving the man in the field at all that day and Tierney replied: "I was thinking about him all the time".

He admitted telling lies when first arrested in Limerick but claimed he didn't know the man was dead until the guards told him.

There was surely some shred of truth in what James was saying, he may have had no intention of killing Vickers that night. But he seemed completely lacking in understanding the consequences of what he did. If it did happen crossing the field it seems strange that James dealt with Vickers and then proceeded to Foley's house. Had he not gone to Foley's that night he may not have been connected to the killing at all and the guards would have suspected it was a robbery gone wrong. It gets worse when Tierney drives back the next morning as he doesn't consider for a second that Vickers still lay in the field. Nor does he consider that he will be seen driving around in the taxi.

Outside the court, Chief Supt Hannigan, Supt Doyle, Supt Murphy and Monica Vickers, with thanks to Irish Newspaper Archives and the Cork Examiner

Michael O'Neill who had travelled from Castledermot, Co Kildare gave evidence for his son. In his policing career, especially as a chief inspector, he had surely encountered a murder trial before. Now though it was his son on trial and Michael understood more than anyone his life was in jeopardy.

Michael gave another account of his son's activity and the accidents he had been involved in. It wasn't until cross examined that anything new was heard. Michael admitted his son was normal enough until after the second motorbike accident. Michael said his son came home one night and challenged him to fight on the landing.

The defence called several doctors in an attempt to prove Tierney was suffering from mental incapacity. Dr Rose near Southampton who had treated the accused in 1928 said he found him unconscious at a convent on that occasion. Dr Rose told the court had he been aware of his medical history he would have considered epilepsy. He believed that an epileptic could suffer from violent outbursts instead of twitching seizures. Under cross examination, the doctor admitted he saw no violence from James and had to discharge him after four days as there was nothing obviously wrong with him.

Dr McDonald of Barringtons Hospital, Limerick who had treated the accused in July of 1936 gave similar evidence. He too would have suggested epilepsy but knew nothing of the medical history. McDonald reckoned that chronic epilepsy would reduce the intellect but he found no evidence of it with Tierney. The doctor was left with no choice but to discharge him on August 3rd.

Dr Hardman a radiologist and x-ray expert who had examined x-rays of Tierney's skull was called. He admitted Tierney's skull was larger than average and that the lower jaw was elongated. He said this was consistent with acromegaly but in such cases, he expected to find a tumour also. When questioned by Maguire for the prosecution Dr Hardman admitted that Tierney could have been born with a long jaw. He also said there was no evidence of a fracture or a blow to Tierney's skull.

Yet another doctor was called but by the defence this time, Dr William Haughton the senior surgeon at Stephens Hospital in Dublin. He had treated James in April of 1934 saying it took 2-3 days before the patient answered questions sensibly. At the time he gave his name as James Edward O'Neill from Castledermot Co. Kildare. Dr Haughton said James was confused for several days but then seemed normal.

Dr J Coyne, the medical officer of Mountjoy, said he had previously been the deputy superintendent of a London Mental Hospital for ten years. He had examined Tierney on several occasions in jail that year and had not found any major mental incapacity. Coyne believed the accused may suffer from acromegaly but could not say he was insane. He described Tierney as "was definitely below full adult standard and rather childish". Since being in Mountjoy in February of that year Tierney had not suffered any epileptic episodes. To the prosecution, Dr Coyne relented that a person suffering from acromegaly may suffer violent outbursts or hallucinations. In such a case he said Tierney may have imagined Vickers was about to attack him and lashed out in what he thought at the time was self defence. The judge asked "on any occasion on which you examined him was he insane in criminal law", Coyne answered simply "no".

Dr Rutherford a mental specialist from Dublin who had thirty years of experience treating mental disorders took the stand. The doctor described the diagnosis of acromegaly as very difficult saying people often suffered from it without knowing. Nowadays it can be diagnosed more easily with a blood test. He said Tierney was sane but suffered from acromegaly with symptoms such as epilepsy. He believed the attack on Thomas Vickers was consistent with Tierney suffering an attack of such symptoms.

Mr Roe for the defence was confident his client would not be found guilty of murder. It was Vaughan Buckley who made the closing speech for the defence. It was a last ditch attempt to save Tierney from the executioner as the medical evidence had not clearly claimed him to be insane. Buckley argued that if robbery was the motive, why did Tierney choose a taxi man and take him to one of the only places in Cork he could be identified.

He argued the notion that Tierney could not tell right from wrong and even going to Foley's that night was childish behaviour. He asked were they dealing with "the acts of a madman or the acts of a cunning intended robber". Haugh suggested he went to Foley's that night knowing there would be money. Earlier he had gone to Mrs Mahomet's and arranged a room for the night, was unable to pay but intended paying later when he had it. The prosecution now said this was evidence that Tierney set out that night to rob and then hide out for the night in Mrs Mahomet's before leaving the city.

Haugh said the most likely scenario was Tierney intended robbing Foley's but Vickers was suspicious of him and followed close behind. At the spur of the moment, Tierney changed his plan, dealt with the taxi man and then went on to Foley's. The prosecution was not sure he intended to kill that night or just rob him, but said that would never be known now.

Justice O'Byrne when he summed up the evidence explained to the jury the conditions for finding a verdict of manslaughter versus murder. He believed there was little to support the notion of self defence and therefore pointed the jury towards an unprovoked attack which meant a verdict of murder. On the plea of insanity, O'Byrne told the jury the onus of proving insanity rested with the accused. In other words, he implied in the eyes of the law every man must be assumed sane until proven otherwise. The judge suggested that Tierney's intelligence was lacking but said this was far from insane. Almost every detail of evidence was gone into again. He questioned why Tierney had arranged an alternative room for that night after staying in the Carbery for two weeks without paying a penny. He asked what was Tierney preparing for that night, did this cunning suggest insanity? Justice O'Byrne's summing up took two and three quarter hours before the jury retired.

They took just over two hours before returning with a verdict of guilty with a recommendation for mercy. Tierney hearing the sentence didn't respond but just stood there silently and besides looking a little pale he was unaffected by it all.

He was asked had he anything to say as to why the death sentence should not be passed but he simply replied "no sir". Justice O'Byrne then let it be known he agreed with the verdict and that the recommendation for mercy would be dealt with. It still left him the duty to pass the death sentence that day. As was usual he put on the black cap before telling Tierney that the 29th of April would be his last.

As the sentence was read out in court Monica Vickers was heard crying. Michael O'Neill was shocked and stunned by what he had just heard. Before leaving court that day the retired policeman was seen shaking hands with the widow.

Close to the scene of the crime in more recent times.

Immediately Mr Roe for the defence applied for leave to appeal on several grounds. Those were that the verdict was not in keeping with the weight of evidence and that the statement Tierney gave on the 26th of November should not be allowed. Justice O'Byrne refused the application for the appeal.

Later that month in the Court of Criminal Appeal the Chief Justice Mr Johnson allowed an application for free legal aid and transcripts of the evidence. It went towards an appeal against the guilty verdict and death sentence. The same legal team of Roe, Vaughan Buckley and Neville were assigned to the case.

The application bought some time for Tierney and he was not sentenced to death on the 29th of April. Instead on the 10th of May, the case came before the Court of Criminal Appeal presided over by the Chief Justice, the President of the High Court and Justice Hanna.

Now Mr Roe based his application on the same five grounds as before,
1. That the verdict was against the evidence and weight of evidence.
2. That the statement made by the accused on November 26th should not have been admitted to evidence.
3. That the learned judge misdirected the jury as to the relationship between the evidence of Dr Hardman and that of doctors Coyne and Rutherford.
4. That the learned judge should not have suggested to the jury that epilepsy if present would have been detected by Dr Ross in 1928.
5. That the weight of evidence in support of the theory of insanity was not fully or sufficiently put before the jury by the learned judge.

Roe addressing the Chief Justice said it was clear from the evidence that Thomas Vickers died at the hands of James Edward Tierney

On the second grounds for appeal, Roe told how Tierney was arrested in Limerick before eleven on the night of the 25th. He now revealed that the superintendents arrived from Cork about 4 am and proceeded to question the suspect. At that point, Tierney was in custody for several hours and had already been cautioned. Hannigan he said went in and asked about ninety questions. Roe argued that this was a peculiar arrangement and that Tierney had not volunteered his statement at all.

When Roe finished his argument the Chief Justice said it was not necessary for Mr Maguire to respond for the Attorney General. The Chief Justice felt he had heard enough and announced that the appeal was to be dismissed. He was satisfied that the statement Tierney gave in Limerick had been volunteered and therefore admissible. He also dismissed the other grounds for appeal saying the trial judge had acted fairly. The date of execution was fixed again, now it was to be Friday the 28th of May.

Roe applied for leave to appeal to the Supreme Court on grounds of the statement being inadmissible but the Chief Justice refused his request.

Within a day a petition had been set up calling for a reprieve for Tierney by the Dublin Men's Association. That very month a petition for Patrick Boylan had received 25,000 signatures and his death sentence had been reprieved. Boylan's case was very similar to this as his defence pleaded insanity which was doubted. Patrick Boylan in a fit of jealousy had cut his eighteen year old sweethearts throat with a razor at a party.

Tierney's only hope now rested with the Executive Council as the Supreme Court's appeal had been turned down. Only days before the date of execution the Executive Council made their decision. They commuted the death sentence to one of penal servitude for life.

James Tierney or O'Neill was only in his mid-twenties and had years to face behind bars. Between then and 1954 eighteen more men were executed in Ireland, many more were sentenced to death but received a reprieve. In 1964 the death sentence was abolished for nearly all cases of murder except for the murder of a Garda.

A Hatchet Job
Clancoolbeg Bandon 1888

Early on the morning of the 10th September at Carey's Cross near Bandon Kate Sullivan, a married woman of fifty years was up early attending to the usual household chores. She lit the fire and went about preparing breakfast. Her nephew, Daniel Burke, was sitting on a form, a sort of workbench and she told him to put down a kettle of water on the fire to boil a few eggs.

Daniel rose from the bench and went towards the fire. Without uttering a word he lashed out at his aunt with a hatchet he had pulled from under the bench. He didn't render Kate unconscious, nor was she lying in a pool of blood, she was surprisingly still standing and conscious.

Her son Patrick had seen it all and he ran to the nearest neighbours, the Mehegan's, for help. Burke was still armed and dangerous looking. As young Patrick went for help his first cousin Daniel pursued him armed with the bloody hatchet. When Patrick arrived at the neighbour's Daniel lingered outside and even made a lash at the door with the hatchet.

Patrick's father Stephen who was working in the fields got news of the deadly attack. He returned to find Burke still armed with the hatchet on the road with his son Patrick. Stephen managed somehow to wrestle the hatchet from Burke with the help of one of the Crowley's before he attacked anyone else. He then went back to his house to find his wife lying unconscious in a pool of blood. Dr Welply was sent for but he quickly realised the woman had serious head injuries from which she might never recover.

In the meantime, the now unarmed Daniel Burke was manhandled by several of the locals who struggled to keep hold of him until the police arrived. He was arrested and taken to Bandon barracks but seemed to be oblivious of the precarious position his aunt was in.

At the petty sessions in Bandon, Daniel Burke was charged before resident magistrate George Cronin with assaulting his aunt. Evidence was given in court that Kate Sullivan's life was in grave danger. Some evidence was produced that day; Daniel was remanded into custody and removed from the court.

Every day the doctor went to Sullivan's house and attended to Kate. Her condition didn't improve and she never once regained consciousness nor uttered a word to anyone. On Friday the 14th of September she succumbed to her head injuries and passed away. Now the charge against Daniel Burke was much more serious but he didn't seem to understand at all.

The inquest was held by Coroner James Somerville on Saturday the 15th of September. As was normal the district inspector Mr Green appeared for the crown. Daniel Burke was not present at the inquest. The jury was made up of twelve respectable men from the locality such as farmers and shopkeepers.

Patrick Sullivan swore he had seen it all that morning. His mother had asked Burke into the house and offered him breakfast. He pulled the hatchet from under the bench he was sitting on and struck her on the head. Patrick fled the house for his own safety and Burke came after him.

Husband of the deceased Stephen Sullivan recalled getting up on the morning of the 10th and going out to dig potatoes before going to work. In the yard he found a man sleeping but did not disturb him. He returned with the potatoes and told his wife Daniel Burke was asleep in the yard. She told her husband to wake him and have him come into the house for breakfast. After they had eaten, he left Burke in the kitchen with his wife while he went to work in the fields.

The next time he saw his wife she was unconscious on the kitchen floor, he lifted her up but she did not speak. Stephen said his wife remained in the same condition until she died the following Friday.

Medical evidence was given by Dr J Welply who had seen Mrs Sullivan on Monday and every day after until she died. The doctor said he found a bruise on the left side of the head two and a half inches long, under which the skull was fractured. Another wound on the other side of the head was similar and he described her face as very battered. Either of the wounds on the head would have resulted in death and he was satisfied they could be inflicted with the hatchet.

The jury duly found their verdict in agreement with the doctors "that the deceased died from wounds detailed by the doctor and that these were inflicted by Daniel Burke".

Officially death was recorded as a fracture of the skull and effusion of blood on the brain.

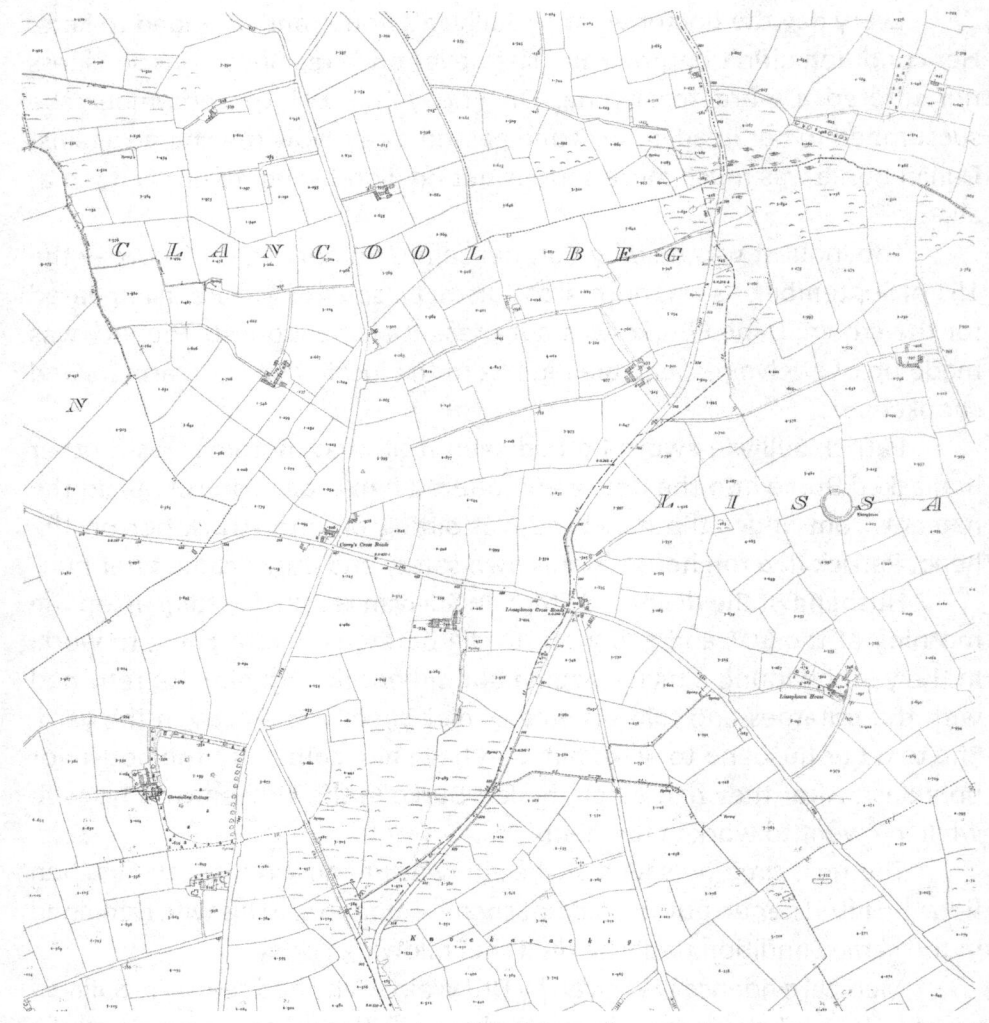

Map showing Clancoolbeg.

    Daniel Burke who was in the Army reserve was thirty years old and had at some point served in India. Since returning home though he had been in the workhouse hospital
    His Aunt Kate was fifty years old and lived with her family in a house, that wasn't built very long near Carey's Cross on the farm of John Crowley Clancoolbeg. The motive for the case seems Daniel Burke was indeed insane. It seems he had fallen in love or became infatuated with his first cousin, Kate Sullivan's daughter. She had however refused to permit the marriage and some said this was why he attacked his aunt.

On the 17th of September, Daniel Burke was to be charged at Bandon Petty Sessions. It was the District Inspector that rose to explain why Burke was not present. A message had arrived from the governor of the prison. The prison doctor said Daniel was suffering from delusions and not fit to plead. It was decided to adjourn and call the case again at the next sitting of the petty sessions. The case came before the Petty Sessions again and Burke was returned for trial at the Winter Assizes.

On Saturday the 8th of December Daniel Burke was brought before the Cork Winter Assizes and charged before Chief Baron Palles, that he killed his aunt Kate Sullivan. Palles said he was only in court to determine whether Burke was fit to plead or not. As he walked into court the accused was escorted by two attendants from the lunatic asylum. It was learned that day that Daniel Burke had been in the Lunatic Asylum since October.

The only evidence given was that of Dr Dwyer the resident medical superintendent of the lunatic asylum. He had been monitoring Burke's mental health regularly and believed he had improved vastly but only in the last few days. Chief Baron Palles was direct with the doctor "is he at present of sound mind and capable of pleading to this charge". The doctor believed he wasn't nor was he fit to defend himself in court. Despite the jury deciding he was not fit to plead, Burke was still asked had he anything to say. He replied, "I have nothing to say only that I didn't hit her". Burke didn't object to the case being postponed to the next Assizes in the spring of the following year.

No record of this is to be found so it is doubtful he was ever charged. If he was found guilty but insane he would have remained locked up indefinitely.

Modern image of Clancoolbeg cross close to the scene of the crime.

A Costly Dowry

Barreragh Courtmacsherry 1884

Long ago in Ireland when a woman got married her father paid a dowry. This was to ensure she would get a husband that could provide for her. The father would go to great lengths to get the money together and negotiate a sum agreeable to both parties. The family who received the sum often used it to arrange marriage settlements for their own daughters. So in effect, a dowry could ripple through the area passing from family to family as marriages were arranged.

It wasn't always for the daughter a dowry was paid. If a farmer had several sons he could pay a dowry to have one of his sons married into a farm. In 1880 Jeremiah McCarthy's father paid £80 for his son to marry Mary Murphy. Jeremiah moved to the townland of Barreragh near Courtmacsherry looking out to the old head of Kinsale. The arrangement with his father-in-law John Murphy was that Jeremiah was now half-owner of the thirty six acre farm and entitled to a share in the profits. When both his parents in law died, he would own the farm outright yet his wife had no rights at all.

What was strange though was John Murphy had three sons, none of whom lived on the farm. All three had left for America and given up any right of inheritance. It was said they left to get away from their father who was known to be a difficult stubborn man. John Murphy had two other daughters older than Mary that were married to local farmers. He would have had to pay a marriage settlement for each of these to get them set up on another farm.

Maybe Jeremiah didn't know what he was getting into when he got married or maybe he was forced into the arrangement. There was no question of building a new house for the newlyweds so the farmhouse was shared and the transition of power was slow to come about. It became obvious that John Murphy wanted the £80 and his daughter married but was reluctant to let another man run his farm. On several occasions, the old man sold goods without consulting his son-in-law. This exacerbated Jeremiah who felt the old man should accept his role in the farm. He knew he wouldn't have a say in the run of things until the old man was dead.

As time went on bitterness developed between the men, with Mary acting as the go between her husband and parents. After several years of marriage, there were no children born to the couple and the rift between the men grew. Simply put Jeremiah wanted control of the farm but the old man had no intention of going anywhere. There were violent outbursts at times between the men with the women in the house trying to keep the peace.

Coming up to Christmas in 1884 living in the house with the two couples became unbearable. Things got so bad that on one occasion Jeremiah broke into the old couple's bedroom and threatened to kill them with a pitchfork. The old man had enough and summoned his son-in-law to court but didn't press charges when it came to it. It didn't stop there though, on another occasion Jeremiah threatened him again with a reaping hook. Mary was also at the receiving end of her husband's anger and got it from him regularly.

The whole situation was known about in the locality and talked about by the neighbours. It seemed like McCarthy let it get to him, he grew more and more angry and bitter towards his in-laws.

One Thursday evening after dinner it erupted in the house once again. Mary went out to feed some leftover potatoes to the hens and her husband objected to it. He said the hens did nothing for him so they shouldn't be fed. Mary was reluctant to feed the hens seeing the mad stare in her husband's eyes but he gave in and let her. It wasn't until she put the few potatoes into the trough for the hens that Jeremiah jumped up from where he sat and reared up on her again.

He kicked the trough and cleared out the hens preventing them from eating. The old man came from another room and told his son-in-law not to break the trough he had made, as he had broken the one before it. Jeremiah wasn't listening now and took his frustration out on the trough kicking it again. The old man tried feebly to get the trough and put it out of harm's way but it was too late. Jeremiah lashed out again and this time he broke it. Still, the old man was concerned about the trough but Jeremiah lashed out with a stick and struck his wife in the mouth.

Then he turned his attention on the old man and grabbing him dragged him across the floor. Mary tried to separate the two men but it was impossible. She picked up the stick her husband had dropped and used it on him but to no effect. He grabbed it back from her and pulled the old man out of the house into the yard.

The two men struggled in the yard, anytime the old man managed to get back on his feet his son-in-law shoved him back down again. The old man got several lashes of the stick and several times fell heavily to the ground with Jeremiah on top of him.

Eventually, Mary managed to get between them and helped her father back into the house. She got him to his room but he fell to the floor. He never uttered another word and they soon realised he was dead. Jeremiah came into the room armed with a pike as if he needed it to defend himself. When he came to realise the old man wasn't responding he retreated to the yard. Did he understand his actions had led to this?

The women knew that John was dead and it was Jeremiah who had caused it. Word spread quickly; a priest and doctor soon arrived to do what they could. The police came from Courtmacsherry and duly arrested Jeremiah McCarthy.

The following day the resident magistrate Cronin went to Murphy's house to take statements from the women. It was an ordeal for them to go back over it all again so soon, made worse with Jeremiah present and allowed to question them. Julia was the first examined and was so weak she made her statement in bed. Despite this, she made clear her son-in-law's ill treatment of them all over the last few years. She said he had threatened her husband's life before. It was normal for a suspect to be allowed to question a witness when giving a statement but often they fell into the trap of incriminating themselves.

> Jeremiah: Was my wife present on every occasion we were quarrelling?
> Julia: She was, he was continually beating his wife and threatening to kill us all.
> Jeremiah: Am I the first person to have struck a blow yesterday?
> Julia: You are, you struck your wife, you had a stick in your hand but I could not say it was with that you struck her.
> Jeremiah: After throwing down your husband the first time did you see him running after me with a pike?
> Julia: No, he did not he had not a pike a stick or a stone but you killed him right before me in ten minutes.
> Jeremiah: after he came in the last time into the bedroom, did he make any attempt to go after me again?

Julia: He never spoke another word after we brought him into the room.
Jeremiah: Did you tell your husband to stay where he was?
Julia: I was calling him trying to rouse him up, but he was dead when he was brought into the house.
Jeremiah: Did he stand of his own accord in the room?
Julia: Not at all, he fell down dead.

Once Julia had given her statement, McCarthy was handcuffed and taken to Courtmacsherry and from there to the county jail. He was remanded in custody for eight days to await the verdict of the inquest. After he left the house that day both women broke down in front of those congregating for the wake. They had suffered for years but seeing John die before them was too much to bear. Would Jeremiah ever darken their door again?

Jeremiah McCarthy must have known then that the mother and daughter would give the same story and he wouldn't stand a chance against it. That day was the last time he could legally be allowed to speak as the suspect could not be questioned in court.

On Saturday the coroner Dr James Sommerville held the inquest at half twelve in Murphy's house. A jury of twelve local men were sworn in to listen to the facts on how Murphy had died. The jury was comprised of foreman James Morgan a local farmer, farmers Thomas Gough of Cullinagh and Thomas E Beechinor from Ballynamona and John Murphy, George T Hayes, Thomas Jeffers, James Donovan, Michael Donovan, Patrick Collins, Jeremiah Neill, Patrick Murphy and Jeremiah Mahony. District Inspector Carr from Clonakilty kept an eye on proceedings for the crown prosecution. Rev Peter Hill parish priest of Barryroe attended and Rev John O'Dea of the same parish.

Mary McCarthy was the first witness called at the inquest; she revealed that relations were so bad her husband would not sit at the same table as her father despite living under the same roof. She had only been married two months when they fell out and that was four years ago.

The coroner asked her a direct question "do you think your husband thought your father was living too long?" Mary agreed saying that was the root of it all. Her husband often remarked when the old man was out that he might not return alive. She described their living arrangements over the last number of years saying there was often trouble between the men. She then described in detail the events that evening that led to her father's death. She said her father never laid a hand on her husband that day and only tried to stop him from breaking another trough.

Her mother Julia Murphy gave a very similar story of the events and how they had suffered at the hands of their son-in-law. The coroner seemed somewhat satisfied with the evidence the women had given.

Dr Henry Garde of Timoleague told how he had carried out the post mortem with Dr Saunders. The only trace of violence he found on the deceased man was on his left temple. The brain appeared healthy and the skull intact. He reckoned the man suffered from heart disease and he described the heart itself as flabby and fatty. The coroner asked was it the condition of his heart that caused the death. The doctor believed the heart ceased due to the stress of the struggle. He thought that a healthy man would have survived a similar beating.

The coroner made it clear though that John Murphy could have lived for a long time had he not suffered such handling. Having heard the medical evidence the coroner addressed the jury saying they didn't need to incriminate any individual in their verdict.

It didn't take them long to conclude though that "the deceased on the 11th of December dropped suddenly dead from disease of the heart and that death was accelerated by a violent struggle with Jeremiah McCarthy".

A magisterial investigation found that there was a case to answer and sent him to trial at the Spring Assizes. He was kept in jail to await his trial which was months away. Many believed he had become obsessed with his domestic arrangements and it had come to affect his mental state.

The following March he appeared before Justice Andrews and pleaded not guilty to the wilful murder of his father-in-law. The prosecution was led by crown solicitor Gregg and queens counsel Green, while solicitor Bushe defended McCarthy.

The only witness with direct evidence called that day was Julia Murphy. As before she portrayed the hardship her husband had suffered at McCarthy's hand. On several occasions, Jeremiah threatened his life with a pike and once with a reaping hook. She also heard Jeremiah say he would take his own life when he was angry.

Neighbour Cornelius Sexton told how he had met McCarthy the evening Murphy died. He recalled how his face was covered in blood and that he asked for a smoke saying it would be his last for some time.

McCarthy told him the blood was from when the old man struck him with a spade.

Dr Garde from Timoleague told how the old man's heart failed under the exertion but the wounds on him were superficial and not the cause of death. He went on to say he didn't find blood on the body.

Two constables were questioned by Mr Bushe and recalled finding a spade and pike with signs of blood on them but they were not produced in court.

Mr Bushe pleaded for his client saying there was not enough evidence to end his life. Bushe claimed Julia Murphy had a grudge against her son-in-law and was willing to say anything. He argued that the old man was the aggressor and McCarthy was only trying to stop him when he was angry.

That day in court the jury returned after deliberating for just forty minutes. The foreman announced that they could not agree on a verdict. It was the evidence of the old woman which the prosecution relied heavily upon; all of the jury did not believe her. Justice Andrews asked was there anything he could do but they thought not. Andrews told them it was an important case and sent them back again.

This time when they returned their verdict was guilty of manslaughter with a recommendation to mercy. Andrews announced that he would consider their recommendation before sentencing and McCarthy was put back into custody.

When it came to sentencing the judge said although Jeremiah was guilty of manslaughter, death would not have occurred but for his father-in-law's weak state. At that point, the guilty party had already spent four months in jail. He then sentenced McCarthy to nine months of hard labour starting from the date he was first jailed.

Going Home from the Fair
Derrigra West Ballineen 1900

About six in the morning a railway navvy called Donovan came running to the village of Ballineen with dreadful news. On his way to work, just outside the village in the townland of Derrigra, he had found a dead man on the road. Sergeant Boyd with his three constables King, Sullivan and Daughton quickly went to the scene. The dead man was known locally as Paul Mahony, a 23 year old labourer. He was lying on his back across the middle of Derrigra road which led to Kinneigh about half a mile from Ballineen.

There were no obvious signs of how he died except for a small cut over his left eye and a mark on his chin. The police examined the scene and believed a struggle had taken place possibly the night before and so suspected foul play.

As the police were there that morning, a man approached but turned when he saw them and fled. To the police, he didn't seem like a man who was completely surprised to see the body but wasn't expecting the police. They felt this man knew something about what went on the night before and must be found.

It turned out Mahony had last been seen alive in a pub the night before, with Daniel Murphy, the man who had fled that morning. Sergeant Boyd and constables King and Daughton set out for Connagh to make an arrest. They went to Murphy's farmhouse and took Daniel, a farmer's son, into custody. They had seen him at the scene that very morning but he fled across the fields. He had also been seen arguing with Paul Mahony in Mrs Donovan's pub in Ballineen the night before. Murphy made no statement to the police and was brought to Ballineen barracks.

No time was wasted, Coroner Neville was informed and he made his way to the village where that very evening an inquest was opened in Fitzgerald's Hotel in Ballineen. The police were represented by District Inspector Davis from Dunmanway who listened intently but also intended to question the witnesses himself.

The jury was made up of local men, the foreman Patrick Fitzgerald a draper, Daniel Deasy teacher, Patrick Donovan harness maker, William Driscoll Blacksmith, Michael Donovan shopkeeper and publican, James

Warren master tailor, publicans John Kehilly, Thomas Enright and David Coakley publican all from Ballineen. Also Abraham Schofield a farmer from Knockaneady, Nicholas Penny, J Shorten and John O'Keeffe.

The first witness was Mahony's employer, Timothy Nyhan, a farmer from Kinneigh. He formerly identified the remains saying he last saw Paul Mahony alive around 11 am the day before. His wife gave Paul 10 shillings that were due to him and he left for the fair, saying he was going to buy a few shirts. Timothy said Mahony had been working for him for about 12 months, before that Paul had worked for Regan's in Nedinagh near Dunmanway. Timothy was also aware that Paul had been in the US navy.

District Inspector Davis began questioning Nyhan, asking was Mahony troublesome after drink. The farmer was reluctant to reply, but did say "he was a very nice decent fellow; he was a little noisy when he was drunk". This wouldn't do Davis at all and he kept asking several times was Mahony quarrelsome after drink. Eventually, the farmer gave in, saying sometimes he was, but he never saw anyone quarrel with him. Davis strongly insinuated that Mahony chose to go to the fair in Ballineen to cause trouble. Even the coroner explained that young men go to town on the fair days as a day out knowing they would meet up with their friends.

Dr Morgan O'Brien Neville from Warrensbrook near Ballineen was called to give medical evidence as he had examined the body in the courthouse with Dr Smyth. Superficially he found a small abrasion above the left eye and another behind the right ear. It was when they removed the scalp that a fracture of the occipital bone at the back of the skull about 2.5inches long was discovered. Removing the brain he found a clot of blood on the right hand side. The heart also had a blood clot in the right ventricle. In the stomach was found undigested food and it smelled strongly of porter. He concluded death was as a result of blood on the brain caused by the fracture of the skull.

D.I. Davis was in straight away with:
"What would the fracture be caused by? By a fall but it should be a fall of some violence.
Would it be caused by a blow? I don't think it was caused by a blow, I don't think it was caused by violence at all.
Could it be caused by a blow? No, because we would have other signs that we have not.
Would it be caused by a blow of a stone or stick or by coming in contact with a car?

I don't think so, it must be caused by coming into contact with the ground. If it were caused by a stick or stone, there would be an external mark and there would be a depression on the brain."
Then, juror, Daniel Coakley began.
"Did the clot of blood on the inside correspond with the external mark? No
When he got this fall do you think his death was very soon after? I would not like to say, he was certainly stunned by the fall"

Under further questions, the doctor struggled to explain what caused the abrasion over the eye. He said the other injury by the ear could be caused by another man catching his ear in a struggle. The doctor agreed that if Mahony was struggling with another man, and was violently tripped onto the road, it could result in the injuries he saw.

It was getting late that evening and all Dr Smyth did was agree with what had already been heard. Davis wanted to adjourn the inquest until Saturday saying he had no more witnesses to call that night. Daniel Coakley suggested there was enough evidence to find a cause of death but Davis was adamant that all the facts had not been heard. They agreed to adjourn until half past five on Saturday evening and in the meantime, Paul Mahony's remains could be buried the following day.

Paul Mahony was found on a back road, just 100 yards from the Derrigra crossroads. On his person was found a purse with 1s 11/2d and also Mahony's discharge papers from the American Navy. It turned out he had served on a ship called the USS Lehigh. He joined the Navy in June 1898 and was honourably discharged in September 98. There was also in his possession a letter from his brother-in-law sent from Somerset New Hampshire. Paul Mahony was originally from Counkilla, North of Drimoleague, where his father Maurice was a labourer and his mother was Mary Kingston. Both his parents were widowers when they married in Drimoleague in 1870.

When the inquest was resumed on Saturday evening, the police revealed further details which explained why they believed Paul Mahony was not alone when he died. When discovered on Thursday morning, a cap had been found folded and placed under his head. Also, his arms had been straightened out neatly and arranged on the body. The police wanted to know who had been with Mahony that night and what they knew of the death. Several of those that had been with Mahony that evening had been questioned but had nothing to add, Daniel Murphy was still in custody.

Paul Mahony lying across the road, illustrated by Claire O'Donovan.

At the inquest, Jeremiah Donovan was called to describe finding Mahony on the road. Donovan lived at Dromidiclough and told how he left home at half five that morning going to work on the railway. About 100 yards from Derrigra Cross he came upon the man's body lying across the road. At first, he doubled back and met a colleague Tom Murray, and then another Railwayman Con Leary arrived. He said the three stood there for a minute looking at the body, and then he went to the Barracks to report it. Donovan did not know Paul Mahony saying he had never seen him before that morning. He told the jury that none of them touched the body, he had noticed the cap under his head but not that it was folded neatly.

Thomas Murray of Derrigra was called to be sworn in but was reluctant. He asked why he was being brought into it. The coroner encouraged him with "take the book man, you have to only tell the truth and what need you be afraid of doing that". Murray was sworn in and told the same account of coming on the body. He said he was agitated that morning and noticed nothing about the body but saw no other person other than those already mentioned.

He did recall being in Ballineen the day before, at the fair, he went after work about six in the evening. He was in town for an hour or so and noticed some young men running about by Mrs Donovan's pub. While in town he noticed Daniel Murphy of Kinneigh passing by the cross but couldn't say what time or whether it was before going to town or after.

Mrs Anne Donovan was next called to tell who was in her pub on the fair day. She saw Paul Mahony between nine and ten that night with Daniel Murphy, Jerry Hurley from Connagh and another of the Hurley's from Dromfeagh. There were a few more in the pub, Buckley from Teenah, Tom Cullinane from Farranmareen, Den Crowley and Dave Crowley from Connagh were sitting by the fire in the kitchen. At the counter about half nine, there was some disagreement between Murphy and Mahony, the publican said it ended after a few words and Jerry Hurley intervened. She cleared the pub about ten that night and took no notice of Paul Mahony leaving, but there were two policemen outside as everyone left.

Jeremiah Hurley was then questioned he told how he sold a sheep at the fair and spent the rest of the day in O'Neill's pub. It was later when he went to Mrs Donovan's and he corroborated who she said was present. Hurley could not recall what Mahony and Murphy had words about but did recall saying to them it was ugly for neighbours to be quarrelling. He thought that it was not long after, that Mrs Donovan cleared the pub and he was the first to leave as he was quite drunk.

After leaving the pub he headed for home, he met Daniel Murphy and Bill Hurley on the road but had no idea where, whether he overtook them or the other way round. All he could say was he spoke to Daniel Murphy on the way home; he could not recall the conversation but seemed sure that Paul Mahony was not mentioned.

The coroner thought this was very unusual, that he was so unsure about the conversation, but still, certain Mahony was not mentioned. Hurley could not recall the conversation with Murphy that night but remained positive Paul Mahony was not mentioned. He then said how he didn't know how far he walked with them but parted with Bill Hurley at Lordan's Cross. The coroner was frustrated with him saying "Why man didn't you say you went home with Hurley and Murphy?" but Hurley thought he had made it clear with "of course I did". So if Hurley could be believed he had gone home with Daniel Murphy who was in custody and passed by Derrigra Crossroads that night.

Patrick Buckley was sworn in and questioned saying how he had also been to Ballineen for the fair and spent much of the day drinking. He too was in Mrs Donovan's pub in the evening with Tom Cullinane. He recalled seeing Daniel Murphy and David Crowley there but not Paul Mahony who he didn't even know. He had no idea when he left the pub that night but had no recollection of Mrs Donovan ordering everyone out. Buckley admitted to being drunk but said he walked a bit of the way home with David Crowley, Denis Crowley, Daniel Murphy and Bill Hurley. He wasn't sure where but could have met them at Liscroneen Cross which was also known as Lordan's cross or nearer the village. He went back to Daniel Murphy's with Bill Hurley and all three of them slept in the same bed.

The following morning he got up and went to Ballineen again but said he went by the Manch road and did not pass the place where Mahony had been found. He said it was only at eight on Friday morning when he got to Ballineen that he heard Mahony was dead on the road. He was asked did he go to the spot afterwards but replied "What would carry me up there" saying that Mahony was neither his friend nor enemy. He knew Mahony for the last few months but had not met him since his mother's wake. Buckley seemed sure that he had not met Paul Mahony in Ballineen on the day of the fair.

District Inspector Davis announced he had no more witnesses to call, yet no more was known than the day before. Coroner Neville now wanted to wrap it up and find a verdict. He suggested to the jury that they merely find according to the medical evidence, which could have been done the day before. The jury had no option but to agree with the coroner who said: "that death was due to fracture of the occipital bone and effusion of blood on the brain". What caused the fracture they were unable to determine and went with an open verdict.

It was still a mystery who was with Paul Mahony on the way home from the fair and what happened to him. All we knew now was Daniel Murphy was most likely not with him as he seemed to have an alibi but the evidence seemed a little contradictory. Murphy was not released though and the following Thursday he appeared at the petty sessions and was remanded for another eight days.

It took a few days for the police to make progress with their investigation. When they had a clearer picture of the events that night, Daniel Murphy was released from custody. On the 25th of April, cousins from Connagh, David and Denis Crowley, were arrested and charged with being involved in the death of Paul Mahony. David Crowley was a married farmer about fifty years of age. Denis was younger in his mid thirties, a farmer's son and like the deceased had returned from America.

It was Saturday the 5th of May before some of the mystery was unravelled in court. At a special sitting in Ballineen petty sessions, David and Denis Crowley were now charged with the death of Paul Mahony before resident magistrate Butler. The accused men were legally represented by solicitor Mr Powell.

First Jeremiah Donovan and Mrs Anne Donovan were called and gave similar testimony to the inquest. The next witness was Bill Hurley from Gortaleen, he was better known as Bill, but his name was Jeremiah. He had not been called at the inquest that was a different Jeremiah Hurley but had been mentioned as walking home with Daniel Murphy and sleeping at his house.

Hurley recalled being turned out of the pub at ten. Those present were Paul Mahony, Denis and David Crowley (the accused men), Tom Cullinane, Daniel Murphy and Jeremiah Hurley from Connagh. He thought that there was also Kelly from Teenah.

They all left together and two policemen followed them out of the village as far as Thomas Tanner's house. Between there and Derrigra Cross they split up, he went ahead with Jeremiah Hurley and Daniel Murphy. Before the three got to Derrigra Cross they heard an argument going on behind them, between David Crowley and Paul Mahony. Denis Crowley and Tom Cullinane were also there. He heard David Crowley threaten that he could kick Mahony. Mahony replied saying nobody would stand up for him and they did not go back to help.

It was further on before Hurley heard anything else that night. He stopped below the entrance to Firgrove where William Hosford lived to light his pipe. It was then he looked back to see Denis Crowley strike Mahony with his fist. He saw Mahony fall violently backwards onto the road and commented to the two who were with him that it was a shame to see it. He saw Mahony get up but he seemed drunker than before. David Crowley then attacked Mahony and grabbed him by the throat. Mahony seemed helpless. Hurley said the night was bright enough that he could see what went on. He didn't explain nor was he asked why he didn't go back, knowing nobody would help Mahony.

The three walked on to Lordan's Cross where Jeremiah Hurley left them. The pair then stopped off at Daniel McCarthy's house in Liscroneen, Daniel Hurley was there before them. They waited for three quarters of an hour for the others to arrive.

When only three appeared, Tom Cullinane and the two Crowley's, Hurley enquired after Paul Mahony. It was Denis Crowley who replied with:" I hit him with my fist below there and left him inside the dyke". David warned him to say no more about it and then told Jeremiah to be heading home.

They all walked to Murphy's cross where the Crowley's and Tom Cullinane left them. Hurley went to Daniel Murphy's house with him and said ten minutes later Patrick Buckley arrived. The three sat around the fire smoking and then slept in the same bed as we already heard.

The District Inspector had enough for the magistrates to send the Crowley's for a trial but chose instead to apply for another remand of eight days. Powell asked for bail for his clients offering £1000 if it was required which was a serious sum of money. The magistrates made it clear there was to be no bail for any sum of money.

The following Saturday the court sat again to hear more evidence. Constable Peter King told of being at Mrs Donovan's when it was cleared on the night of the fair. He recalled how some left the pub when the publican asked but he had to go in to get a few out. King said that it was David Crowley, Denis Crowley and Tom Cullinane who remained and were reluctant to go until he asked them. Even after the pub was cleared Denis Crowley made another attempt to get back inside. The constable told how he followed the group as they walked west out of the village that night as far as Thomas Tanner's house.

Dr Neville gave the same account as he had at the inquest. He described in detail the injuries he found. Before he finished District Inspector Davis asked "Were there signs of suffocation?" Powell tried to object to that question with "That is a most unfair question". It did seem a little off considering the doctor had made no mention of suffocation at the inquest. Strangely Dr Neville agreed with "The position of the blood in the heart indicated suffocation". Powell tried to move away from that by asking the cause of death. Dr Neville said death was caused by blood on the brain but then added "Death was probably hastened by suffocation". Dr Neville didn't believe the blow Mahony received caused the death, but the fall would have. He then referred to the testimony of Jeremiah Bill Hurley saying the throttling Mahony received from David Crowley would have caused the suffocation.

Sergeant Boyd was called next and described in detail the scene he found on the road that morning. He talked about the night before when Mrs Donovan's pub was cleared. The sergeant went on to tell of going to David Crowley's house making enquiries a few hours after the body was found. He clarified that at that stage he had no suspicion of Crowley, nor any intention of arresting him that day. In fact, Crowley wasn't arrested for several days afterwards. Powell knew where it was going and objected to the conversation the Sergeant had with David Crowley saying it could not be used as evidence. The debate went on for some time, Powell was adamant that anything David Crowley had said the day the body was found was not given voluntarily and therefore could not be evidence.

However, the sergeant was allowed to proceed and he said at the time he was not satisfied with the answers David Crowley gave. David Crowley told him he had left the pub on the night of the fair at nine. Boyd then brought in Constables King and Daughton asking Crowley "Did you see these men outside the pub at ten?" The Sergeant told the court that at this point Crowley became very pale and his wife intervened with: "Don't be too hard on him, can't you see the state he is in". Boyd then said that Crowley's wife gave him a chair to sit on but he fainted just as he sat down.

Powell again objected to what the Sergeant was saying with "The man had been drinking heavily the previous day, I object to this being taken down". Magistrate Butler wasn't sure what he should do and suggested adjourning to ask the Crown Solicitor for his opinion on the matter. Davis obviously wanted it to be allowed saying "If the man fainted would it not be taken as evidence". Butler was unsure what he should do with it and asked the Sergeant "Did he actually faint?" Sergeant Boyd couldn't have been clearer with his answer "His wife drew attention to his colour and put him in a chair and he fainted in it".

Butler still didn't know what he should do, he was keen to finish up the evidence that day and make a decision but now he knew he couldn't. No matter how much Davis pushed it, Sergeant Boyd's testimony was not allowed but would be held over and a decision made about it.

District Inspector Davis was examined next and described in detail the scene he found on the road that morning. He said Jeremiah Bill

Hurley showed him the spot where Denis Crowley struck Mahony; it was 38feet from where the body was found. He found large stones there, one particularly sharp and jagged which could have caused the injury to Mahony. Once the police gave evidence of arresting the Crowley's, the prosecution rested their case and Powell was asked did he still object to Boyd's testimony.

Powell's answer was "Indeed I do", and the magistrate suggested submitting it to Mr Wright for his legal opinion. Powell again argued the police had no right to examine a man they had no charge against and then later use it against him as it had been taken without caution. The court was adjourned for a week and in the meantime, District Inspector Davis was to consult Mr Wright. At the last minute, Powell chanced "Would you consider bail?" but Davis strongly objected and the Crowley's were taken back to jail that evening.

A week later back in court District Inspector Davis had his reply from the Crown Solicitor and read it out for all to hear. Mr Wright's reply was "In my opinion, if the Sergeant held out no inducement to Crowley to make a statement, even though such were made in reply to questions, it is admissible. The circumstances under which the statement was made, as to the demeanour, uneasiness etc of the prisoner are also admissible".

Powell objected, quoting case law but Davis argued that the case could not be compared. Then the defence solicitor said it straight, a cunning member of the constabulary could go first and fish out whatever information he could get from a person of interest and then arrest him afterwards. The argument went on for some time with Powell continuing to quote other cases. Eventually, the magistrates ruled that the statement would be admissible and Powell's objection to it was noted in the records.

Sergeant Boyd was called to resume his testimony from the week before. He told of questioning David Crowley, who he knew was not telling the truth about the time he left the pub. He pointed to Constable King and asked Crowley did he see him in the pub at ten. Then he asked, "Did you not see Mrs Donovan take the pint out of Tom Cullinane's hand at ten o clock?" Boyd said at this point David Crowley appeared pale and nervous, making no reply to him. Crowley's wife intervened telling the Sergeant he was going too far, she caught her husband by the arm and put him into the chair. Now Boyd said that David Crowley appeared to be in a half fainted state and he asked no further questions to him. Davis asked "Had you any suspicion on him at the time?" but again Powell objected saying a suspicion the Sergeant had could not be evidence. The sergeant then made it clear that he did not arrest David Crowley that day.

Sergeant Boyd described finding documents on the body. One of which was an honourable discharge from the US Navy. Powell again objected now he had a problem with the word honourable being used as it could be mistaken for the deceased man's character. The certificate of discharge was ruled as admissible.

After all the objections Powell declined to cross examine Sergeant Boyd. The defence also had no witnesses to call and Powell reserved his defence. He did make one observation on the evidence, saying that what the chief witness Jeremiah Bill Hurley said was not corroborated at all. He asked why the men such as Daniel Murphy who were also on the road that night were not called. Powell claimed no jury would convict on such evidence and applied again for bail for his clients.

Davis strongly objected to bail saying it was hard enough to get evidence. He hinted that with the Crowley's out on bail, some of the witnesses might contradict themselves at the trial. The magistrate refused bail, saying if the accused were convicted at a trial the time spent in jail before the trial would go towards the sentence. Powell however argued that if they were to be acquitted at the trial the time spent in jail would be unfair. Magistrate Butler told Powell to apply to the Queen's Bench and then returned the two men for trial at the next Assizes and they were taken back to jail that night.

At the Summer Assizes in July of that year, David and Denis Crowley pleaded not guilty to killing Paul Mahony on the 11th of April. It seemed a contradiction but Mr Wright the crown solicitor who had advised on the admissibility of Sergeant Boyd's statement was now prosecuting, assisted by Mr Moriarty and Mr Cullinane.

The defence now had Mr Brereton Barry and Patrick Lynch with local Dunmanway solicitor Mr Powell.

When the long panel of jurors were called that day they amounted to 47. The defence was entitled to challenge 20 jurors without cause and as many more as they could give a reason for. The crown was allowed to have jurors standby without giving any reason. Even when the defence agreed to only challenge 12 there were still concerns about the number of jurors.

It was decided to adjourn until the next assizes and bail was agreed for the Crowley's. Justice Kenny set bail at £40 each and two sureties of £20 each were to be put up.

It was March of the following year before the Crowley's appeared in court again. This time the charge was manslaughter before Justice Baron Palles in the county court. Both men pleaded not guilty to the indictment against them. Now Mr Seymour Bushe led the prosecution with Mr Moriarty and Crown Solicitor Mr Wright. Brereton Barry led the defence with Patrick Lynch and Mr Powell.

As was normal Seymour Bushe opened the case stating the facts as he saw it and alluding to the evidence that would be heard in court.

They began with Jeremiah Bill, the principal witness on whom the whole case hinged. He gave a very similar account to what had been heard before. It was under cross examination that he admitted to going round to Jeremiah Hurley's house at ten that morning, to discuss what they would say to the police. He knew then that Paul Mahony was dead and Daniel Murphy had been arrested.

Barry asked:
"Did you say to him "you and I must clear Danny Murphy between us"? I did.
What had Danny Murphy to be cleared of? Of killing Paul Mahony.
Who said Danny Murphy killed Paul Mahony? Nobody said it.
Why did you want to clear him of it if nobody said it? To do justice.
But sure nobody had said he did it? No.
Can you give any reasonable explanation why you said to Jeremiah Hurley that he and you should clear Danny Murphy? I said he could free him if he liked.
Nobody had accused Danny Murphy at that time? No."

So basically Jeremiah Bill admitted going around to his namesake's house that morning when he heard the news to get their stories straight. If he was telling the truth would he have needed to do that?

When Mr Barry pleaded the case for the defence he put forward the notion that it was Daniel Murphy who had attacked Paul Mahony that night. Barry suggested he wasn't out to find Murphy guilty but wished to prove that the Crowley's were innocent of the charge against them. He claimed Hosford's gate was wrenched from its hinges and used to transport the body but could not prove it. A donkey was also used that night and Barry called to the owner Coakley to say his donkey was missing in the morning. Barry's problem was he had no actual witnesses to prove his version and no one to say Murphy did it.

Barry called several witnesses, Cornelius O'Leary who lived along the road heard Murphy say that night "Take off me, let me back and I will let Paul Mahony see what I can do to him".

When Justice Chief Baron Palles summed up he asked the jury to satisfy themselves beyond all reasonable doubt that the prisoners were the men who caused Mahony's death. He made it clear that the defence had taken a most unusual course and he believed an illegal one to suggest Murphy was involved instead of their clients. The judge made it clear to the jury that they were not there to decide on the guilt of Murphy that day but said it affected what they were there for.

On the evidence against the accused, the judge did concede that it depended on Jeremiah Bill Hurley and was only corroborated by Murphy. He made it clear to the jury they had to believe these men and everything they said to secure a conviction.

After three quarters of an hour, the foreman announced that there was no chance of the jury agreeing on a verdict that day. Wright conceded that there was no point in sending the Crowley's before another trial at that Assizes so he proposed to adjourn and try again at the Summer Assizes. Bail was agreed and set to the same amount as before.

In July it was Justice Andrews who presided over the retrial in the county court.

Mr Seymour Bushe, Queen's Counsel, still led the prosecution with Mr Moriarty and Crown Solicitor Wright. The defence team also remained the same.

When Bushe opened the prosecution case he gave the day's events at the fair and how all the men walked home together. He would prove that Denis Crowley struck the deceased to such an extent that Mahony was violently blown to the ground. When he regained his feet it was David Crowley who attacked Mahony and throttled him by the throat. He said Paul Mahony was a fine young man who had served in the US Navy with distinction. Bushe gave a brief account of the events leading up to Mahony's death.

Hosford's gate and the bend on the road below it.

They all left the pub together and walked west out of the village. By Tanner's house, Buckley had left them and they split into two groups. Ahead were the two Jeremiah Hurleys with Daniel Murphy. Not far behind was the deceased, Tom Cullinane and the two accused men.

After Derrigra Crossroads, Jeremiah Bill stopped below Hosford's gate to light his pipe, while his two companions went on a little. He looked back and witnessed Mahony struck by Denis Crowley which would explain why the others did not see it. There is a bend in the road at that point which makes what Jeremiah Bill said all the more plausible.

Bushe tried to justify why Tom Cullinane had never given evidence saying he was drunk that night, but in reality they all were. No matter how drunk he was, Cullinane surely knew what occurred after all he was at the scene that night.

In court, Jeremiah Bill Hurley gave pretty much the same account as he had several times before. He did reveal that not only did he know the Crowley's but they were cousins of his, he was friendly with them and had a drink in Fitzgerald's pub that day.

Under cross examination by Mr Barry, he could not explain why he didn't go back when he saw Mahony attacked. He did say the following day he didn't go back to the scene. He had heard that Dan Murphy had been arrested and instead he went to his namesake, Jeremiah Hurley. He claimed now that he told Jeremiah Hurley that they must make a statement to free

Murphy, but Murphy remained in custody for two weeks. He denied when questioned that he told people it was one man who killed Paul Mahony and also denied saying the Crowley's were innocent.

Daniel Murphy gave an account that corroborated Jeremiah Bill Hurley's version. Murphy told of going to the scene the following morning saying he was surprised to see the police there so early; he fled through the ditch and across the fields. Murphy claimed it was one of the Crowley's that had asked him to check in the morning if Mahony was dead. He also admitted that when he ran from the police he went straight to Jeremiah Bill Hurley's house. Murphy also told that Buckley had since left Ireland and gone to America.

Jeremiah Hurley from Connagh who was also on the road that night was next examined. From his evidence, nothing new was learned that day he merely corroborated with what had already been heard from Murphy and Jeremiah Bill. After that, all the prosecution had to call was Sergeant Boyd, the doctors and evidence of finding the body and arresting the prisoners.

Barry spoke for the defence as he had before. He still maintained that the blame was being put on his clients, who he said were innocent. The Crowley's with Tom Cullinane were the first group along the road he claimed. He said Paul Mahony followed behind with Murphy and the Hurleys. He had several witnesses to call who would attempt to prove what he had said. The defence had not suggested this time that Daniel Murphy was the guilty party just that the Crowley's were innocent.

The defence then called Anne Donovan the publican but she did not go back over the night she cleared the pub. Instead, she recalled Jeremiah Bill Hurley coming into her pub on the day of the petty sessions. She heard him say the Crowley's never killed Mahony and that he put two innocent men in jail. He also said that if asked he would say Paul Mahony was alive beyond O'Leary's. Anne reckoned he had said this twice in her pub, once on the day he returned from the Assizes in Cork back in March and again on the day of the Petty Sessions.

Denis O'Leary who lived in Derrigra West, between Ballineen and Lordan's Cross was next called. He was going to bed on the night of the 11th of April the year before when he heard voices outside. It was 11 o'clock and he heard the voices of the Crowley's and Cullinane joking on the road as they passed by.

Later that night about 1 in the morning he heard other voices coming along the road from Ballineen. One he heard saying "Oh fie, why did you do that" but it was not any of the Crowley's. Denis told that the place the body was found was further towards Ballineen than his house which was further along the road.

Cornelius O'Leary was next produced, brother of the last witness. He also heard voices on the night of 11th April 1900 at about eleven. Cornelius however said he got up and looked out the window; it was Dan Murphy and Bill Hurley passing by. He described the men as having a hold of each other and Dan Murphy saying "Take off me and let me go back and I'll let Paul Mahony see what he can do to me". He said a few yards behind them was Paul Mahony and Buckley a few yards behind him.

To clarify O'Leary's cottage was further along the road to where the body had been found, so if Cornelius O'Leary was right then something else happened on the road that night that was not being heard in court.

Another local man John McSweeney, a labourer from Derrigra West, told that he had passed Hosford's gate that night in April at about half nine and saw nothing out of place. The following morning he passed again and the gate was thrown against the ditch it appeared that below the gate several men had been on the road.

Another man who lived near the scene of the crime, Patrick Coakley was called. He told that about eleven that night Patrick Buckley arrived at his house asking to borrow his donkey to remove a man on the road. Outside on the road, he saw several men standing about talking but couldn't identify them. Coakley said his donkey was not in the stable the next morning, it was found wandering two days later.

When Justice Andrews summed up, he revealed nothing of his own opinion and warned the jurors to consider the evidence carefully. It took only forty five minutes that day for the jury to reach a verdict of not guilty and the Crowley's were discharged.

This was an unusual case and showed how the law denied the accused men of having a say and giving their version of events. It seemed a case of either the Crowley's or Murphy and if the Crowley's had given evidence against Murphy first would he have been in the dock on trial? Murphy had been arrested first but Jeremiah Bill Hurley admitted agreeing with his namesake about what they would say and they seemed to have stuck to it. It's hard to see the allegiances between the witnesses but everyone was out to protect themselves and not get the blame for it. Someone moved the body that night and when they didn't tell the police, had to keep up the lie. They didn't just leave him in a panic that night, someone stayed, moved the body, lay him on his back and propped the cap under his head maybe in the naive hope he would be alive in the morning.

After the Wedding
Ballygarvan 1871

One Sunday in February a local farmer named Daniel Coveney married Catherine Fitzgerald. Daniel was from Glinny, north of Riverstick and Catherine was from Kilanully, just east of Ballygarvan. Records show that unusually, the marriage ceremony took place at her father Daniel Fitzgerald's house and a party was held there afterwards.

Some of the wedding party ended up in Daniel Twomey's pub in the village of Ballygarvan. The drinking went on for most of the day and into the night.

At 6 am on Monday morning the 20th of February, a farmer named Bowen passed by the chapel with his servant. They spotted something suspicious in the ditch; it was the body of a woman, bent over with her feet drawn up under her. At first, they thought she must be drunk.

Then in the darkness, they noticed how her clothes below the waist had been pulled up leaving her exposed. The area all around appeared as if it had been trampled upon by several pairs of boots, yet the woman wore none. Her face lay down in the mud as if it had been forced there when she died.

The farmer's servant thought he recognised the woman and petrified he ran off to inform the neighbours. It was one of the neighbours who lived nearby, Ellen Sullivan, who arrived and covered the body. She also found a white handled knife nearby. It had been trampled into the ground with all the activity of several pairs of footprints.

The local police constable was informed and he organised the body to be removed from the roadside. The coroner was also informed to conduct the inquest.

Constable Lohan wasted no time investigating the crime and all the goings on since the wedding the night before. He quickly established enough facts to arrest several young men that had been seen with the woman the night before. They were all local men who had been in the pub that night, Timothy Burns, Denis Deasy, Michael Buckley and Jeremiah Daly.

That very night coroner Eugene Horgan opened an inquest to establish the facts of how the woman died. A jury of local men were sworn in; John Ahern a farmer from Ballinphelic was the foreman, James Sheehan publican, George Rice farmer Rathmacullig and Daniel Murphy farmer Adamstown. Also Timothy Dillon, J Burns, J Moloney and J Cooney. Then there was two Timothy Murphy's and two Michael Murphy's.

The woman was identified as Mary Lynch aged between fifty and sixty. Many had only known her as Mary and she seemed to wander about relying on the charity of people. She drank and was homeless but caused no harm to anyone.

Dr Fowler had made an examination that day and told the inquest that he could not be sure how she died nor could he prove she had been raped by the men. Some evidence was heard that gave the woman's movements that Sunday.

The jury decided on an open verdict saying the deceased came by her death from a severe fall, exposure to weather or an attempted violation. Her death record simply said Mary Lynch aged fifty, cause of death: found dead unknown.

But there was a breakthrough in the police investigation that evening after the inquest. One of the four men arrested, Jeremiah Daly was willing to inform against the others. He claimed to have been there and witnessed what happened, but took no part in what went on. Daly was released from custody while the other three were remanded till the next hearing in court.

On Monday the 27th of February there was a special sitting of the petty sessions at Ballymartle. There before Resident Magistrate Starkie, the three men were charged that they feloniously assaulted and ravished Mary Lynch resulting in her death. It was constable Lohan who led the prosecution and the accused men were defended by Mr Alfred Blake.

The prosecution called several witnesses that had seen people on the road by the chapel that night but failed to identify them saying it was dark.

The local tailor David Coghlan had been in Twomey's public house on Sunday with his father. He had noticed Buckley and Burns drinking in the pub with a woman. Later that night at about seven he passed by the chapel and witnessed two people lying in the dyke, the nearest was a man but he couldn't say about the other.

John Bowen the farmer told of coming on the body by the side of the road that morning. His servant Thomas Dooly backed up the statement of his master but added that he at first thought it was a black sheep after lambing in the dyke.

The body was found on the roadside beyond the church

Julia Forde an old woman who lived near the chapel saw two men with a woman pass her door. She saw the woman fall and believed she was drunk but the men helped her up. The old woman heard her screeching further along the road but failed to identify any of the men.

The crowds in the courthouse and outside had come to hear one person that day, Jeremiah Daly. He had become the approver and was now willing to tell all. Daly began by saying he saw all three men drinking in Twomey's pub that Sunday. He left about eight pm but the three were gone before him.

As he passed the chapel that night Buckley caught hold of him on the road. At the same time, he saw Deasy lying in the dyke with a woman. He said Burns was also in the dyke with the woman. Con Crowley was just standing around and not involved at all.

When Buckley grabbed Daly he said to him "come here and have some of what is going on" and at the same time tried to throw him down onto the woman. He claimed he didn't get involved with what was going on saying to them "shame on you boys, this is bad conduct"

The defence asked Daly how much drink did he have that day. Daly had been to the wedding and drinking porter all day, he told Blake "could not say how many pints, I drank so many of them". Still, he insisted he wasn't drunk describing himself as "I was sugach" he was saying he was fresh and well able to know what was happening.

Blake then asked of the conditions Daly agreed to on becoming an approver:

Were you asked as a condition of your being left off to become a witness against these men? I was sir.

Were you told nothing would be done to you if you gave evidence against the prisoners? I was sir.

Magistrate Starkie: Who told you that? Constable Lohan, it was before I was discharged he said that to me."

Constable Lohan then tried to interrupt but was prevented by Blake, who continued asking:

"Was it before the inquest? It was sir."

The constable now managed to interrupt saying "was it not after the inquest witness, it was after the inquest". Blake now realised he was getting somewhere saying "a word cannot be believed from this fellow". He tried asking again once more:

"Was it before or after? It was before", the courtroom laughed out loud at this.

The constable questioned Daly again who now said he had given evidence before the inquest but then changed his mind saying it was afterwards. Any further evidence seemed to be difficult to obtain from Daly; he was later described as a "half idiotic creature". He came across to the court as a man trying to merely save himself by blaming the others. Approvers often came across like this even when they gave concise evidence but Daly certainly failed to do that.

The next witness was Con Crowley from Ballinphellig who was also in Twomey's public house that Sunday evening. Going home he met two men in the ditch near the chapel. A naked woman was lying on her back and he said the last witness Jeremiah Daly was in a certain position with the woman. He said it was a shame what was being done to her. He also saw Burns and Buckley nearby standing around.

Crowley said he met Daly afterwards and Daly told him he had "done so and so" to the woman three times. He had also met Burns later in Barrett's public house and his cap and coat were dirty. He claimed that he did not see Deasy on the road at all that night.

Blake reserved his defence and the three men were remanded back to custody until the next court hearing.

The following day in court it was Dr Fowler who was examined. As at the inquest he was not sure of the cause of death. Normally more than one doctor carried out the post mortem to give a second opinion which was lacking here. The doctor said he had found very few signs of violence on the body. Death could have been the result of an accident or maybe violence or could have been from exposure. Dr Fowler had done nothing at all that day for the prosecution's case. He said that death was from nervous shock resulted from one of the causes he had mentioned but couldn't be more definite.

A local man Michael Brien who worked in the nearby pottery for Mrs Allman was called. Brien told of seeing the woman in Twomey's pub that Sunday evening. He also told of hearing Buckley saying at the pottery on Monday that "Daly had acted in a certain way towards a woman and that Burns waited on the road with a similar intention".

Blake asked could he examine Constable Lohan about whether he had asked other witnesses to give evidence against the three. What he was trying to get at was whether the constable offered a deal to anyone else besides Daly. The questioning of the constable however was not allowed.

Again Blake reserved his defence which made no sense as the evidence was somewhat lacking and he could easily have taken advantage of it. The magistrates didn't take long to decide that day; all three were returned for trial at the next Assizes.

Blake applied for bail but was refused as he had been before.

The three were called before the Cork Spring Assizes that year on the charge of violating and murdering Mary Lynch but the case was postponed until the following Assizes.

At the end of July that year in the County Crown Court of the Cork Summer Assizes, the Ballygarvan case was called. By now it had become known as the Ballygarvan outrage and the three men were indicted for felonious assault which resulted in the death of Mary Lynch.

The crown case was led by Sir Colman O'Loghlan, with Mr Green Queens Counsel and Mr O'Hea. The defence was now represented by Gerald Fitzgibbon and Mr Alfred Blake.

In opening the case O'Loghlan made no bones about it that the case rested on the testimony of Jeremiah Daly. He asked the jury to take the evidence of Daly not as an approver but as a witness to the crime. He also asked that the jury listens to the other witnesses who corroborated Daly's account.

John Bowen and Constable Lohan both told of the scene at the side of the road near the chapel. They described in detail the ground around the body which showed there had been a struggle and a great amount of activity by several people.

Jeremiah Daly was examined by O'Loghlan and he stuck to the same story as before. Close to the chapel that night he met Buckley on the road who said to him "come here and have a share of what's going on". He saw a woman in the ditch and that Denis Deasy "was ill treating her". He couldn't describe in detail what was going on but said Burns then "ill treated her". He had heard her crying out as he walked along the road. Daly denied doing anything to Mary Lynch saying Buckley had flung him onto her but he got up out of it. He walked away that night with Con Crowley and Buckley, as they left he heard her still screaming. Burns and Deasy remained behind.

Under cross examination by Fitzgibbon, Daly revealed he had been living in Ballybough Barracks in Dublin for the last couple of months. It was referred to as Ballybough College, a safe place where informers were kept to prevent interference.

Fitzgibbon asked Daly about the conversations and arrangements he had with Constable Lohan.

> "Did he tell you if you would swear against the others you would be let off? He told me to tell the truth.
> Did he tell you, you would be let off if you gave evidence? He told me to tell whatever I knew.
> Had you any talk with Constable Lohan? I had, Constable Lohan called me out after the inquest and asked me what I knew about it. I said I knew nothing about the occurrence.
> Did he ask you to give evidence? He did not.
> Did he tell you that if you told what you knew you would be left off? He told me to tell what I knew and that's all I know about it.
> Where is Con Crowley? I don't know.
> Was he up in College with you? He was not, I did not see Con Crowley for three months, he was not in Dublin with me.
> Did he swear against you? He might swear what he liked against me, but I was innocent.

Did Crowley swear while you were a prisoner that you were one of the parties engaged in this outrage?"

O'Loghlan objected to this question and the judge ruled in his favour. O'Loghlan then told the court that Crowley would be a witness for the crown but he had gone to America.

A juror asked, "why did you not summon assistance that night" saying that there were houses nearby but Daly claimed he was in fear of being threatened by the others. The juror unsatisfied, said that he was not alone, he had Con Crowley and the woman, he could not understand why he didn't put up a fight against the three others. Daly couldn't explain himself and just said: "I went away sir".

Justice Fitzgerald then intervened with "you and Crowley were there not taking part in this outrage, why if you were a man did you not interfere to save the woman?"

Daly still couldn't really explain himself saying "I didn't want to interfere with them sir if they left me go home quietly, I was afraid I'd be hurt".

The next witness David Coghlan was also in Twomey's public house that Sunday. He saw Buckley and Burns on the road that evening with a woman heading towards Fivemilebridge. Coghlan was taking his drunk father home, by the Chapel, he met two men lying in the ditch and another standing around.

Dr Fowler said he examined the body and found scratches on the legs and face. He had not found any signs the woman "had been violated" but then he revealed that he had never done a post mortem. It was yet another blow to the prosecution. Fowler concluded that death was due to nervous shock but this proved nothing.

John Barrett a publican from Fivemilebridge told the court that the accused Timothy Burns worked for him. He "partly guessed" there was something up with Burns that night, suggesting his clothes were dirty.

Barrett's lack of clarity annoyed the judge who uttered "tell the truth like a man. Was his coat dirty or was it not?" The publican gave in "well it was dirty sir, I saw the deceased in my house that evening".

It was all pointless though as it went nowhere towards proving that Burns had committed any crime, he could have gotten his coat dirty anywhere. If anything it showed Justice Fitzgerald's frustration with the lack of evidence in the case.

That was all the prosecution had to offer and Fitzgibbon grabbed his chance to argue the case for the accused. He referred to O'Loghlan's opening speech where he had asked the jury to consider whether the men had done it or not. Fitzgibbon now asked the jury to consider whether the woman had been abused at all. He claimed there was no evidence to prove it, suggesting it was merely the imagination of the crown. He went further suggesting that if there were relations between the men and the woman it must have been done fully with her consent. Then he backtracked a little saying the prosecution had failed to identify his clients as even being with the woman.

As Justice Fitzgerald summed up the case, he told how Con Crowley had since emigrated to America but did not connect this to guilt on his part. On the subject of Daly's evidence, Fitzgerald couldn't hide his doubts with what was heard. He left it to the jury to decide for themselves but strongly suggested that a conviction could not be upheld on his evidence alone. He also didn't see how Daly's account of refusing to be involved corroborated with any of the other witnesses. It all depended on how credible the jury believed Daly to be and whether or not they thought he was telling the truth.

After only a short time, the jury returned with a verdict of "not guilty" and the three men were free to leave.

When all was said and done everyone walked out of the courtroom as free men. Jeremiah Daly cannot have been popular afterwards, but the question remains, was he telling the truth? Others had implicated him but the crown had decided to take his evidence to get a conviction against the others.

Mary Lynch had died in suspicious circumstances and the men certainly knew more. One can't help feeling that if it was someone higher up the social ladder such as a farmer's daughter the law would have been more severe.

The young men would have known though that they would not have gotten away with it if the woman was someone else. The language used in court shows how unable the law was to deal with it. The furthest anyone was willing to go was "saw him in a certain position with the woman" or "attempted violation". The medical evidence was also desperately lacking. Nowadays advances such as DNA alone could secure a conviction. It wasn't just the times in this case though; Dr Fowler seemed completely unable to find the cause of death. The police should have known this and got a more qualified doctor. It certainly is one case that having the inquest so quickly was of an advantage to the accused.

Did they rape the woman that night, were they present when she died? It is obvious there were people with her because of all the footprints around the body and she was left naked below the waist. Whether they did or not, or who they were, there certainly was a complete lack of respect for the woman due to her perceived lowly position in society. Then again society at the time had less respect for women than it does now.

Murder at Killeady Hill
Killeady Hill Ballinhassig 1826

On Sunday 12th of November 1826, two men called to a house belonging to a Mr Saunders near Killeady Hill looking for lodgings for the night. The men were both carrying spades and appeared to be travelling workmen. They were refused a bed and so they moved on.

A little later that evening, a cry was heard not too far away that a man's body was found badly mutilated in the dyke of the roadside. As the locals were deciding what to do a stranger walked calmly along the road towards them. He announced that the man lying at the roadside was a friend and relation of his and that he had seen off the attackers. He had just chased away several of them across the fields.

The locals asked for help to take the body to the nearest house but at first, the man refused, seeming afraid to touch it. Then he came around and between them the body was removed to the nearest house.

The locals soon became suspicious of the stranger. One remarked that he had been seen earlier on the road with a spade but where was it now? He said it had been left at his lodgings but was very reluctant to go and prove what he said. He then suggested it might have been stolen. Somehow between a few of them, they managed to detain the stranger for the night but he refused to give the name of the dead man despite admitting he was his friend and relation.

In the morning police constable Thomas Haynes arrived at where the man had been held for the night. The man was asked again about where the spade was. He still said it was at his lodgings. The police took him to Riordan's house not far away and he claimed a spade there as his own. The woman of the house Mary Riordan denied he was lodging in her house at all nor was the spade his. Her husband also said he had not seen this man before.

Marks of blood were found on the man's clothes. He explained he had gotten these when he helped lift the body from the roadside but the police were not convinced. When the locals found two spades and a flail in a ditch not too far from where the body had been found, their suspicions were confirmed.

The stranger and his friend were believed to be going in the direction of Skibbereen or Bantry before the incident occurred. They had been working away as farm labourers closer to Cork. The police eventually learned that the suspect was named Daniel Mahony and the deceased was Edward or Edmond Fitzgerald. Reports at the time described a deep wound at the back of Fitzgerald's head while others reckoned the head was almost severed from the body.

It was Monday before the coroner James Daltera arrived to conduct the inquest of how the man met his death. A jury of twelve local men was sworn in to view the body and reach a verdict of how he died.

It seemed a straightforward enough affair, the man who was still unknown at this stage, had a tremendous wound on the back of his head so bad that the head had almost been severed. The cause of death was obvious enough and no doctor was called to give evidence as a post mortem had not been carried out. The coroner carried out a superficial examination and then questioned the locals who had found the body.

The jury returned a verdict of wilful murder against Daniel Mahony who was in custody. Back then it was enough for him to be sent for a trial before a proper judge and jury.

On the 6th of April 1827 at the Cork Spring Assizes Justice Torrens presided over the county court. Daniel Mahony was called and charged with two murders by the same means, one was Fitzgerald the other was an unknown man and there was precious little evidence.

When produced in court Mahony was said to have appeared wretched with hardly a scrap of clothing. He was in his late twenties but with a high forehead and sunken eyes, making him seem such a frightening looking character. He had no legal representation arranged so Mr Freeman and Smyth who were in court offered to fill the role.

The evidence against Mahony was circumstantial but the attitude seemed to be if he didn't do it then who did.

The first witness called that day was Mary Kelleher who worked for Mr Saunders. After dark that night two men came to the door looking for lodging for the night but she told them there was none and sent them on their way. She now identified the accused as one of the men. She said that Mahony had a flail and both men carried a spade. She thought it was about a quarter of an hour after they left that she heard a man was dead on the road nearby. The following day she saw the dead man and recognised him as the other man who had called to the door the night before.

Barrett's pub with Killeady Hill in the background.

      Bartholomew Sullivan, who found the body recalled the night of the 12th of November. It was about eight when he came upon a man in the dyke about two fields away from Saunder's house; Sullivan said the man was not dead. He was about to lift the body when the accused arrived and said he saw the four men who had carried out the attack. Sullivan offered to go after them but Mahony persuaded him not to bother as they were too far gone.

      Timothy Murphy told the court he lived within three fields of Saunders' house. On the 12th of November, the last witness came to his house saying there was a man on the road. He went with him to the scene and it was then that the accused came strolling calmly down the road towards them. Murphy told how Mahony at first refused to help with the body and seemed very reluctant to touch it at all. It was when they did lift the body that something tied inside the shirt fell out and in it, they found 21 shillings. He also said the suspect really didn't want to be detained that night but was forced to against his will until the police arrived. When they asked the name of the dead man Mahony told them he did not know it as they were only friends.

It was the next morning that Murphy found two spades, a flail, clothes and a hat in the ditch across from where the body was. He noticed blood on one of the spades and the flail.

Labourer James Connolly was then called and testified that he had been working with both the deceased and accused the Saturday before the killing. He positively identified the bloody spade which was produced as belonging to Mahony. Justice Torrens asked how could he be so sure as it was only a common spade. Connolly pointed to a mark on the handle saying he had seen Mahony put it there to distinguish it from the others.

James Daltera was called to give evidence of being at the inquest and having examined the body. He described a deep cut at the back of the head and said it could have been done with a spade. A cut and fracture were also observed above the left eye which could also have been the result of a blow from the spade.

The policeman Thomas Haynes, Mrs Riordan and her husband all told the court how Mahony had claimed a spade in their farmyard. The Riordan's had never seen him before nor had he made arrangements to lodge for the night.

The defence had no witnesses to call and Justice Torrens proceeded to sum up the evidence. Torrens did give him the benefit of the doubt a little, suggesting that a disagreement may have taken place between the travellers on the roadside. There was no evidence for this but Torrens told the jury if they believed there was any kind of provocation the charge could be reduced to manslaughter. He also noted how the dead man's money all 21 shillings had not been touched so the motive was not robbery.

It took no time at all that day for the jury to return a verdict of guilty. Justice Torrens then had to do what many judges dreaded so much, sentence Mahony to death. The judge reminded him of the terrible deed he had carried out and that now only one option was open to him. It was normal to also tell the prisoner to devote what little time he had left to prayer and not waste his time thinking of a reprieve.

It was possible to get a reprieve then but only if new evidence was found, there was no real appeals process nor was time allowed for it. Back then death sentences were handed out for far lesser crimes but then quickly reduced to transportation for life. Not the case for murder though, taking a life meant another must be forfeited. In the 1820s the Murder Act of 1751 was still law and in existence to deter would be murderers.

According to that act, those found guilty of murder must be executed two days after sentencing unless it fell on a Sunday, then the person would get an extra day. Most shocking for people back then though, was that the murderer was denied a Christian burial after execution. Instead, the body would be hung publically in chains or more commonly dissected for medical research. This was one of the only ways for medical schools to obtain bodies legally and demand far outstripped supply.

Finishing his speech that day Torrens told the condemned man that the following Monday would be his last. He was to be executed at the "new drop" recently constructed outside the county gaol.

On Monday morning Daniel Mahony was led out to the gallows. He was attended to that morning by Rev O'Connor. At half twelve Mahony took his final steps up onto the scaffold and died in an instant without a struggle. A large crowd had gathered to watch the spectacle but it was all over in seconds. His body was sent for dissection at the county infirmary.

What Made You Do It
Rathnaroughy Innishannon 1882

On Saturday morning the 25th of March Thomas Haynes set off for Bandon with his wife Ellen in a horse and cart. They lived with her mother and sister, Hannah who were left at home to look after the young children.

All day was spent in Bandon getting the necessary supplies but also having a few drinks and it was early evening when they set out for home. On the way, they had one last stop in Innishannon, as they were now so close to home. Several more drinks later and Thomas drew the attention of the police. In that age old Irish way though, they believed he was under the influence but not drunk and left him off. It seems in Ireland then, one needed to be completely incapacitated to be considered drunk.

It must have been about nine, dark with hours when the couple set out again for home. It was a short journey now and they would not be too much longer. Country roads were not like they are today. There were no headlights or streetlights, it was much darker and any lamp cast long shadows.

Haynes and his wife were not the only ones on the road. About nine o'clock a horse and cart pulled up the hill at Rathnaroughy and came on what they thought was a man lying on the road drunk. Further on a horse was also on the road so the driver told his son to catch hold of it.

Before he did Thomas Haynes stepped out of the shadows and told them to move on as he had it under control. Without a question or another word spoken they did just that and went on as it was late.

Further on up the hill, they heard a horse approaching from behind, it was Haynes alone on the horse. He now asked for help, saying it was his wife; she was on her feet but not quite right. They went back with him and saw Mrs Haynes on the road. As they approached she went through a small gap and fell down. An attempt was made to lift her up but Haynes' horse bolted and he ran after it rather than see to his wife. The occupants of the cart must have assumed that Ellen was drunk, but now with her husband out of earshot she spoke clearly. She was well aware of who was helping her, saying his name several times. Ellen pleaded with him to not tell a soul of this and he agreed nobody would know.

Ellen was brought out onto the road and sat by the roadside while arrangements were made to get her home. Her husband had by now returned with the horse. The man who helped her took his cart home but a woman & boy remained with Ellen. The boy offered to take Haynes horse to get a cart, and eventually, he agreed. When he returned with the cart, Ellen's mother Mrs O'Brien and a servant Denis Murphy were with him. Between them, they tried to get her into the cart but discovered her body was lifeless. It was her mother who said it first, but then blood was spotted on her face. She was dead.

Once her body was lifted onto the cart, they all got in except Haynes who walked behind. He became upset, crying about how he would not manage without her and what would happen to the children. They got her home and into the house, in the light it revealed she was cut all over her hands and face. Not cuts from falling about the road in ditches though, real deep cut wounds, that must have been inflicted on her.

It was early on Sunday morning before a doctor arrived and examined the body. The local police constable arrived and cautioned Thomas Haynes before arresting him. Thomas had given no explanation to what had occurred that night. At the time he seemed like a man who didn't know what happened himself but was only just beginning to realise as the fog of drink lifted. The police constable noticed that Haynes hands and clothes were covered in blood.

The morning light revealed marks of blood stretching 200 yards along the road far from where Ellen died. The tracks of blood proved the location where the incident must have happened.

Ellen Haynes was only in her twenties and was tragically seven months pregnant at the time. She had married Thomas six years previously in December of 1876, she had been Ellen O'Brien. Both their fathers were farmers living in the townland of Killaminogue. Thomas's profession was stated as a farmer, he was twenty six when they married, and her age was given as nineteen. She could have been younger though as her age at death is recorded as twenty three, which would have made her only seventeen getting married. They were married in the Catholic Church in Ballyheada near Halfway. The couple had allegedly eloped and maybe this was why they didn't marry closer to home. Some even suggested that Haynes was a protestant but records show this is not true so the eloping story has no actual foundation. Thomas had an older brother John who remained at home on the family farm with his parents.

The village of Innishannon, image courtesy of the National Library of Ireland

With the marriage, Thomas Haynes came into what was described as a comfortable farm of eighty acres from Ellen's family. It was an unusual arrangement as Ellen's father was only fifty three when she married and he left his farm to his son-in-law. William O'Brien died three years later and Thomas had the farm to himself. Over the course of the next few years three children were born, Thomas in 1877, William in 1879 and John the following year.

Later that Sunday, when he was sober Haynes, was brought before resident magistrate Cronin and information was taken from those who had encountered him on the road that night. Afterwards, he left Innishannon for the county jail.

An inquest was held on Monday 27th in Haynes farmhouse by coroner Horgan. Cronin was present as was County Inspector Maguire. Haynes was not brought to the inquest nor was any person present to legally represent him.

The jury comprised of respectable men from the locality, foreman John Horgan, John Phipps farmer Farnahoe, John Connell farmer Killaminogue, W.H Daunt, William Murphy, John McCarthy, John Sullivan and John Buckley. James Lucey farmer from very close to where Ellen had died, P Roberts, John Flynn, William Buckley, Denis Daly, John Crowley and John Deasy.

The first witness at the inquest was Daniel Regan from Clouracaun who told of seeing a figure on the road on Saturday night. Haynes told him "pass on boys". Daniel said he was with his son Samuel, servant Humphrey Hennessy and Mrs Sullivan in his horse and cart. He didn't think much of it at the time but clearly recognised Thomas Haynes.

A little further up the hill, Haynes came after them on his horse saying "I want you to come down Mr Regan, there is a woman here and there is something wrong, many a thing occurs to women that we men do not understand".

Daniel went back down the road and Haynes said "she is on her feet now" but saw the woman going through a gap and falling again. He explained that initially, he didn't follow her thinking Mrs Haynes was drunk and trying to avoid him. Daniel said he advised Thomas at that point that the best thing would be to take his wife home.

He then opened up the gap with Haynes and saw the woman lying on her side. Daniel recalled her husband saying it was a shame to see her like this but never said what had happened to her. An attempt was made to lift her but Haynes' horse bolted and he went after it.

Daniel described how Ellen knew who he was and referred to him as Mr Regan several times and said: "don't have any talk of this". He didn't think she was drunk from the way she spoke to him but at the time didn't know what was wrong with her. Her husband said she was not that bad and that it was just roguery on her part.

When she was brought back onto the road though, he reckoned she seemed weak and sat on the dyke with Mrs Sullivan. Daniel's son, Samuel, suggested he go home which he did. His son remained and offered to get Haynes cart. What Daniel failed to explain was why he didn't use his cart to take Ellen home that night and why he left alone.

Samuel Regan was called to give his version of that night. He said at first Haynes would not allow him to go for the cart with his horse. When Samuel returned with the cart he noticed how Ellen was covered in blood. He mentioned how Haynes made no explanation at all.

Mrs Sullivan was called next; she said she had walked back to the scene with young Samuel. At the time Haynes was sitting in the dyke supporting his wife. She recalled Thomas saying "I don't know what ails her". Mrs Sullivan said it was her that put her hand on Ellen's forehead and said "Tommy she is dead, you ought to go for the priest" but he said nothing. She asked Haynes what had happened and he claimed he only met her on the road and had not seen her since Innishannon.

Dr Alexander Alcock told the inquest that it was half three on Sunday morning before he got to Haynes house. He found Ellen covered in cuts, one on the forehead he said was deep about an inch long and another over the right eye. Her neck was all scratched as was the left arm, while the right arm had a wound between the fingers.

Dr Alcock then went on to the post mortem he had carried out with Dr Welphy and Dr Cole. They discovered another deep cut that went to the bone but had not penetrated the brain. The doctor said Ellen was within four or so weeks of giving birth. Examining the womb, they discovered the waters had broken and her baby girl was dead. There were several more bruises and wounds on the arms and legs. These he thought were the result of falling or being dragged about the road. Alcock went as far as to say that "the little creature appeared to have been terribly mauled".

He concluded that the wound to the head was enough to kill her but that the blood loss from the womb would have killed her faster. Death he said was due to the shock to the nervous system by the injuries she sustained.

One of the jurors questioned the doctor about what could have caused the head wounds. He believed it was something sharp and cutting such as a knife. To the magistrate he said there was no possibility the injuries could have been self inflicted; the bruises could have been done by kicking or dragging her on the road.

Dr Welply was also questioned and agreed on the injuries Ellen had sustained but he didn't agree that the head wound could cause death. Instead, he suggested it was a blow of a blunt instrument that resulted in death.

Hannah O'Brien who was Ellen's sister gave evidence of her marriage to Thomas Haynes. A few months after Ellen was married she began arguing with her husband. Hannah said he treated her badly for no reason, sometimes hitting or kicking her.

She recalled the last row the couple had on the 9th of March. On that occasion, Thomas ordered his wife to carry a bag of corn but she refused saying she was busy. Hannah then saw Thomas make a kick at her and when he missed he threw a bucket of water at her. She heard him pass some remark to Ellen several times that day threatening to kill her. Hannah stated that Thomas normally carried a pocket knife but for the last few days he had been looking for it to cut his tobacco.

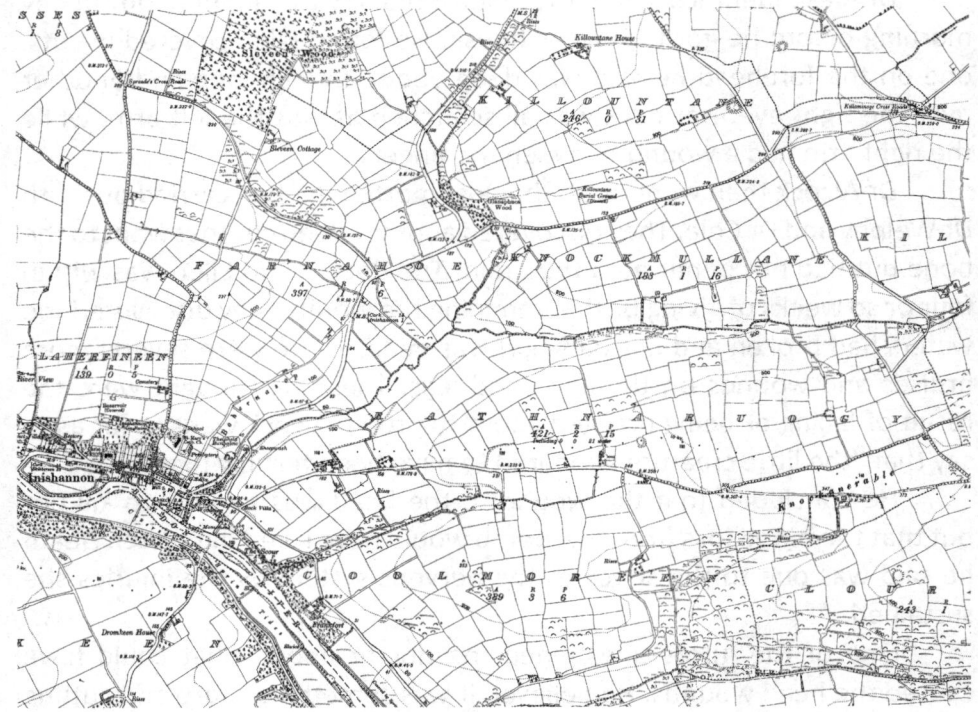

Map showing Rathnaroughy just outside Innishannon

The result of the inquest was that the deceased Ellen Haynes died at Rathnaroughy on Saturday the 25th from a shock to her nervous system and from haemorrhage resulting from injuries she had received. In their opinion, these injuries were inflicted by her husband Thomas Haynes.

The evening of the inquest, the funeral took place and Ellen's remains were brought to Templemichael graveyard about two miles away. A huge crowd attended the funeral; all were still in shock about what was alleged to have happened.

At this point, the murder weapon believed to be a knife belonging to Thomas still had not been found despite the police searching the area.

People were truly shocked by what had occurred so near to them. None more so than the parish priest Fr Holland. The priest wrote to the Cork Examiner saying how deeply affected his parishioners were but relieved that it did not occur in their parish. Holland satisfied himself that since the start of what had become known as the land war there was no such trouble in his parishes which were, Innishannon, Knockavilla and Brinny. All that bothered Holland was the fact that the Haynes were from Killaminogue and were not parishioners of his. He specifically wrote in the newspaper to remind the public of the fact it did not happen in his parish of Innishannon. Killaminogue was in Templemichael parish but maybe Holland was unaware the murder occurred in Rathnaroughy which was in his parish. What the parish priest really should have been concerning himself with was some compassion for the Haynes family, especially their children.

Thomas Haynes was brought back to Innishannon for a special sitting of the court before resident magistrate Cronin. Haynes was charged with the wilful murder of his wife Ellen on the 25th of March. The crown prosecution was conducted by Mr Bryan Galwey. Haynes had not employed a solicitor to speak for him so this meant that Haynes would be given the opportunity to cross examine any witness himself. Normally though, those that did this had to be careful as they often only implicated themselves further.

It was Haynes servant Denis Murphy who explained how Haynes left for Bandon with a horse and cart but returned on horseback. Murphy had been instructed to meet his master at five that evening at O'Brien's in Innishannon which he did. He had brought a horse for Thomas and would take home the horse and cart himself. Ellen it seems would have to walk home from the village unless she went with Murphy.

Young Denis said he stayed about half an hour in Innishannon and left alone, getting home about half six. The next time he saw Mrs Haynes was when she was dead on the roadside four hours later.

He said that he had seen Thomas kick and hit Ellen on a few occasions. Sometimes by night, he heard her call out from bed for the priest. When asked by the prosecution Denis said that Thomas Haynes always carried a small knife.

Then Haynes began asking

"How long is it since you saw a knife with me? I did not see one for a fortnight with you.

What reason did I tell you to bring the mare to Innishannon? You said you wanted to go to a funeral. "

So far so good, but Haynes put his foot in it saying he could call several witnesses who all could prove he bought a knife in Bandon to cut his tobacco. The prosecution would have wished to ask Haynes questions such as where was that knife now but they were not allowed to question him at all.

More witnesses were called; John Murphy who was in Gallivan's pub in Innishannon with Mr & Mrs Haynes, an hour and a half after dark that night. He said it seemed like Thomas had a lot of drink taken but Ellen was sober. She left Gallivan's pub first carrying something under her shawl. About 10 minutes later Thomas left on horseback. John said he had even held the horse for Haynes in Gallivan's yard. Then he walked with Thomas as far as O'Driscoll's pub and saw him head towards home.

Again Haynes began his own defence by questioning the witness

Did I ask you at any time where my wife was? You did.

Where was that? At Gallivan's or Miss O'Driscoll's.

But Haynes kept going and replied to him with "At Gallivan's and I told you I did not know that she had left". Then it was Magistrate Cronin who asked did you hear the wife ask him to come home? Murphy replied that he had but one of the other magistrates James Payne objected saying it was not relevant. Cronin turned on him and scolded him for it with "Well Mr Payne, you have not followed out this case with me on the part of the crown or studied it like I have". But Payne insisted. What Cronin was reminding him was that he was the magistrate in charge employed by the crown. Payne was a magistrate by name due to his rank and could come and go as he pleased. He didn't have to be there.

The local blacksmith Michael O'Connell said he also passed on the road that night. Haynes approached him saying "come here Mike O'Connell my wife is sick". But then two men on horseback passed by and Mike went to Ellen who was lying against the ditch and Mrs Sullivan was with her. It was a dark night and he lit a match to see what was wrong. The flame revealed Ellen's face was covered in blood and he got some on his coat. He was shocked and said to Haynes "she is all destroyed" but got no explanation. Michael tried to prop her head up against the ditch but there seemed to be no life in her and her head dropped back down.

The blacksmith accused Haynes right there on the road with "begor Tom you must have killed your wife and struck her with a knife". Haynes he said made no attempt to defend himself and only said "Oh poor Elly Brien, poor Elly Brien".

Several more witnesses were called that had only passed them on the road that night or heard a woman's scream from a distance. There was a complete lack of evidence against Thomas Haynes but nobody was in any doubt it was him all right.

Mr Galwey for the crown approached the bench and proposed that all those witnesses at the inquest not be called today. He suggested that their statements be read out and any further details could be added.

Cronin did not believe that this was legal at all and said as much. He said the depositions could only be used if they were given in the presence of the accused man and he was allowed to question them at the time. This had not been the case as Haynes was not at the inquest and if he was, he would not have been allowed to cross examine. Cronin was right though it was not the correct way to do it whatsoever.

Galwey, though, was sure it was, and Payne backed him saying it was the easiest thing to do now. Cronin quoted the law and made it clear he was very opposed to it but Galwey insisted.

Cronin eventually gave in agreeing to go on if Galwey would take full responsibility for it. Daniel Regan's account given at the inquest was then read out for the court. Regan who was present had nothing to add to it and Haynes didn't question it either. It was Cronin who intervened asking Galwey did he see now how wrong it was.

The statement they had just heard included details of a conversation between Regan and the deceased while the accused was not present. This he said was allowed at an inquest but was not legal evidence in court.

Galwey persisted with his course and the other statements from the inquest were read out. When asked, Haynes had nothing further to add nor did he have a statement to make. Galwey had made an error and lost an opportunity to call the witnesses. Having Haynes carry out his own cross examinations would have only revealed more information for the prosecution.

Cronin clearly wanted to hear more that day still and believed there was a prima facie case to be made against Thomas Haynes. So he returned him for trial at the next assizes; there was no question of bail.

At the Cork Summer Assizes, it was Mr Justice Barry who presided over the county crown court. The crown was well represented with Sergeant Sherlock, Mr Greene, James Murphy, Mr Moriarty and Crown Solicitor Mr Gregg.

Now it was serious, Thomas Haynes could no longer rely on himself to question the witnesses and had to be legally represented. His life hung in the balance and any judge had to see that his defence case was fully argued. It seems strange but judges generally disliked when an accused pleaded guilty because they were denied the chance of hearing the evidence. At least when they got to hear the evidence, it made it a little easier to send a man to the gallows.

It was months later in the county courthouse far removed from the scene of the crime and yet it was packed with eager listeners. Sergeant Sherlock opened the prosecution case, telling everyone how dreadful a crime it was. He said a 23 year old mother of three who was heavily pregnant was cut down in her prime. She was blameless, respectable and sober. He said Thomas was an alcoholic and it was his behaviours and actions that brought about this terrible deed.

Sherlock detailed how the prosecution could prove where Haynes was seen on the road that night with his wife. The medical evidence would also show what had happened to her that dark night.

Denis Murphy again gave the events as heard before. He told of living in Haynes house, the last year and a half. He slept in the loft directly above the married couple and heard arguments going on by night. Denis had heard him strike her from his bed and Ellen crying saying she would tell the priest. Once he heard them row about a churn and Thomas struck and kicked her. He had never seen Ellen strike her husband.

Under cross examination, young Denis was made to say that he had only ever heard two or three arguments. In the pub in Innishannon that night Denis thought nothing was amiss and they seemed friendly towards each other. Ellen often accompanied her husband to fairs and markets.

Witness John Murphy had met the couple outside a pub that night about nine. His recollection was she was sober and repeatedly asked her husband, to come home with her. She eventually left alone and Thomas went after her ten minutes later.

The prosecution now had many more witnesses to call than before, John Quinn told of meeting a man and woman lying in the dyke by the road that night. He also came upon a horse but didn't stop nor take any notice and kept going. Several more told of hearing a woman's screech.

When it came to Daniel Regan's evidence the defence objected to the conversation Regan had alone with the deceased that night. The judge ruled that it should be allowed but noted the objection. Regan revealed his cart was about 150 yards further along from where Ellen died but he still didn't explain why it wasn't used to take her home.

The blacksmith Michael O'Connell repeated his statement to the accused that night "Tom your wife is dead and you killed her, you must have struck her with a knife, the blood is coming so fast." He said Haynes denied it saying he had no knife.

Mrs Catherine Sullivan described the scene she saw on the road. She walked back down the road with Samuel Regan to see what was keeping Daniel Regan and didn't know what was wrong with Ellen. So she asked Thomas "was it the way she fell off the horse" but he said, "no, I never saw her since she left Innishannon till I saw her in that spot".

Hannah O'Brien described her sister's relationship with Thomas Haynes. She explained living in the house with her sister and husband was part of an arrangement or marriage portion when Ellen had married.

The examination started with:
"Did they live happily? They did not.
Justice Barry: That is too general.
Did you see him assault her? Frequently, I often saw him kick her."

Hannah went on to describe the assaults and the threats Thomas had made to her sister.

The doctors again proved that Ellen Haynes had died from terrible injuries inflicted from a knife, there was no possibility it was from falling about the road.

The prosecution was struggling for witnesses that could actually prove Haynes had killed his wife. So instead they called someone credible to prove it indirectly. They called Thomas Poole, the land agent of Haynes farm. He had been to see Thomas Haynes in jail to ask what he wished to do with the farm. He said Thomas had become the tenant of the farm when he married Ellen; her father had been a tenant before that. In jail, Haynes told the agent he wished to make a will and would need a solicitor. It was Murphy who asked was there any mention of his wife that day. Poole said he could not help it and asked: "what made you do it". He claimed Haynes said, "I was mad".

Poole had never told anyone this before, not even the crown solicitor. It was only the evening before that he received a subpoena from a policeman ordering him to court.

This closed the prosecution case, there had been nobody called that saw Haynes with the knife in his hand nor had the murder weapon been found.

In the afternoon it was Mr Lawrence who made a speech for Haynes. At first, he bowed to the prosecution's greater experience. Lawrence did not seem confident at all in his ability to save Haynes from the hangman. He said the prosecution had attempted to portray the accused as a cruel husband. He claimed the sister was bound to be biased and all the servant had heard was two or three arguments in a year or so.

He also mentioned the knife or lack of it, the prosecution claimed a knife was used but there was no evidence of this. Lawrence also challenged the medical evidence saying Ellen's most serious injury was the rupture of her womb. He suggested this was from a fall off the horse, yet there was no evidence she was even on the horse that night.

Lawrence asked why would Haynes kill his wife and then be the first to help her and ask for help from others. He strongly suggested a fall from a horse and some rough handling whilst trying to help her resulted in her injuries.

On the evidence from the land agent, he was scathing saying "it was not the evidence of a confession but rather the creation of a disordered mind, the fiction of a perturbed and irrational intellect".

Lawrence addressing the jury gave in a little saying if they must find that Thomas Haynes actions led to the death of his wife then the verdict should be manslaughter. He even went so far as to say if this was the case Haynes actions were a sudden outburst which he immediately regretted. Even though Lawrence was trying to allow for all eventualities to save his client from the noose, he may have been better off claiming Haynes was not responsible.

Murphy replied for the prosecution, clinging to the evidence that Haynes treated his wife in a "cruel harsh and unnatural way". Murphy said it was really a double murder as her unborn daughter also lost her life.

Finally, Justice Barry summed up all the evidence that had been heard. He was clear that what was against Haynes was merely circumstantial and he went into this in great detail. He said, "no witness was produced who saw him raise his hand in anger or violence to his wife that day". It was the series of circumstances that led them to allege he had killed her. Justice Barry explained that with circumstantial evidence the jury had to satisfy themselves that no other person had done it. He went on to say if they were satisfied the circumstantial evidence was as good as the most credible eyewitness.

It was more a case of if he didn't do it then who did. If he had not done it then surely he would have given a reasonable explanation of what occurred that night but he did not. Justice Barry gave no credence to Lawrence's notion of reducing the verdict to manslaughter. He seemed adamant that if Haynes killed his wife even in a sudden madness he was guilty of murder.

When the jury retired it took only fifteen minutes for the foreman to return saying they believed Haynes did not intend to kill her but all agreed he was the man who did it. The foreman asked if this made any difference but Justice Barry said it did not. The judge remained firm saying Haynes inflicted the injuries, it was not just a push that killed Ellen but violence inflicted with a knife, he was still in favour of it being murder and asked the jury to give it more consideration.

This time the jury was only absent for thirteen minutes and they returned this time with a clear verdict. Haynes appeared to be in a state of panic he looked about at the jurors and the verdict was read out "guilty of murder". The foreman then addressed the judge saying they recommended mercy as the jury all believed it was not premeditated. Justice Barry said it would be taken care of but he didn't seem convincing.

The clerk of the court then asked the condemned man the usual question, had he anything to say as to why the death sentence should not be passed on him. Haynes, however, had nothing to say.

Lawrence applied to have the judgement arrested as his client had not been asked to plead for the charge. It was the clerk of the court that showed the entry in the book where Haynes had pleaded not guilty the day before.

Justice Barry then moved to pass sentence and put on the black cap. Addressing Haynes he began "Thomas Haynes you have been convicted of the crime of wilful murder, and of the justice of that verdict, no sane man who had heard the evidence can entertain a particle of doubt".

Barry went on reminding Haynes of his dreadful crime saying he slayed not only his wife but his unborn child. Haynes became visibly upset and broke down. It only got worse for Haynes when Barry reminded him that the recommendation of mercy would come to nothing and he should not waste his time on it.

Putting on the black cap he told Haynes "It is now my duty to pronounce upon you the dreadful sentence of the law. The sentence and judgement of the court is and I do adjudge and order that you Thomas Haynes be taken from the bar of this court where you now stand, to the place from whence you came the common gaol of the county of Cork and that you be taken on Tuesday the 22nd August in the year of our Lord one thousand eight hundred and eighty two to the place of execution. And that you be there hanged by the neck until you are dead and that your body be buried within the precincts of the prison in which you shall have been last confined after your conviction and may the Lord have mercy on your soul".

The condemned man seemed to attempt to reject the sentence when he cried out "oh god" but he was led away.

Within days it was expected that Haynes would get a reprieve based on the jury's recommendation, despite Justice Barry thinking otherwise. In jail with only a few weeks to live Haynes was said to be bearing up well and coming to accept his fate. He had turned to religion as those in his terrible position so often do.

A petition was sent to the Lord Lieutenant asking for Haynes sentence to be commuted to that of imprisonment for life. In early August word was received that a decision had been made on the pending executions. Laurence Murphy was reprieved due to his weak mental state, having been convicted for the murder of an old woman he worked for near Killeagh (see Murder Most Local, Historic Murders of East Cork). In the case of Thomas Haynes, the reply was the more common one "the law must take its course". The date fixed for the 22nd of August still stood and time was now running out for Thomas Haynes.

The well known executioner William Marwood was otherwise engaged and not available to travel to Cork. A shoemaker named Longhorn had previously offered his services and now this offer was accepted. Longhorn was also a Methodist preacher and when his name was associated with execution he lost that post. It turned out Marwood became available again due to his victim receiving a reprieve.

On Monday night before the final day, Haynes lashed out attacking one of the warders by throwing him on the ground. He was quickly restrained by several more warders before he did any more harm. Was this finally further evidence of the outbursts he was capable of and which had killed his wife? Later, he became calm and tranquil resigning himself with what would come in the morning.

Reports for the County Gaol stated that Thomas Haynes slept soundly for his last night. On the morning of the 22nd of August, he got up and put on the black suit he had worn weeks before at his trial. His time that morning was spent in the prison chapel until the bell was heard at a quarter to eight. Haynes who was being watched closely was seen to feel it now that his time was near. Moments later they gathered outside the chapel door, warders, sub sheriff, deputy governor and prison doctors. Haynes was led out to the yard, held by the warders as his eyes were shut. The procession came to a halt when Marwood stepped out from a doorway and began his part. Marwood was an executioner for ten years and he didn't appear like the man of his reputation that day. Marwood had executed nearly two hundred, with 26 of those in Ireland. He was almost a household name, having developed the long drop method.

Marwood went about his job swiftly pinioning or restraining Haynes feet and arms with straps. Thomas complained it was too tight but they moved him on towards the scaffold, his eyes still tightly shut. The condemned man now had a deathly pale appearance and his body visibly shook. At one minute to eight Haynes was placed on the trap door upon the scaffold. Only a few decades before thousands of people would have gathered to witness the drop but now it was held in the privacy of the prison yard.

In the next minute, the white cap was pulled over his face and the noose placed over his head. A final adjustment of the noose and rope and at the stroke of eight the bolt was pulled with a click then a bang. In an instant, it was an apparently lifeless body dangling there on the end of the rope.

That day Marwood had selected a new white hemp rope and calculated the drop sufficient to cause death to be 7ft 4in. Death was instantaneous according to the doctor but pulses from the heart could be felt for thirteen minutes. An hour later the body was cut down and placed in a rough coffin made in the prison. It was not known whether any of his family or neighbours came to the gaol that morning but nobody had visited him in jail.

Some alleged that Haynes foul temper and treatment of his wife was related to the sunstroke he suffered in America years before. It seems his temper was known around the area and was even worse after drink. It was also rumoured that Thomas Haynes had another brother who worked in a drapery shop in Dublin. He supposedly fled the country when he heard what had happened as the name Haynes was not a common one and people knew he came from Cork.

For the family living in Killaminogue, it wasn't so easy, Thomas Haynes parents were still alive. His father Thomas died in 1894 and his mother Mary in 1900. The census of 1901 shows brother John as the only Haynes left there. His sister Hanora and her husband Timothy Looney now also lived on the farm.

As for Thomas Haynes children, they had their mother's family and left the area.

Jealousy and Revenge
Ballymah Waterfall 1851

In Cork, we all know well the Chetwynd Viaduct as we pass under it when driving to Bandon and further west. The viaduct was built between 1849 and 1851 for the Cork Bandon and South Coast Railway and it's the biggest reminder that the railway existed.

This story is set further along the rail line before the Waterfall station in the townland of Ballymah on the rail works.

When one thinks of the navvies working on the line the great expansion of rail in America springs to mind. It was the same in this country and men flocked for such work despite the arduous work and dreadful conditions.

Thursday the 19th of June was the Feast of Corpus Christi, the workmen went to mass but returned to work afterwards. Later that day there was a disagreement on the job and several of the men walked off. As they left that day, threats were made against the others that remained especially the ganger.

Those that remained most likely thought the troublemakers would not be seen again and would move on to another railway job elsewhere but they were mistaken. The following Monday morning at six, some of the men returned to Cutting No.8 in Ballymah. Some say they returned looking for work while others said the men were looking for a fight but we will never know for sure. On that summer's morning, the three men sat there on the rail line smoking. After about fifteen minutes of chatting between themselves without any trouble, the ganger Richard Green came up behind them and struck one of the men twice on the head with the handle of a pick. The man that fell was Edward Farrell the ringleader of the row. A third blow was landed on Farrell's chest and Green calmly walked away home without saying a word.

Farrell's companions ran for their own safety while he lay on the ground in convulsions. One said he saw Farrell's brains on the ground as he left but after five minutes or so all signs of life ceased and Farrell died where he lay.

The police were sent for and by the time Constable John McManus arrived the ganger had left but he was easily found at home and duly arrested. It was Mrs Green who handed over a pickaxe handle, the murder weapon with her husband's name inscribed on it.

The inquest was held on Tuesday 24th of June by Coroner Richard Foott.

The railway works contractors had hired a solicitor, Mr Julian, to represent their interests in the case.

The first witness at the inquest was John Sullivan who had been with Farrell when he was killed. Sullivan's version was that they went back to the railway looking for work that morning. He also claimed they had been fired the Thursday before for leaving work to attend mass. Green was not sacked though and he recalled Farrell abusing him as he left. Both men threatened each other with Green saying "I could kick every whore bully in Cork" and Farrell replied, "I could kick every cuckold in Cork".

Sullivan was adamant though that on Monday morning, not a word was exchanged with the ganger. He just came up the bank from his work at the railway cutting and gave Farrell two deadly blows to the head in quick succession. As the man lay on the ground a third blow was given to the chest and right arm.

Cross examined by Mr Julian, Sullivan told how they had been lodging with Green until the falling out on Thursday. He also revealed how it was Farrell who was the most vocal and the ringleader amongst them.

The second man who had come to the works on Monday morning with Farrell was William Lyons. He gave a similar account to Sullivan and said he was shocked and horrified when the attack occurred. So frightened was Lyons that he hid in a gully having seen Farrell's head split open and his brains spilling out. He admitted that it was his companion Sullivan that went for the police.

Another Navvy by the name of Michael Connolly gave a conflicting version of events for that Thursday. He said it was Farrell who challenged Green to fight him but he refused. Green allegedly said he had got the better of Farrell in a fight before and wanted to mind his own business.

When it came to the events of Monday Connolly agreed that there had been no words exchanged before the blows were given.

Mr Richards whose job was the timekeeper on the railway works told the inquest how he spoke to Farrell early on Monday morning. He asked what had brought him back and claimed the reply was that they were there to start a row and were not looking for work at all.

Dr Yelverton Haynes gave evidence of having carried out the post-mortem on Monday. He found two serious head injuries and said either of which would have resulted in death. The skull was fractured so badly that the brain had been cut into.

The jury's verdict was "that Richard Green feloniously, wilfully and with malice aforethought made an assault on Edward Farrell and gave him mortal wounds of which he died". The coroner ordered that Richard Green be held in the county jail to await his trial at the upcoming Assizes on the charge of wilful murder.

Richard Green was a fifty eight year old married man and we know he had a house in the vicinity of the railway works. He had at some point taken in some of the workmen as lodgers and this it seems was the source of the discord between them.

By August most of the work on the railway had been completed and the line to Bandon was ready to be tested. Unrelated to the murder there were several protests and attempts to block the train by putting rocks on the track. Several men were convicted of obstruction for such behaviour in Ballymah near the scene of the murder.

Also that month, Richard Green came before Chief Baron Pigott at the Cork Summer Assizes charged with wilful murder. Pigott who was originally from Kilworth Co. Cork was known as a very able and fair judge. At times though, he went into such details that cases tended to go on for much longer than necessary.

The prosecution case was represented by J. Plunket, Queens Counsel, Mr Coppinger, Fitzgerald and O'Hea. Mr Brereton had the unenviable position of defending Green.

As before at the inquest, the labourer William Lyons recalled the 19th of June when he said they were sacked by the ganger for going to mass. He still maintained that it was looking for work they were when the men returned to cutting No.8 on Monday morning. He recalled again the men sitting about on the bank smoking a pipe that was passed amongst them. It was the argument the week before that Lyons believed was the cause of the killing.

When cross examined Brereton attempted to introduce the notion of intrigue between Farrell and Green's wife. Even going as far as suggesting Green had found Farrell with his wife, they had all been living under the one roof. Lyons denied this but it was proved that in the heat of the argument the week before Farrell called the ganger a cuckold. If the defence could prove an affair with Green's wife it would demonstrate provocation. It was their only chance of reducing the charges against the ganger as nobody could deny he had done it.

Several more railway labourers gave a similar story as to how Farrell was killed that Monday. The medical evidence was given by Dr Yelverton Haynes who had examined the remains for the inquest. He described two wounds on the top of the head and another over the left ear. He found extensive fractures in the skull where the skull had cut into the brain in several places. The weapon produced in court he believed could cause such injuries when used with extreme force.

When the prosecution rested their case Mr Brereton made his speech to convince the jury that there was more to it. He said Green had been extremely aggravated and mocked by Farrell about his wife's unfaithful conduct. He called two witnesses to prove this theory.

The first was John Callaghan who told of hearing Farrell taunting Green the Sunday morning before the killing. He alleged that Farrell boasted of having sex with Green's wife and drove the ganger into an infernal rage.

Jeremiah Roche also gave evidence concerning the Sunday before the murder. He had heard Farrell referring to Green as a cuckold but said that Green was not present at the time.

When questioned by the prosecution Callaghan told of meeting Farrell at the chapel gate on the Thursday of Corpus Christi. Farrell mentioned that morning his intention of going to the ganger to clear the name of his wife. It was also alleged in that conversation that Green had beaten his wife "black and blue".

Coppinger for the prosecution countered the argument of the defence saying that if an affair had occurred it proved conclusively of premeditated malice but said it went in no way towards reducing the charge to manslaughter.

The judge summed up all the evidence that had been heard at great length. It didn't take the jury long to reach a verdict of guilty of murder. Despite their verdict, they recommended mercy be shown to Green. Instead of the judge putting on the black cap that day and passing sentence it was left till the end of the Assizes for Green to realise his fate.

The station at Waterfall near to the murder scene, years later, image courtesy of the National Library of Ireland

On the 20th of August, Richard Green appeared again in court. Interestingly before him that day several men were sentenced for lesser crimes of causing death accidentally or manslaughter. For the time the sentences handed out were lenient, with the most being two years of hard labour.

For Green, it was far different as he had been found guilty of wilful murder. Putting on the black cap the judge asked him was there any reason why the death sentence should not be passed on him. Richard Green seemed like a man who had not the first idea what was going on. The only reply he could manage was that he was sorry for what he had done.

Chief Baron Pigott continued in his speech that so many judges dreaded having to do, telling a man that his life was to end. Pigott pointed out that it would serve as a warning to all men of Green's class not to do such things. He then pointed out the difference in the eyes of the law when the crime could be reduced to manslaughter. The judge revealed that despite their verdict the jury was of the opinion that Green had not intended to kill. Hearing that, Green desperately interjected with "I did not my lord".

The judge went on saying it was all pointless now as the jury's opinion was not reflected in their verdict. He was left now with the rules of the law, saying "your jury have recommended you to mercy; I have not the power to award it". The recommendation for mercy he said would be forwarded to the correct authority which was the Lord Lieutenant. The judge warned him though not to hold out much hope for mercy. Instead, he said to use the time he had left to reflect on what he had done and make amends with his maker.

It was later announced that the sentence of death was to be carried out on the 10th of September. By then Green was put out of his misery, Pigott did what he claimed he couldn't do and arranged for the death sentence to be commuted. Instead Green was to be transported for life, Australia still being the chief destination.

Transportation as a punishment ended within a few years but the death penalty remained until the 1960s. Some convicts in Australia were granted a "ticket of leave" after a few years for good behaviour. It normally was 10-12 years for a life sentence before this was allowed. This enabled the convict to get a job and live some kind of normal life. Their family could then join them in Australia but the ex-convict could not leave Australia or even board a ship. We don't know what became of Richard Green. He was fifty eight when arrested so ten or twelve years of hard labour would have taken its toll on him, especially in the Australian climate.

The Cork and Bandon railway expanded over the next decades and spread to towns and villages over all of West Cork. In the 1920s the railway was taken over by the Great Southern Railway but by then the heyday was over. In the 1940s the railway was incorporated into the CIE network. By the 1960s competition from the road network made it unviable according to CIE and the railway in West Cork closed forever.

Plenty More Fish in the Sea
Fisher Street Kinsale 1873

Today Kinsale is very well known as a tourist destination but it wasn't always that way. Go back in time and the town was a trading port. It was such a strategic and valuable port that it was well protected by the British. For a long time though, Kinsale was far better known for fishing particularly mackerel fishery.

By the 1870s, every year the mackerel caught off Kinsale was worth a fortune. Most of it never touched Irish soil and was loaded straight onto waiting steamships and landed in Milford Haven or Holyhead. From there it was taken to cities all over the UK. To demonstrate how much mackerel was caught in 1870 alone the Great Southern Railway earned £11,000 from the carriage of Kinsale mackerel on their trains. That would be worth several million in today's money. Some reckoned that up to £75,000 worth of mackerel could be caught off Kinsale in a single week when the prices were right. The following few years saw unprecedented catches of mackerel with boats returning loaded to the gunwales becoming a regular sight. There were times though when the mackerel were virtually worthless due to lack of transport. The Kinsale mackerel fishery had one thing going for it, that it generally coincided with lent when fish was more in demand.

In 1870 there were 95 Manx, 25 English, 18 French and 58 Irish vessels engaged in the mackerel. The following year it increased to 197 English and Manx, 49 French and 70 Irish boats, the foreign boats were twice the size of the Irish.

1872 was no different with record catches again. Some boats had 17,000 fish in one night. With every year more fishermen arrived in the town from as far away as Scotland and France. The Manx fishermen came in their droves as did the men from the east coast of Ireland, Cornwall and Wales.

In 1873 the season opened well on the 18th of March with over 300 fishing smacks and many of them had over 4000 herring each with many more vessels still to arrive. That year there were 181 Manx, 42 English, 92 Irish, 2 Scottish and 70 French boats at the mackerel. There were fifteen steamships and seventeen sailing ships employed taking the mackerel to England.

The price paid by the buyers was always a contentious issue, that year the price per six score or box quickly dropped from 28s to 15s 6d. In early April there was said to be over 500 vessels fishing for mackerel and catches were good. One Thursday night, 400 tonnes were caught and quickly loaded onto four waiting steamers and six sailing ships and sent to the London market for Monday morning.

All seemed to be going well in Kinsale until Monday morning when the fishermen getting ready to go fishing, saw a notice by the pier.

It read:

We the undersigned fish merchants and fish buyers hereby give notice that on and after Monday next the 7th instant a deduction of 6d in the pound will be made on all fish bought by us during the season.

It was signed by no less than 37 fish buyers which were almost all those present in Kinsale. Normally fish was auctioned between the buyers to achieve the best price but now the buyers were working together to reduce the prices. The first to reject the buyer's demands were the east coast fishermen particularly those from Dublin. The Manxmen generally seemed satisfied to be fishing, but, once they changed their mind they quickly became more adamant than the others, that prices must be restored or the boats would not return to sea.

Things quickly escalated in Kinsale, the buyers sent the four empty steamships to Cork fearing they might be damaged by the fishermen. One steamer left Kinsale towing twenty fishing boats with 100 men that worked for one fishing company.

On Tuesday the 8th of April meetings were held between the two sides. Rev Kelleher Rev Daunt the rector, J Lordan Chairman of the town commissioners and Mr Popham manager of the Munster Bank were present but no agreement could be made as the only buyer present was from Messrs Benson and Wood. Many tried to intervene, such as Rev Daunt saying that more money was being lost by not fishing at all. After all the 6d was just a 2.5 per cent reduction but the fishermen were having none of it. When one fisherman said that in other places the buyers paid the fishermen a bonus it did little to resolve the matter. A committee was formed with fishermen from Dublin, Howth, Arklow, Peel, Port St Mary, Lowestoft, Kilkeel and Kinsale and suggested a 3d reduction in the pound which pleased the fishermen but the buyers would not give in and demanded more. Soon there were six thousand men idle in the town with just twelve police to keep order.

The tradesmen (such as carpenters painters plasterers) then went out on strike. They were demanding three shillings to bring their weekly wages to 27 shillings. Ships carpenters also asked for an increase of sixpence a day. When they got it they went back to work. A few of the French vessels broke ranks and went to sea. When they returned their fish was landed in the town to satisfy the great Lenten demand. As if this wasn't bad enough, the fishermen learned that a local buyer Mr Cahill had struck a deal behind their backs with the Frenchmen.

The peaceful strike then turned ugly very rapidly, hoards of fishermen descended on the pier as the Frenchmen were landing their catch. Boxes were trashed to pieces and fish scattered everywhere but at least no one was hurt. It didn't stop there though as the fishermen felt cheated by the buyers and they march into town calling for action. Mobs went around to the buyer's lodgings demanding that they sign a document agreeing to the old terms. Several buyers caught off guard felt compelled to give in and agreed but only because they were forced to.

Riots in Kinsale when the French landed their catch

At the house of Mrs Stamers on Fisher Street (now called lower O'Connell St), there was no answer to their knocking but they knew buyer George Lawrence stayed there with his wife. At this point, the mob became more unruly and decided to batter the door in to achieve their demands from Mr Lawrence. In the heat of the moment, a log was found across the road and driven through the front door.

The twelve police in the town led by Sub Inspector Hojel and Head Constable Edgeworth arrived on the scene. Three men were trapped inside the hall of the house as they tried to break through the door to the upstairs.

The police quickly arrested the three men, Nicholas Kelly, John Russell and John Crowe but when they emerged onto the street the mob turned on them. A shower of stones were thrown at them and Constable Delany was knocked out. For their own protection, it was now the police with their prisoners that became trapped in Mrs Stamer's house. The inspector warned those outside to behave themselves or face the consequences but they demanded the release of the three prisoners. The showers of stones began again and by now there was not a pane of glass intact. The fishermen made several attempts to retrieve their friends with inspector Hojel asking them to withdraw from the street.

Fisher Street Kinsale or Lower O'Connell Street as it is now known, image courtesy of the National Library of Ireland

Outside cries were heard to close in and get the three prisoners. Inside Hojel's orders were to fix bayonets and prepare to fire. All of a sudden five or six shots were heard at intervals fired from the hall and the bow shaped windows upstairs in Mr Stamer's house. The first few shots did nothing to quell the crowd but with one of the last shots it was heard a man had been hit.

It was only when a company of soldiers from Charles Fort arrived that the mob cleared from the street and dispersed in all directions. The injured man had been hit in the groin and was in dreadful pain. Some of the fishermen took him to the Workhouse hospital but he didn't make it. On the way there the thirty something year old fisherman James Gorry from Peel in the Isle of Man died.

The soldiers and the police maintained a presence on the streets of Kinsale that night but there were no further outbreaks of trouble. Instead, there was a gloom of sadness in the town, that it went as far as it did and a man lost his life. That night George Lawrence and several more of the buyers lodged in the police barracks fearing for their lives.

The following day there were more meetings between the fishermen and the buyers, chaired by Mr John Lordan. The buyers now agreed to reduce the rebate demanded to 4d. Some fishermen agreed and were willing to go back to sea. But the remainder of the fishermen were steadfast on a reduction of 4d. They were now divided over a single penny or put another way 0.41% of a difference in price between them.

By Thursday several of the buyers agreed to withdraw their demands for a reduction of 6d in the pound. Thousands of fishermen came ashore from their boats and paraded triumphantly through the town. It was not forgotten that a man had lost his life in the struggle. That evening Coroner Eugene Horgan opened the inquest in the town.

The jury was made up of respectable men from the town; the foreman was Dr George Dunne of Newman's Mall. The remainder of the jury was, from Market Street T Horgan merchant, William Murray a Chandler and shoemakers Michael Kiely and John Supple. From Main Street Charles Bateman an auctioneer, Michael Penny Draper and David Mahony publican. From the Guardwell was Joseph Williams pawnbroker and T Barry publican. From The Glen was Robert J Jagoe, Corn Merchant and J H Williams a Maltster. There was also Michael Herlihy a publican and T Crowley a Merchant from Fisher Street. County Inspector Barry was also present.

Head Constable Edgeworth was the first witness examined that day and his examination took the whole day. He described in detail arriving in Fisher Street that day and seeing Mrs Stamer's door broken in. He found two Howth fishermen John Russell and Nicholas Kelly in the hall and arrested them. He then heard that outside Constable Michael Delany had been seriously hurt and found him out cold with his face bleeding. Dr Dorman arrived to attend to the wounded man and advised them to take shelter in Mrs Stamers. Mr Hubbard also pointed out a man who was involved in breaking the door. Edgeworth said he arrested this fisherman who turned out to be John Crowe of Kinsale.

A mob had now gathered at both sides of the house and he reckoned there were about 300 in total. He warned them to stop throwing stones and back off but instead, they called for the release of their comrades. When the stones continued, he asked Inspector Hojel for permission to load their guns but was told: "not a while". Instead, he ordered three men to fix their bayonets and protect the front door from an attack.

It was Inspector Hojel who gave two constables the order to load and the three prisoners were taken upstairs for their own safety. Hojel warned the fishermen several times to stop or they would be fired upon but the stones continued. He then heard Hojel say "do not fire, I'll try my revolver, it will only pinch them and not kill them". At this point, the coroner intervened saying it wasn't true, a revolver could kill.

Edgeworth continued saying he heard the inspector say to a man on the street "if you do that I'll shoot you" then "if you throw that stone I will fire at you". He heard Hojel pull the trigger but the revolver did not fire and then a rifle shot was heard from the hall. The stones still rained on the house and another shot was fired.

The fishermen then warned them to give up the three prisoners or it would be worse for them. Three shots were fired from the hall, two from the window and two more by the inspector with his revolver. It was after the fifth shot that he heard a man had been hit on the street.

Under cross examination, Edgeworth admitted to firing two shots that day but swore that neither of them took effect. He didn't hear the men upstairs being explicitly ordered to fire; those in the hall were instructed to fire at the ringleaders.

County Inspector Barry asked, "are you certain that were it not for the shot you fired your life would have been in imminent danger?" Edgeworth maintained that he only fired in self defence.

Edgeworth said he had been ordered to fire at the ringleaders and could have hit one if he wanted to. The first shot he fired to the right of a man and knew he missed. The second time he aimed at a man throwing a stone and then fired at his ankle. He knew if he missed the arm the bullet would go into the crowd. He said the second shot also missed as the man turned and ran.

The boats went back to sea on Monday the 14th of April but some of the smaller ones had to return to port due to the weather. Of those that stuck it out, 1000 fish was the biggest catch of the boats, fetching between 28 to 35 shillings a box. Many had predicted that the buyers would leave the town due to the trouble but the fishing returned to normal and had just missed one of the best weeks fishing.

The inquest was resumed on Tuesday the 15th when Mr Peter Hubbard who worked as a clerk to one of the fish buyers corroborated what the head constable had said. He believed it was necessary to fire shots that day saying that otherwise, the mob would not have broken up.

A Wesleyan minister Rev Ludlow also lived at Mrs Stamer's house and he said when the fishermen came first to the house, they were allowed in. Mr Lawrence signed the papers they asked agreeing to drop the demand for a price reduction. There was no trouble until the fishermen returned for a second time asking Mr Lawrence to sign his name to a list.

This time their knocks on the door were not answered and they took the law into their own hands and battered the door in. It was then Lawrence fired a shot from an upstairs window. He thought the shot was also necessary but did say the crowd was generally good humoured until the shots were fired.

A local woman name Bohan also maintained there was no trouble until the shots were fired.

George Lawrence was questioned and admitted to firing a shot from a six shot revolver. The gun he said was loaded with a ball and belonged to a friend of his, Mr Smith.

Later that day the funeral took place in the town and was attended by masses of fishermen and townsfolk. The funeral cortege to the graveyard in the town was quite a sight with fishermen walking four abreast behind the coffin. The magistrates, fearing trouble, issued instructions that all pubs or anywhere alcohol could be purchased were to close at four that evening until the following day.

Coincidentally almost exactly a year before a sixty eight year old fisherman, Thomas Gorry, had also been buried in Kinsale. Thomas also from Peel in the Isle of Man died from inflammation of the lungs while fishing on the Manx lugger *Lynx*.

When the inquest sat again on the 22nd of April it was Sub Inspector Hojel who was examined by Mr Julian. He recalled the riot and how they were trapped in the house when at times he said the stone throwing was furious. He did reveal that there were breaks in the action and the fishermen allowed the doctors to come to the house to attend to Delany who had been struck. The injured man was taken back to the barracks through the mob and then it intensified.

Hojel was clear that he could not have given up the prisoners saying he could have lost his job if he did. He ordered three men to fix their bayonets to protect the hall door. He heard someone in the crowd say "come boys close in, make a rush there are only a few of them". It was only after this he maintained that he ordered his men to load their weapons. When the other men went upstairs, he told them to fire, but only if it was necessary and not to allow anyone to enter the house. Several times he called to the crowd to stop throwing stones and back away but they did not.

The inspector was in the hall with the Head Constable and instructed him to fire after his revolver had failed to. He said the first three shots did not deter the crowd, he heard one say "don't be afraid they are only blank" and they kept closing in. Hojel believed it was the third shot fired from the hall that hit one of the men outside.

One of the jurors asked Hojel for the name of the man who fired the fatal shot but he refused to say. Instead, the inspector said he was responsible for every shot that was fired that day. He insisted that it was necessary to have fired on the crowd to protect the lives of those in the house.

A juror Michael Kiely asked:

"Have you any authority to fire on the crowd without a magistrate? I have.

I thought you should have a magistrate and the Riot Act read? You could fire yourself to protect your life if it is in danger."

Then Mr Julian read the 696th rule of the police code:

"Firing to be effective. Whenever the necessity of firing shall, unfortunately, arise it ought to be at the leaders of a riot or the assailants of the police and if possible with effect. Firing over the heads of mobs engaged in an illegal pursuit must not be allowed. As a harmless fire, instead of intimidating will give confidence to the daring and the guilty, while comparatively innocent persons in the rear might thereby be injured. Care must be taken not to fire upon persons separated from or not assisting the rioters or assailants."

Period map of Kinsale showing Fisher Street and the harbour.

Dr William Hornibrook was called to testify the medical evidence. He had seen James Gorry the night of the riot at about half past ten but by this time he was dead. He found a gunshot wound on the right side of the man's groin.

The following day he carried out the post mortem assisted by Dr Vickery. He discovered that the bullet had entered the groin and passed through the hip exiting at the right buttock. He believed from the direction of travel of the bullet that the shot was not fired from upstairs but from the same level. The doctor could not tell for sure if it was fired from a revolver or rifle as he had not seen the bullet but reckoned from the wound it was a larger bullet. At that point, the inquest was adjourned until the following Tuesday.

From this evidence, George Lawrence, the fish buyer, could be ruled out of being the one who shot James Gorry, as he had fired from upstairs. He wasn't to get away entirely though. In April Mr Lawrence was charged with having an illegal revolver on the night of the riot.

On Tuesday the 29th April when Coroner Horgan concluded the inquest, there was not much interest in the case and only those required attended. The police were represented by solicitor Mr Julian and the Crown prosecution by Mr T Rice.

After some discussion with Julian about the adjournment which he had disagreed with, the coroner asked were there any witnesses to be called from the fishermen, to give their side of the story but no one came forward. Mr Julian suggested that it would now be cowardly to make insinuations against the police and not come forward with the evidence.

Rev Daunt apologised, he had asked for the adjournment and had intended to ask the deceased man's relatives to attend. He had failed to meet them as he was busy on Sunday and the fishermen had gone to sea on Monday.

Mr Julian made an eloquent speech for the police saying they were the finest bunch of men with not a bad one in the whole country. He could see no other verdict the jury could reach but justifiable homicide.

"We find that James Gorry came by his death from a gunshot wound inflicted by the Constabulary in the discharge of their duty on the evening of the 8th April 1873. At the same time, the majority of the jury are of the opinion that the police might have extended their forbearance a little further and that the want of magisterial aid was apparent". On his death records, death was recorded as a gunshot wound fired by police, justifiable homicide.

There had been a magisterial investigation but not into the conduct of the police and the shooting. Over the course of three days in April at the Kinsale Courthouse, four fishermen were charged with being involved in the riot before Resident Magistrate Cronin. They were John Crowe and Patrick Foley from Kinsale, Nicholas Kelly and John Russell of Howth. The fishermen were represented by Mr Alfred Blake and County Inspector Barry with Mr Julian were there for the police.

The evidence heard was generally from the police constables but this time they identified the accused men as being part of the riot. It was Mr Hubbard who had pointed John Crowe out to the police and repeated again that he had seen him in the hall of Mrs Stamers.

At the end of the day's proceedings, Mr Julian announced that he had been speaking to some of the fish buyers about the matter. The buyers believed that the fishermen should be let off lightly and dealt with by a magistrate.

Blake then revealed that a petition had been sent to the Lord Lieutenant pleading leniency for the fishermen. It had been signed by all the clergy, gentry and the Town Commissioners. Julian felt there was no point in petitioning the Lord Lieutenant at this early stage. On the question of bail, they could not decide and instead adjourned until Monday.

On the third day of the investigation against the four fishermen, more evidence was heard. This time Constable Ryder from Ballinhassig told how extra police, like himself, were drafted into the town when trouble was expected.

He admitted to firing one shot thinking it was the third or fourth fired that day. He would not say whether he fired at a person or hit James Gorry. Ryder denied seeing any man hit or falling on the street that evening and he thought his shot was the last fired.

His orders that day were to fire at the ringleaders and not into the crowd.

Foley was identified as being one of the men going about the town forcing the buyers to sign the document. Constable Myles Murphy testified to arresting Kelly when he caught him in the hall of Mrs Stamers. He said John Crowe intervened as Kelly was arrested and would not leave; he was then arrested by the Head Constable.

After the evidence against the men had been heard Mr Blake addressed the court. He did not appeal for leniency instead he gave in saying he knew they would be returned for a trial before a jury. He reserved his defence until then but asked that the men be allowed out on bail. The court adjourned that day granting bail at £60 and two sureties of £30 for each man.

Everyone wanted things to go back to how it was before the trouble. With 4000 visiting fishermen and several hundred locals, it was a big injection to the economy at the time and in everyone's interest to catch the fish while they were there. It was better for all that the whole affair be forgotten about. There wasn't a magisterial investigation into the police conduct as the inquest jury had recommended. The police stuck together and never revealed the name of the man who fired the fatal shot. If they had, the inquest could have returned a verdict against the policeman and the coroner could have issued a warrant for his arrest. It would not have made any difference anyway as no further legal proceedings would have been possible against the policeman. Had it been proved George Lawrence fired the fatal shot it might have been a different outcome altogether. Months later Lawrence pleaded guilty to the charge of illegally being on the possession of a firearm but was released when agreeing to be bound to the peace.

The four fishermen charged with riot and the assault of Constable Delany were brought before Justice Morris at the Cork Summer Assizes. All four pleaded guilty and for once Mr Teeling for the defence agreed with Colman O'Loghlan for the crown that the men should not be punished severely. It was also agreed the men should be released on a bond of £20 each and would be called again before the court if they got into any trouble.

The fishing in Kinsale quickly went back to normal and in May that year the mackerel fishing was very heavy with boats heard of catching up to 20000 in a single night. Prices fluctuated greatly between 30 shillings per box to as low as a few shillings. Some buyers got caught when they sold in the London market and only fetched 4s per box having paid much more for them. The buyers still complained about prices saying they would prefer to pay a fixed price between 15 -20 shillings per box rather than risk the sudden price changes. Some of the boats didn't go to sea knowing they could make a big catch but struggle to cover their cost due to the low prices.

By June the fishing was coming to a close for the year and some of the buyers had left for Arklow and the herring season there. The boats followed suit and by the end of the month, only the local Kinsale boats were still pursuing the mackerel with average catches and moderate prices being paid. It would be March next year before the Manx, Cornish and Frenchmen would be back again for the mackerel.

In the 1890s the Kinsale mackerel fishery steadily declined but each year the Manxmen returned albeit in far fewer numbers until the outbreak of World War I.

What is amazing is that back in the 1870s it took several hundred boats with nearly five thousand fishermen to catch a few hundred tonnes of mackerel daily. Never mind all those employed ashore packing the fish or the crews on the steamers. Nowadays a modern 40m pelagic vessel can catch the same amount of mackerel with a crew of just six men. Maybe ten truck drivers would replace the thousands of men that were required to pack and ice the fish before. Fishing is so efficient now by the standards of the Kinsale Fishery that modern boats are only allowed to fish for a handful of days a year. The small boats that fished off Kinsale back in the 1800s would never have made a dent in the fish stocks compared with those of today.

An Unlucky Horseshoe
Ballynalouhy Ballymartle 1895

On Sunday the 9th of June, a large group of men were at a road bowling match between Tom Butler and Michael Walsh. When they were near Skeugh Crossroads, about 2 and a half miles east of Innishannon, a disagreement broke out. It was about where the bowl had left the road and should be marked. Daniel Crowley took it badly saying "you sons of bitches you want to scheme me out of a bowl". He threw off his coat in a field and called on several men to fight him. He exchanged a few blows with one man but it came to nothing serious and the bowling resumed. In the afternoon the group went to Mrs Delea's pub, The Rising Sun in Ballynalouhy, near the train station.

Road bowling at the time was illegal. Some judges despised the activity saying it was dangerous. One court case that year in Ballinspittle resulted in several being fined for road bowling, clearing or marking the road, and even aiding and abetting road bowling, all were fined several shillings or a week in jail.

After the pub, another row broke out on the road below Ballymartle Railway Station. This time there were more men involved. Daniel Crowley was again in the thick of it but what sparked it off this time is unclear. It wasn't going to settle down so easy though, especially with many having drink taken. Insults were thrown with Crowley being called one of the worst things in the country at that time, a "landgrabber". This applied to anyone who had taken on an evicted farm, which Dan Crowley's father had several years before. Daniel Crowley was seen with his coat off challenging anyone to fight. On one side you had Daniel Crowley, his brother Patrick as well as Jeremiah Crowley with his brother Daniel Crowley junior. On the other side, you had the Deasy's, John and his brothers Con and Michael but there were many more involved.

More than one man got a beating that evening, but John Deasy seemed to come out the worst, despite his brothers being there. He was seen leaving with bloody clothes and some noticed he was bleeding from behind the ears. Deasy walked home with his brother Michael and thought little of the bleeding at the time. It wasn't until Wednesday that his condition had deteriorated rapidly and on Thursday was so bad two doctors came to see him. Seeing his head injuries they knew he needed serious medical help and he was sent to the South Infirmary immediately and operated on soon after.

The Rising Sun pub looking towards the railway bridge.

As this was a serious injury, the police began an investigation and made several arrests. The four Crowley's were arrested; Daniel did not attempt to deny his involvement and claimed he was driven to it. He realised though that it was getting serious and he could lose his job as a porter at Ballymartle train station. On the 14th of June, the four men were charged with grievous assault and remanded into custody.

Late on the night of Sunday 16th John Deasy died in the South Infirmary. He had been suffering for seven days. Deasy was 23 years old and from Killaminogue, which was halfway between Innishannon and Ballymartle.

The inquest was held by Coroner Alfred Blake in the South Infirmary Hospital. County Inspector Gamble, with District Inspector Harrell of Kinsale, were present for the crown, while the four Crowley's were represented by solicitor Dr Wynne.

There was no shortage of witnesses at the inquest as there had been a big crowd at the fight near Ballymartle Train Station on the 9th. Several had seen exactly what had occurred and recalled Daniel Crowley senior striking John Deasy with a weapon.

Dr John Reid, a surgeon at the South Infirmary, detailed John Deasy's condition. He said Deasy was admitted to hospital at 3 pm on Thursday the 13th of June. He immediately saw he was suffering from a compound fracture of the skull and knew it would be necessary to operate. He described Deasy as semi conscious before the operation. Reid carried out an operation he referred to as Trepanning, drilling into the skull to release the blood pressure on the brain. His condition improved the following morning but it was short lived and he never regained consciousness.

On Sunday his condition deteriorated rapidly and he died on Sunday evening. Reid was confident that everything medically that could be done, was done. Reid also carried out the post-mortem and told of the abscess discovered on the brain under the fracture. Reid answered the Coroner explaining that the abscess was caused by the skull being driven into the brain. To District Inspector Harrell's questions, he described the wound as roughly triangular shaped, an inch long by a quarter of an inch deep. He believed a sharp hard instrument struck extremely hard would produce such an injury.

A juror curiously asked would a horseshoe attached to a belt do it and Dr Reid agreed it would.

Dr Wynne pleaded with the jury to return an open verdict per the medical evidence. He suggested the matter would be dealt with at a magisterial inquiry at a later date.

One of the jurors asked was it not normal to have the accused present at the inquest. Coroner Blake replied that it was the custom years ago but not anymore. Blake also explained that it was another reason why they had to be more careful with the verdict. The jury went with the coroner's suggestion and returned an open verdict.

The charges against the four Crowley's were about to get a lot more serious. Several times they were produced before a magistrate and remanded to custody.

On the 28th of June, all four men were brought before resident magistrate Colonel Pearse at the Ballymartle Petty Sessions. They were charged that they on the 9th of June feloniously and wilfully with malice aforethought killed and murdered John Deasy. District Inspector Harrell from Kinsale led the prosecution while Henry Wynne solicitor from Cork defended the Crowley's.

As before Dr Reid gave the medical evidence and told how John Deasy had died. The only other witness that day was William Donoghue from Farlistown. He revealed it was he who was struck by Crowley in the first row over the bowling. Later that evening he did not see much of the fight except when he saw Dan Desmond knocked down and saw all four of the Crowley's were involved.

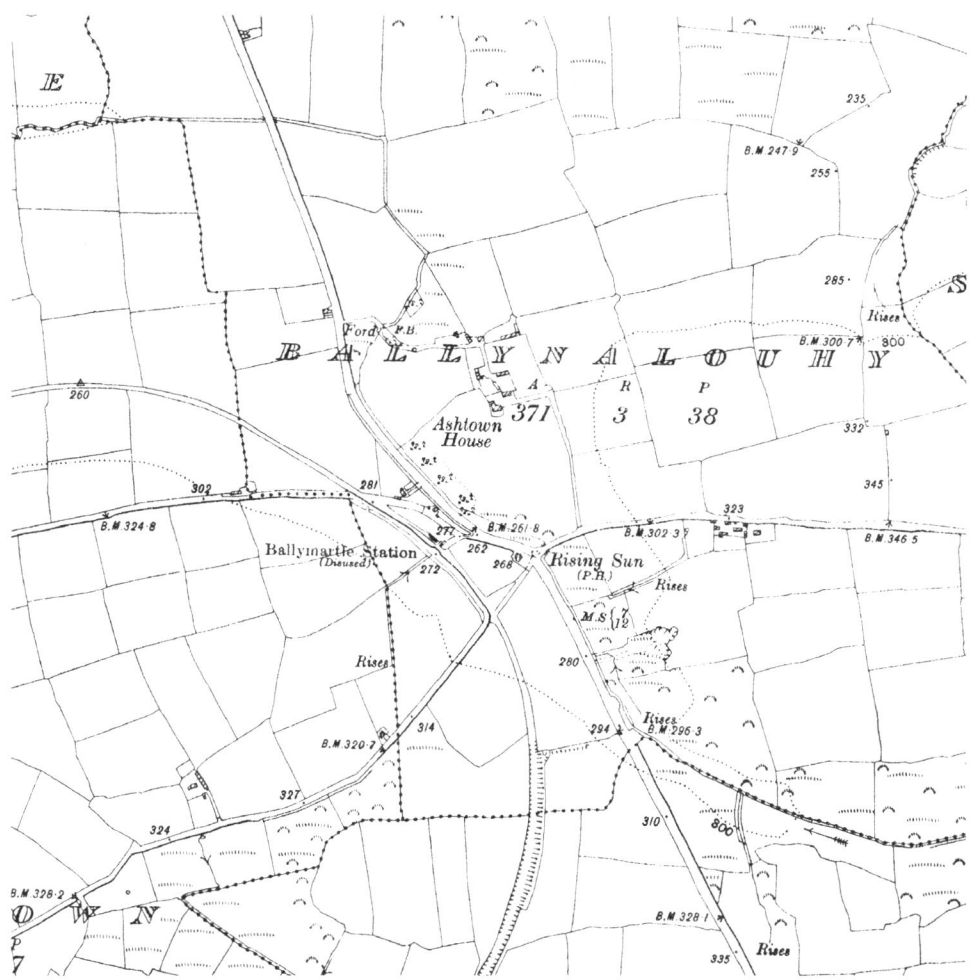

Map showing Rising Sun pub and Ballymartle Station.

It took another special sitting of the court in Ballymartle on the 1st of July before a decision was made. There was no shortage of evidence that day and it certainly seemed that the Crowley's were not popular as everyone was willing to testify against them. Called that day were James

Crowley, Mary Daly, John Desmond, William Buckley, Con Carey, Daniel Desmond of Derrynagashel, Patrick Kenneally, Michael Sullivan, Jerry Byrne, John McCarthy Farlistown, William Hogan and Daniel Murphy. It seemed that nobody was going to speak for the Crowley's. All these witnesses had seen bits of the fight and Daniel Crowley with a weapon in his hand. Some had seen John Deasy leaving covered in blood and it was also heard how a bit of a horseshoe attached to a belt was found near the scene.

Brother of the deceased Michael Deasy recalled the row breaking out between the Rising Sun Pub and the Railway Bridge about eight that evening. He made out that it started between Daniel Crowley and Dan Desmond and his brother only intervened to help Desmond. When the fight broke out he saw Daniel Crowley laying into his brother John with a belt and witnessed John staggering away afterwards. Michael did confirm though that it was only Daniel Crowley Senior he saw striking John, he did not see the other three accused men attacking John at all.

Sergeant John Byrne from Bandon told of meeting Daniel Crowley Senior at Ballymartle Station on the 13th of July where he worked as a porter. He warned Crowley by saying "this is a serious thing you have got into". Crowley voluntarily gave a statement and with no objection from the defence, it was read out in court.

"I had to do it, we are boycotted since we came here, and I never go out without a weapon. Last Sunday when I came down they were beating my brother and I was glad to have the weapon to defend us. It was a piece of horseshoe tied to a piece of a leather strap. I knew I would want a weapon, that is why I carried it. We took an evicted farm here a few years ago. If I had a revolver the matter would be worse for the three of them were attacking us. Since we came here they are at us every place we go. It was the belt I was wearing I used on him and I broke it and lost half of it. That is why I am wearing this (pointing to an old brace he had around his waist). I will lose my job on the railway too, but sure I may never come out. I think I struck only two of the Deasy's with the belt but they were all beating me though I have no mark."

Dr Wynne made a plead for his clients that day saying no jury would prosecute for murder in this case. He couldn't deny Daniel Crowley's involvement and even admitted he would not get bail but he asked that the charge sent to trial should be manslaughter. For the other three, he argued there was not a shred of evidence against them and they should not be detained another day.

Colonel Pearse seemed like he did not want to be the one to make a decision that could later be criticised. He said it was for a higher authority than him to decide. On the matter of releasing some of the accused as there was not a shred of evidence against them Pearse remarked how they were all together that day and he was reluctant to separate the charges against them. He returned all four men for trial at the upcoming Assizes on the charge of murder; at least it was only a few weeks away. On the applications of bail, he wouldn't make a decision either but was sure the Queen's Bench would grant it. What he did do was remind everyone that a life had been lost and that it was a serious matter.

It's easy to imagine Daniel Crowley Senior as an older man but he was only twenty two years old. He had been born in Shanacrane to the North West of Dunmanway but had moved to Ballynamaul when his father took on the farm that many others would not. The other two Crowley brothers, Daniel junior and Patrick had been born near Kilmeen. It is safe to assume that they were all seen as outsiders in the area and occupied farms that locals had been evicted from.

After a few weeks in jail, the four Crowley's appeared at the Summer Assizes before Justice Andrews. The charge against them was reduced to manslaughter so they were saved from the threat of a death sentence. The men were now represented by Mr Brereton Barry and Dr Wynne, while the prosecution had Mr Moriarty assisted by Mr Wright Crown Solicitor.

When Moriarty opened the case for the prosecution he told the jury the case before them was straightforward except for the defence which he called "false". He said it would be heard that Dan Crowley claimed he lived in fear and needed to go about armed with a belt with a piece of metal tied to it. The defence would also claim that Crowley was merely acting in self defence. Moriarty remarked that it was an unusual weapon to carry about for defending oneself. He also asked was Crowley in such fear of his life that he went to a bowling match and the pub afterwards.

The same evidence was produced that day, how Daniel Crowley was seen striking the deceased with a weapon. Under cross examination, more than one witness admitted that Daniel Crowley had been struck by several men before he hit John Deasy. It was also heard that the crowd threw Daniel Crowley over a ditch but one or two denied this.

The picture Mr Barry tried to paint was that Daniel Crowley was defending himself against a crowd. He called a brother of the accused Timothy Crowley for the defence. Timothy recalled his brother Daniel swinging the belt with the horseshoe to keep the crowd away from him. He told how there was more on the Deasy's side and the Crowley's were outnumbered.

The jury decided in half an hour that Daniel Crowley Senior was guilty of manslaughter but recommended mercy due to being provoked. The three other Crowley's were found not guilty and acquitted of the charge. It was the following day before Daniel Crowley was sentenced to fifteen months in jail with hard labour.

John Crowley's defence of being boycotted seems a little farfetched. If he was boycotted in the true Irish sense he would not have been at the road bowling that day. In some areas, boycotts were so bad that the "landgrabber" was completely ignored by all in the community and needed constant police protection. In one case in the North of the county at Sunday mass, the whole church emptied at the sight of a boycotted man. Daniel Crowley certainly wasn't popular by any means and the term "landgrabber" was an easy insult to get him going in a row. The crowd did seem to be against the Crowley's but the Deasy's certainly didn't bargain for how far he would go.

Daniel Crowley was transferred to Tralee Prison and his sentence was to end in October of the following year.

A Perilous Profession
Passage West 1851

In 1851, Passage West was alive with foreign sailors from all over the world. When they came ashore in their droves, they wanted drink and women. The women arrived nightly in the village to meet the demand and extract what money they could from the sailors for their services.

On Thursday night the 9th of October a Greek soldier caused a scene by saying he had been robbed by a woman. She denied taking ten shillings from him but was still locked up for the night. The woman's name was Mary Mahony, known as a lady of the night who had come from the city to ply her trade on the foreigners. She had arrived on the 7 o'clock train that evening in the company of another woman.

Before Mary was turned out of the barracks the following morning, news arrived that caused the police to run off in a hurry. It turned out the body of a woman had been found in a field near the church. The police went back to the barracks to talk to Mary as she had been near the church the night before with her "friend" and two foreign sailors.

The woman's body was dreadfully mutilated with one injury being described as a cut from ear to ear. Despite this Mary was brought from the barrack to the field where she identified the woman as Julia Hayes. Only minutes after parting with her the night before, Mary was arrested but not before she saw Julia going towards the church with a man.

She said the week before they had also met the same sailors and Julia had been threatened with a knife. Mary was taken aboard several foreign vessels by Constable Heany until she identified the man Julia had been with the night before. His knife was nowhere to be seen but his handkerchief had recently been washed. Several other sailors aboard the same ship who possessed knives were also arrested and taken into custody. When the police came ashore with the foreign sailors, they also arrested two men from Passage. By 7 am that Friday morning all the arrests had been made and not only was Mary Mahony not released but four more women were taken into custody for being involved or having some knowledge of the death. In all Constable Heany had thirteen men and women in custody.

The following day the body still lay in the same position despite having suspects in custody. It seems that the local magistrates had not been informed and in turn, the coroner also had no knowledge of it. Eventually, the body was moved to an unoccupied house in the village.

Initially, Julia's wounds were said to have been inflicted on her face but it was actually more the neck and throat. She had been stabbed three times into her neck just under the ear on the right hand side. On the other side was a larger gaping wound that had hit the carotid artery and severed the windpipe. She must have lost a massive amount of blood quickly and death would have been instantaneous.

The inquest was finally held by Coroner Foott on Monday morning. By then the police had arranged over twenty witnesses which seemed quite a lot for an inquest.

Local man Michael Sullivan found the woman's body in the field near the church early on Friday morning but knew nothing of the circumstances as to how she came to be there.

Mary Mahony was then called. She said she lived in the Coal Quay in Cork and had known Julia for about three years and had seen her get on the 7 o'clock train to Passage on Thursday evening. They separated when they arrived in Passage but met again about an hour later. She said Julia had a foreign sailor with her, Mary knew the man as she had seen him before but did not know his name.

She admitted being with that sailor the Monday before, on that occasion he threatened to stick her with his knife if she did not give him money. She was afraid of him and parted with two shillings and two pence.

Mary said while walking towards the church on Thursday evening she warned Julia what he had done to her on Monday. Julia was not bothered by it saying, he now had money on him and she was intent on getting it from him. Mary then looked at the accused men at the inquest and pointed out the man Julia was with, he was a man by the name of Donoger.

It all seemed straightforward until an English sailor named Richard Greenwood said he had seen Julia Hayes with a man near the church gate. It was just a few minutes before nine according to Greenwood. When asked to identify the man he saw with Julia he pointed out a different man who was also one of those in custody.

Close to the church in Passage where she was last seen alive.

One of the magistrates Parsons Boland tried to clarify the matter saying he had been talking to the Police before nine and heard that Mary Mahony had been arrested. He suggested enough time must have elapsed for Julia to be seen with another man. A policeman then verified from his notes that Mary Mahony had been arrested at ten minutes to nine.

Mary Mahony was recalled and reckoned it was three minutes from when she was arrested and last seeing Julia. She maintained it was quarter to nine when she was brought to the barracks.

When the inquest resumed on Tuesday morning it was heard that a coat with dry bloodstains had been found aboard one of the ships. The coat was known to belong to Donoger. He also had a wet handkerchief which appeared to have been washed but also had what looked like blood spots.

After some discussion, it was agreed that the coat should be sent for analysis to a chemist, Mr Gordon in Patrick Street.

Local woman Elizabeth Flynn said she saw Julia Hayes talking to a tall man near the church about nine on Thursday evening. Donoger was a low sized man and so could not be described as tall. Elizabeth was speaking to Richard Greenwood at the time she saw Julia with that man. Elizabeth lived nearby and reckoned if any noise was made that night she would have heard it. It was very possible though that Julia died so quickly she didn't have the time to cry for help.

Revenue officer James McQuaide said he was aboard the Greek ship called San Georgio on Thursday evening. Four seamen came aboard but

Donoger was not aboard that ship. He noticed one of the men had some sign of blood on his nose and he wiped it away immediately. Constable Heany intervened telling that the man with the blood was Stephano Mercovich. He had been the man who had helped Mary Mahony when threatened by Donoger.

So Mary was recalled again! She confirmed that Mercovich had been there when the other man threatened her. On Thursday night she had seen Mercovich heading towards his ship before seeing Julia with another man.

It seemed that Mercovich was not the man but it all got even more confusing when a man named McCarthy was called. McCarthy was aboard the San Georgio on Friday morning and spoke to Mercovich then. He suggested that a Greek man must have committed the murder but Mercovich suggested it was a Roman from one of the vessels further upriver.

McCarthy saw Mercovich lending his knife to someone Friday morning and thought he noticed signs of blood on it. He said it to Mercovich at the time but was told: "this knife never killed anyone, it has been blessed by the pope and if stuck in the mast of a ship would quell the greatest storm". He did remark that when the police boarded the vessel several knives were found but Mercovich's knife was not.

Patrick Geary believed he saw Julia Hayes standing about the Square in Passage about half nine on Thursday night and she was not in the company of any man. Geary was on duty that night and his job was to convey the seamen to and from their vessels lying at anchor in the channel. He told that about one o'clock that morning he took two men with two women to a ship. He identified Donoger as being one of those men saying he was wearing a red cap at the time.

The next witness Eliza McMahon, was one of the women who spent the night aboard a foreign ship. She had known Julia Hayes for several years and last saw her at the Square about eight that night. Eliza left with Petrinelly and went to a pub where she stayed until eleven. Then she had supper in another house and later met up with another woman and Donoger. It was afterwards that the four of them went aboard the ship where they remained until six the following morning.

Eliza recalled seeing Donoger also at the Square about eight on Thursday evening but said he left with a girl called Ann Hare. She reckoned he was gone for about three quarters of an hour and remained in her company when he returned.

It was Wednesday morning at the inquest when Ann Hare was questioned. She also lived in the Coal Quay, was not married and had gone to Passage on the seven o'clock train that night. Ann admitted that she had been to Passage the last few nights and Julia was with her on the train.

She left Julia that night about half seven but later saw her talking to Mary Mahony at the Square. Mary was at the time accusing Donoger of taking money from her and he gave Julia a push away. Ann said Donoger left with her and they went up by the Church where she spent three quarters of an hour with him, then they returned to the village together about half eight. Ann gave an account of her every move for the remainder of the night until six the following morning saying that Donoger was with her all the time.

She had seen Julia going towards the church that night with a tall man, she thought he had a loose fitting brown coat on but reckoned she would not be able to identify him again. Ann did point out one of the accused, Stephano Mercovich, saying he would be about the right height.

Frances Fitzgibbon, a publican in Passage, corroborated Ann's version of events for later that night. It seems that when Frances was first questioned by the police she denied they had been in her pub that night. Now though, when prompted by the sergeant, she recalled clearly that they were there and maintained that she was now telling the truth.

Another woman, Ann Dwyer, was produced who recalled being in Fitzgibbons pub on Thursday night about half past eight. She pointed out her companion from that night amongst the accused men. It was Giovanni Berglovich a man with a big beard. Ann reckoned she drank two glasses of rum with him and he had the same.

Frances Fitzgibbon butted in with: "That is not true, that man was not with her, all they had was a glass of porter and a glass of rum". Ann Dwyer insisted she was with him "He was there with me and we had two glasses of rum". Mrs Fitzgibbon was still equally as sure saying "I solemnly swear that is not the man who was with her, I know him perfectly well, and the man with the large beard was not with Stephano on that night."

John Gordon described in detail the tests he had carried out to determine if the coat, handkerchief and knives had traces of blood. The means available back then were a far cry to the DNA analysis that can be done today and Gordon struggled to prove with any certainty that the marks were indeed human blood.

*View of Passage West decades later,
image courtesy of the National Library of Ireland.*

Patrick Fitzgibbon contradicted what his wife had said. He recalled Berglovich was on his own in the pub that night about half past eight and was sure he wore a red cap with a blue tassel on it.

Richard Greenwood at this point was recalled and again said Giovanni Berglovich passed him on Thursday night with a woman heading towards the church. He afterwards saw the pair passing Fitzgibbon's pub. About nine he passed Berglovich, who was then with Julia Hayes, heading towards the exact spot in the field where Julia was found dead.

Before the inquest resumed on Thursday morning the Coroner, Jury, Police and several of the witnesses went to the scene of the crime in the field up near the Church. When they returned to the Courthouse there were now several more mentions of sightings of Giovanni Berglovich on Thursday night. Shipwright Timothy Hayes saw Giovanni Berglovich standing around the square sometime after nine.

Dr Benjamin Johnson was called to give the medical evidence as he had carried out an examination. He found three wounds on the right side and one significant gaping wound on the left side of the neck. He said the wound on the left was over two and a half inches, big enough for him to get two fingers into it. On that side, both the internal and external jugular veins were severed along with the carotid artery. The windpipe was also cut. The woman would not have been able to speak or call out as she died. All the cuts were done with a sharp instrument such as a knife. He reckoned that she would certainly have been dead within two or three minutes.

After some deliberation, the jury returned a verdict that "the jury find and present that the deceased Julia Hayes came to her death by reason of the several and respective wounds inflicted upon her by one Giovanna Berglovich, that is one large gaping wound on the left side of her neck and the right side three wounds considerably smaller. That the said wounds divided the windpipe above the thyroid cartilage and also divided the passage for the conveying food to the stomach and the large vessels of the neck namely the internal jugular vein the external on and the carotid artery. The jury upon their oaths do say that the several wounds were inflicted feloniously wilfully and of his malice aforethought by the said Giovanni Berglovich on Julia Hayes on the 9th of October of which said mortal wounds she immediately died at a place called the Copse in the townland of Pembroke in the parish of Marmullane, barony of Kerricurrihy in the county of Cork".

Giovanni Berglovich a sailor from the Greek sailing ship San Georgio was committed to jail on the warrant the coroner issued as a result of the verdict. He would be called at the next assizes and tried before a jury.

Before they left that day the jury wished to thank local magistrate Morgan Allen and Constable Heany for how the investigation had been carried out and for producing such an amount of witnesses.

The case came before the Spring Assizes that year but the crown prosecution asked for it to be postponed to the next Assizes.

It was July before there was any more news of the case. Now at the Summer Assizes, it was decided by the Crown not to proceed further in the case feeling the evidence was insufficient to secure a conviction. Giovanni Berglovich was duly released after nine months in jail. The crown could have disposed of the case back in December and must have known then how it would turn out. Postponing the case several times when the evidence was circumstantial was common and a crude method of serving justice without producing evidence before a jury. Maybe if Julia Hayes was not a prostitute more would have been done. Men had been hung on less evidence but in this case, most of the witnesses for the prosecution were prostitutes. They must have worried that what these women said would not be believed by a jury because of what they did for a living.

Caught by the Coat
Graball Crosshaven 1872

Close to Camden Fort in Crosshaven, an Artillery soldier came running up the road shouting that a local man had been murdered. He called to a house where there were two Sappers from the Royal Engineers. The first thing the informant was asked was why he was out in his shirt and where was his tunic. He replied that his tunic had been left back at the barrack.

It was dark so they got a light and went to the scene of the alleged crime. An old man named Timothy Murphy was found outside his house stark naked with blood streaming from his face and head. Nearby was a blood stained boulder, the assumed murder weapon.

The only other occupant of the house was nine year old Mary Buckley, a relation of Timothy was not there. The two Sappers grew suspicious at the Artillery man's somewhat dishevelled state, especially about his tunic. He insisted that his tunic would be found where he left it at the fort. With the light of a candle, one of the Sappers probed into Murphy's tiny cabin and not far away found a tunic matching that of an Artillery soldier, blue with a red collar.

The Artilleryman was McDonnell from the 57th regiment and he could not account for why his tunic would be in the old man's house or how he was the one that discovered the crime. Even before the alarm had been raised the two Royal Engineer Sappers took the law into their own hands and detained McDonnell on suspicion of some involvement in the murder.

The young girl was found by a neighbour Mrs Bassett. She met a soldier taking the child towards the shore under the pretence of taking her to see her mother. The woman didn't realise some dreadful crime had been committed and so the soldier took his chance and fled.

It was only when they went to move Murphy back into his wretched hovel that they realised he was not quite dead but in a dying state. By the time the police made it up the hill from the village, it was all over. Constable Fitzpatrick arrived to find the suspect apprehended and a doctor sent for.

Murphy was put to bed that night, unable to tell who had attacked him. The young girl however was able to tell that two men had broken into their house and it bore all the signs of it. The door had been pulled from the hinges and thrown aside to gain entry. Inside everything was thrown about like somebody was searching for something.

It was the following morning before a doctor arrived to Murphy's house. Dr Pearson seeing the head injuries knew he could do little and recommended Murphy be sent to hospital.

At ten that morning, a neighbour put Timothy Murphy into his cart to begin the journey of over fifteen miles. It would now take a car only fifteen minutes but it took them much longer. The journey was extremely slow. The driver walked with the horse so as not to worsen Murphy's condition. He stopped regularly to check the patient but a mile from Kinsale realised Murphy was dead. They carried on to the Kinsale Workhouse but were refused entry, so the only option was to head back to Crosshaven.

In Camden Fort that Monday there was a parade of all soldiers for the purpose of identifying the man who had taken the child the night before. Unfortunately, neither Mrs Driscoll nor the young child could pick out the man.

Murphy's wretched hovel was known as a house of ill repute, so much so he was known as old Fagan. The oldest profession is said to be prostitution and where there are soldiers there is great demand for this service. The prostitutes were said to live in the caves and shore near Camden Fort. Murphy allowed them to use his cabin to prepare food, most likely in exchange for something.

Graball with Roches Point in the background.

Mary Buckley the young girl who lived with him was in some way related. Her mother was said to be one of the women who offered their services to the soldiers of the fort but had previously been sent to prison.

It was Wednesday when Coroner Horgan arrived at Crosshaven and opened the inquest to investigate the circumstances surrounding Murphy's brutal death. The artillery soldier John McDonnell was still in custody and remained the chief suspect. His accomplice had still not been found.

A jury of twelve respectable local men was quickly sworn in and went to view the body first. The jury was made up of John and Michael Kennefick, Denis and John Mackesy, Denis Noonan, Edward Graham, John Cullinane, William J Slattery, John Lynch, Patrick McNamara, James Coleman and Jeremiah Sullivan.

Several magistrates attended as did police county inspector Thomas Barry.

The first witness that day was Murphy's neighbour William Driscoll who had known Murphy all his life. He detailed how he took Timothy to Kinsale on Monday escorted by two policemen. Driscoll said they followed the doctor's instructions stopping regularly to give Murphy a drink of new milk and spirits. He had been careful and walked the horse slowly to Kinsale. All the time Murphy moaned from the pain of his wounds which Driscoll told had not been dressed by the doctor. Driscoll described his shock when he discovered that the old man had died as he had expected Murphy would survive his injuries.

Royal Engineer Sapper Henry James Smyth who had been informed of the attack on Sunday by McDonnell was also questioned at the inquest. Smyth reckoned it was about nine when he was called. He went to Murphy's and found him outside, completely naked with blood pouring from his head. Before that night Smyth did not know Murphy and had never been to the house before. He also did not know McDonnell.

He became suspicious of McDonnell and asked him about his missing uniform. When he went into Murphy's house he found not only an Artillery man's tunic but also gloves, belt and cap. Smyth said he didn't get much of a response from McDonnell at the time and he seemed to be under the influence of drink. With the help of another sapper, he detained McDonnell and sent for the police. He also had the presence of mind that night to stop anyone else from going into Murphy's house.

One of the magistrates commended Sapper Smyth for his actions that night. Constable Fitzpatrick told how the uniform found in the house not only matched McDonnell's missing items but also fitted him correctly. At this point of the proceedings, the coroner had no option but to adjourn as the post mortem had not yet been carried out. Dr Pearson who had attended to Murphy sent word for a Dr Curtis from Cork to come and assist.

Back then the inquest was usually held the day after a suspicious death, often it was a reasonably quick affair, with a verdict in a matter of hours. Once a verdict was found the family could begin the funeral cortege to their burial plot. The inquest verdict could influence the legal proceedings against a suspect. A coroner's warrant alone was enough to arrest and detain a suspect.

The inquest was resumed on Friday the 26th of July which was almost a week after the events of the night of 21st July. The post mortem had now been carried out. By that time another soldier from the 57th regiment called Griffith had been arrested. He was suspected of being the man who led the child away. By now McDonnell had gotten legal counsel, a solicitor named Mr Julian.

The first witness called that day was Matthew McCabe a stone dresser who lodged in Mrs Driscoll's house. He had passed by Murphy's house sometime after eight and heard a child crying. At the time a soldier in red uniform was standing outside the house, McCabe heard a drunk soldier inside.

He told Mr Julian he didn't go inside to see what was going on as he knew it was a "bad house".

Sapper James Lacy told the inquest that he was going back to his barracks on Sunday night with his wife. It was as they passed by Edward Fitzgerald's farm he heard women talking saying "old Fagan had been killed". He knew they meant Murphy as he had known him for two years.

When he got closer to Murphy's house he saw Sapper Smyth and McDonnell who he didn't know at the time. On the ground was Murphy stark naked and unable to tell what had occurred. With the help of Smyth, they got Murphy into his house, detained McDonnell and stopped others from entering.

Mr Julian cross examined Lacy making the point that McDonnell didn't try to hide his identity nor did he flee.

Surgeon Dr George Davie was called as he had attended Murphy on Sunday night. The doctor described the head injuries he found on both sides of the head. A stone was produced and Dr Davie agreed such a stone could produce those injuries. The doctor stayed with Murphy until two in the morning but before leaving the symptoms had worsened.

Davie went back three hours later to discover Dr Pearson attending to him. He heard from Pearson that Murphy had vomited porter and thought this a good sign. Pearson also believed the injuries were only superficial. By eight that morning both the doctors thought Murphy was fit enough to travel to hospital, yet serious enough to need it.

There were several questions from jurors and Mr Julian suggesting that it was the wrong decision to send him on such a journey. Obviously Julian would say anything to show a possibility of something else killing Murphy rather than his client.

Dr James Curtis who had assisted in the post mortem maintained that it was not the journey that killed Murphy. He said he would have died anyway. He defended the doctor's decision saying there should be an ambulance and that the road should be better. Curtis reckoned the best place to send Murphy was to the South Infirmary saying he could have been taken to Queenstown by boat and train to Cork. It was 1904 before the train went directly from Crosshaven to Cork.

Graball Bay looking towards Fort Camden,
image courtesy of the National Library of Ireland.

Mrs Bassett the woman who took the child from the soldier was next called. She said that on Sunday night McDonnell and another soldier called to her house looking for drink. When they realised there was no drink to be had they both left and a while later she heard screams coming from Murphy's house. She went out and came upon a soldier in a red coat taking the child towards the shore. Mrs Bassett said she questioned the soldier about what had happened and he said: "a blue coat was inside squeezing her". Then she asked where he was going with the child. The reply she got was the child told him her mother was down by the rocks. When she went to take the child from the soldier, he willingly left her go. When asked to identify the suspects Mrs Bassett recognised McDonnell saying how terribly drunk he was that night. The other soldier in custody was not the man who was leading the child away that Sunday night.

Neighbour Margaret Driscoll told of being in Murphy's house before the attack had taken place. Seeing the door off the hinges she went in to find Murphy in bed and a soldier with his coat thrown in straw on the floor. The old man asked her to sort out the door for him but she refused and left.

Sometime later she heard Murphy had been killed and went back to the house. The same soldier was standing outside near Murphy. She said this was before the two sappers arrived on the scene. Margaret recalled saying to him "I think it was you killed the man".

Evidence was also produced that the uniform found in Murphy's house was that of McDonnell's as it had his name and regimental number on them. Mr Julian quickly cut in to say that there was no blood found on the uniform or on McDonnell at the time. There was blood on the stone which was found and on the ground where Murphy was found.

A third day was needed at the inquest before a verdict was reached. On Saturday it was decided that the soldier Griffith from the 57th regiment was to be discharged as there was no evidence against him.

Anne Mills who lived near the scene of the crime recognised John McDonnell. She said he came to her house between nine and ten on Sunday evening saying an old man had been killed. When both the Sappers were taking Murphy into his house Anne accused McDonnell of beating the old man. As drunk as he was, he denied it telling her another soldier had done it and ran off. Anne said she did believe at the time he had done it but McDonnell told her he didn't want to leave the old man in such a state without telling the neighbours. Ann had seen his hands that night and there was not any blood on them.

She admitted to Julian that looking back, McDonnell's behaviour and appearance that night were not like that of a man who had committed such a crime. She had threatened him that the police were on the way and he didn't seem bothered saying he had done nothing wrong.

Ten soldiers from the 57th regiment were led into the inquest to find the man who was seen taking the child. Sergeant Kerosin from the 57th regiment picked out one man he suspected. He said that Cornelius O'Brien had seemed guilty and he kept an eye on him for several days. Mrs Bassett was recalled to see could she pick out the man, she thought O'Brien looked like him but couldn't be sure.

Several more witnesses were called that day but none could pick out one of the soldiers. Sergeant Finley then proved that O'Brien had been present at roll call on Sunday night and had been in the barracks for some time.

When all the evidence was heard Mr Julian proposed calling the suspect John McDonnell to give evidence in his own defence. District Inspector Barry strenuously objected to such a thing happening and the foreman agreed it was most irregular.

Barry argued there was no point in hearing from a man who had been charged with the crime.

Mr Julian then made a speech for his client which would normally be saved for a magisterial investigation. Usually, the inquest was only concerned with how the death occurred but not so much with who had done it.

First Julian called four gunners who had been drinking with McDonnell on Sunday night. Each of them said that they left the public house about nine and agreed McDonnell was drunk but none saw him talking to another soldier.

Julian addressed the coroner and jury in a speech that was more akin to that of an Assize Court. He argued that there was no evidence at all to prove his client was guilty but he had two points to prove his innocence. He asked the jury were McDonnell's actions that night those of a guilty man when he raised the alarm, gave any help he could and even went for a lamp.

Then he gave a version of events according to his client. In it, he admitted that McDonnell was very drunk and went to Murphy's house with a soldier from the 57th regiment. So drunk was McDonnell he said that he lay on straw in the house while the old man argued with the soldier. It was only because of the soldier he had gone to Murphy's at all that night. He slept for a while, woke suddenly and went to raise the alarm. Julian maintained there was nothing at all to prove the guilt of McDonnell he was just there at the time.

If McDonnell was as innocent as Julian made out, why did he not just tell who the soldier with him that night was? He didn't make any attempt to explain how McDonnell got into the house when the door was off the hinges and entry had been forced. After all, if his version was to be believed he would have been shocked and appalled at what had occurred while he slept on the straw. Was he just so drunk that he didn't have the sense to realise what he had done and inadvertently seemed innocent by hanging around?

It took the jury over an hour to reach their verdict "that Timothy Murphy died at Clontead, Kinsale in the barony of Kinsale on the 22nd July 1872 from the effects of injuries on the head inflicted on him by some person or persons unknown to us on the night of 21st July". When the verdict was heard Coroner Horgan read it again to McDonnell and ordered him to be discharged.

County Inspector Barry quickly cut in saying if McDonnell was to be discharged he would be rearrested again immediately to wait for an investigation.

By now it was safe to say that John McDonnell had been in Murphy's house the night he was attacked. Did McDonnell do it or had he been so intoxicated he didn't know who had? This was where the evidence was lacking, from the time he was seen thrown inside the house to when he raised the alarm. It does seem that if he had been the guilty party he would have run off instead of informing others.

John McDonnell was unmarried and thirty seven years old, he had originally come from Templetown Co Wexford near Hook Head. When arrested he gave his address as the Army Barracks, Crosshaven and replied to the question of friends/relations with "has none".

On Friday the 2nd of August at the special sitting of Carrigaline Petty Sessions the case was heard. There was great interest in the proceedings and the court was packed with the public hoping to hear something that had not been revealed at the inquest. Several magistrates attended.

It started that day with several witnesses questioned about the "improper house" that Murphy kept. Questions were asked as to how the old man managed to survive without an income but one witness denied Murphy was reduced to begging. William Driscoll who had taken Murphy to Kinsale and knew him all his life said it was the neighbours who supported Murphy. He was aware that such women frequented Murphy's house but said the old man didn't earn his living from it.

A little boy Patrick McNamara who lived near Graball was called as he had seen a soldier outside Murphy's house that Sunday night. He failed to identify the soldier as John McDonnell. One of the magistrates cut in asking the boy who his mother was, Patrick replied that she lived at Graball Bay. A police inspector then replied for the boy saying how his mother was a beggar and had only recently come to Crosshaven. He said the boy had a sister who was poorly and the family moved there for her health. The crowd in court took his meaning and burst out laughing at this.

The witnesses and evidence heard that day was pretty much a repeat of that of the inquest. Several of the witnesses admitted when cross examined by Mr Julian that McDonnell made no attempt to run that night nor did his actions seem guilty.

Again Mr Julian pleaded the innocence of his client saying how sending him for trial would commit him to jail for at least eight months. There obviously was to be no Winter Assizes held in Cork that year. He said if it had happened a month before the case would by now have been dealt with at the Summer Assizes. Julian was banking on the fact that a jury would not find him guilty and he would be discharged.

Julian described McDonnell's nineteen years career in the army as excellent except for his drunkenness. He suggested that in this occurrence it was McDonnell's failing for drink that had got him in this case, otherwise, he was innocent.

The magistrates having heard the case left the courtroom to reach a decision. It took them a long time and when they returned no agreement had been made. The magistrates were equally split between sending him for trial or not.

Now they looked to the Crown Prosecution as to how the case should proceed. They were informed the normal course in this situation was to consult the Law Advisor. Mr Julian jumped at the chance and suggested his client should no longer be kept in custody.

It was agreed to send the evidence to the Law Advisor and McDonnell was remanded back into custody. Later in August John McDonnell appeared again before the Carrigaline Magistrates. This time they agreed to send him to trial at the Spring Assizes but unusually for a case of murder allowed him out on bail.

What happened from there we don't really know as John McDonnell doesn't seem to have been brought before the Assizes the following year. Did the crown prosecution just drop the case against him or did McDonnell disappear? Most likely there was no new evidence against McDonnell and the crown realised a jury would fail to convict.

Was he just caught in the middle of it and helplessly drunk when the murderer ran away? Men had been hung on less evidence in the past, with the jury safe in the assumption of who else could have done it.

Why had the child Mary Buckley not been produced or was she traumatised from what she saw? The soldier leading the child away that night had a blue coat and had been abusing her in the house. McDonnell was an artilleryman whose blue coat was found in the house. Yet McDonnell said he slept while the soldier argued with the old man. If the child had seen Murphy killed she would surely have told Mrs Bassett once she was safe in her care.

Did McDonnell and the soldier go round to Murphy's that night looking for a prostitute? They forced entry into the house and in their drunken state, it is possible young Mary was the source of their attention. Her cries were heard from outside and without killing her, the only way to silence her was to take her away. Was it then that the old man's skull was beaten in with the stone?

Whoever the soldier was he must have been sure that McDonnell was not going to give him up to save himself. The soldier avoided detection but could have come forward and given information against McDonnell thereby putting himself in the clear.

In August of that year, an application was made to have Mary Buckley sent to an industrial school. She was at the time under the care of Mrs Driscoll a neighbour. Mary was as much a victim of the crime as anyone and could be in better places than a house of disrepute but was an industrial school any better?

What the killing did do was draw attention to what was going on up the hill in Crosshaven near the fort. Constable Fitzgerald was reputed to previously have done what he could to suppress what was happening.

The village of Crosshaven a decade or so later, image courtesy of the National Library of Ireland.

Some claimed that the Police in Crosshaven was woefully undermanned considering all the activity. The Police force was five in total, Constable Fitzpatrick and four others. One was an orderly stationed in the barracks, two were normally occupied patrolling the beach and two more were left to cover the district. They argued this was seriously insufficient to maintain law and order especially with all the visitors and soldiers in the village.

The history of Camden Fort is well known, it is especially famous for the Brennan torpedo. What is sometimes overlooked is the effect a large military installation has on the surrounding countryside. It brings activity and prosperity to the area but there is a downside to it too. This story shows the darker side which is often forgotten in history but is what actually went on. Certainly, there was prostitution in the area but nobody was arrested for it around that time. There were however women arrested in Cobh and Kinsale for prostitution around that time.

So it seemed at first that McDonnell was caught red handed falling about outside Murphy's house, his clothes inside. Then again he had no blood on his hands or clothes. Had he been found with blood on his hands he could have been hung for it yet may not have done it at all. He may only have woken inside the house and went out to help the old man. All the parts were there yet it lacked any witness who saw what happened that night.

The Cost of Chivalry
Passage West 1859

In 1859 Passage West was a busy port alive with hustle and bustle. The streets were filled with the sounds of foreign voices, seamen from the ships discharging their cargo. These seamen crowded into pubs and establishments in the town enjoying themselves before heading off on another perilous journey that would take them all over the globe.

The port brought with it advantages to the local economy, but there could also be another uglier side when trouble broke out. One dark Sunday night, 30th January, in a laneway off the main street a man lay dead. He was a local labourer. Nearby was a gang of foreign sailors who denied any knowledge of the occurrence.

When the police arrived it was discovered that the man had been stabbed in the chest. It didn't take much questioning to learn that an altercation had taken place outside Calloway's public house on Strand Street.

Head Constable Heany led the police; he rounded up several foreign sailors in the town and even boarded several ships. In total before that night was out, he had eighteen sailors locked up. The dead man was now identified as Thomas White, married with six children and lived in the town.

The following day, Monday 31st January, an inquest was held in Passage West courthouse by Coroner William Honohan to determine exactly how Thomas White met his death. The jury consisted of William D'Esterre Parker foreman from the Green, Patrick Sweeney, Stephen Wilson owner of the American Hotel on the Quay and William Penny. Also John Flynn, publican, David Ludley, D Cadogan, Jeremiah Fitzgerald, Thomas Barry, Patrick, Thomas and John Sullivan.

Before any evidence was heard the jury went to the house of Thomas White who lived behind Toureen Terrace. They all viewed the body and duly returned to the courthouse.

Head Constable Heany questioned the witnesses as he was leading the police investigation. Some of the accused men were represented by Mr Michelli from the Austrian Consul as many of them were Austrian.

The first witness was Randal Crowley; he had been with the deceased man the fatal night along with Daniel Lynch and Mary Mulcahy. They had been to a christening that afternoon and were going home together about nine. Passing Calloway's pub they got into an argument with several foreign sailors. Crowley said it was over a remark one of the sailors made to Mary as they walked past. Crowley did not see his friend Thomas White being stabbed. The truth was Crowley had fled at the first sign of trouble leaving his two friends Lynch and White to deal with it.

When Mary Mulcahy was called she said that the sailors didn't say anything to her, they may have pushed into her but it was not intentional. She went on to her mother's house and was there when the trouble broke out. After a while, she returned to see what was keeping them only to find a crowd standing around a man lying on the ground. It took her a while to realise it was Thomas White and that he was dead.

The third man Daniel Lynch had also not witnessed the stabbing but he did see Thomas White being struck outside the pub. He pointed out Bruno Lorenzo as one of the men who struck Thomas, an Italian seaman from the Genoese barque Marietta. Mr Michelli translated to Lorenzo the allegation that had been made against him and he was heard to say "non e vero" meaning it is not true.

Lynch had been in the thick of it for a while at least with his friend. At one point he witnessed that four men had White against a wall. They managed to break free and ran down a laneway with the foreigners in pursuit.

Lynch told how he got as far as a Blacksmiths called Bowen but White had not been so lucky. Looking back he saw that the foreigners had caught up with Thomas and surrounded him. Lynch got away onto the street and went into a pub for safety. A few minutes later someone came in looking for a candle saying there was a man on the ground outside. He went out and realised that it was White who was lying dead in the laneway.

Then the chief witness Catherine Calloway was called, she was a young girl and the niece of publican William Calloway. She told how a crowd of Italian sailors had been in the pub before nine on Sunday evening. At about quarter to nine, the Italians were put out of the pub and she heard fighting on the street outside almost immediately. A few minutes later one of the sailors came knocking at the door, he had forgotten his cap. The girl said she let him in and he asked for a knife to cut his tobacco. It was

Bartolomeo Pisarello she said returned to the pub. He then made another attempt to get a knife from the press saying "Peter is in plenty of fight" or some words to that effect. She pointed out "Peter" as Bruno Lorenzo who Lynch had already identified as the man he saw beating White.

Young Catherine identified seven of the eighteen men, as being in the pub that night. She thought there had been about ten in the pub before they were put out.

Sailor William Bennett, from the American ship E.Z, told the inquest he had found the body who appeared to be dead and not that far away he saw a crowd of foreign sailors who seemed very excited as if they had been in a fight.

Police constable John Connor who had been involved in the search for the foreign sailors said he found a cap belonging to Pisarello in the gutter and the constable said he could have lost it in a struggle. He had searched the ships and found several knives but found no signs of blood on any of them.

Medical evidence was given by Dr Benjamin Johnson who had that morning carried out the post mortem. He found a small wound on the man's left hand side under the eighth rib. It was inflicted by a small sharp instrument such as a knife. The object that entered the body near the breastbone punctured the sac surrounding the heart and then hit the left ventricle. The doctor concluded this wound was sufficient to result in instant death.

After hearing the evidence the jury returned a verdict of wilful murder against Lorenzo, Pisarello and their five fellow crew members Giovanni Ginocchi, Angelo Tassino, Bartolomeo Baralino, Collotto Antonio and Andrea Farragona. The coroner duly issued a warrant to keep the men in custody until a magistrate investigated it further. The seven men were then sent to the county gaol. The accused were all men from the Genoese sailing barque Marietta.

A subscription was set up for the family of the dead man. Not only had the White family lost their breadwinner but his wife was in poor health and had six children to look after.

A few weeks later in the County Court of the Cork Spring Assizes, the seven sailors were brought before Justice Baron Green. They were all put forward of the charge that they did feloniously and with malice aforethought kill and murder Thomas White on the 30th of January.

The prosecution announced though that the charge was to be reduced to manslaughter. Rev George Brennan who may have spent time in Rome acted as an interpreter for the Italians. They had little to say, nor would they be asked much. None of the Italians objected to anyone in the jury box nor were they bothered about not having a few foreigners in the jury.

Mr Coppinger opened the Crown's case and went into the facts. What evidence was heard that day was merely a repeat of the inquest. No new witnesses had been found in the meantime nor had any of the Italians turned against each other.

Somebody had stabbed Thomas White in the darkness and now it seemed we would never know who for sure. At the inquest, Lorenzo and Pisarello seemed to be singled out as being more involved than the others but now before a jury; it seemed it was all seven or nothing.

When Baron Green summed up what he had heard in court that day it was easy to see where it was going. He had grave doubts about the circumstantial evidence and made it known to the jury. In his mind, the sailors were present that night but their guilt had not been proven sufficiently by the Crown. The jury returned a verdict of not guilty and all seven sailors were free to leave.

It was a sad case where a man lost his life in what seemed to be a complete misunderstanding. The men believed some insult or gesture had been made to Mary Mulcahy and without asking her, defended her honour. The Italians at the same time had just been thrown out of the pub and were ready for a fight. The two sides certainly clashed but bloodshed could easily have been avoided that night. It wasn't as if he was beaten and died afterwards. The single stab wound exactly in the right place strongly suggested intent.

It was all too late for the White family who was left to fend for themselves. The widow with her six children was now at the mercy of the charity of others.

A Day Out Gone Wrong
Fountainstown 1884

The area surrounding any army barracks or fort would often benefit from a positive economic impact, but could also lead to more crime. The soldiers were the source of much of the trouble when they went out socialising and looking for entertainment. Often the conflicts were between the soldiers themselves, especially with drink taken but sometimes the conflict was with the locals.

On the 19th of October, several soldiers had the Sunday off and headed to Ringabella for the afternoon, which they often did. It was a long walk from Crosshaven but they crossed on the ferry at Fountainstown which was much quicker than walking to Minane Bridge. The four friends that left the fort together that Sunday were Privates Jordan, Walsh, Garney and Corporal Ashworth.

Before getting the ferry they met up with several young women, two sisters Margaret and Catherine Lynch, Helena Murray and Ellen Callaghan. They all went to Desmond's Public house and had four or five gallons of porter between them. Walsh and Garney left at half six. There were still a few artillerymen left in the pub in their distinctive blue uniforms. It was dark when Jordan and Ashworth left Desmond's with the women and headed back to catch the ferryboat.

On the short journey across, they chatted with two sisters and another young woman. There were several local men on the ferry boat that night who had also been drinking in Desmond's for the afternoon. When the boat landed on the sand in Fountainstown the soldiers helped the ladies out.

They were only a few yards away from the boat when the local men turned on them. One pointed out the corporal saying "that's him".

It seems there had been some disagreement earlier in the pub but the soldiers hadn't thought anything of it. The men closed in around them, the two soldiers had no chance of escape. What happened next on the beach in the dark was unclear for some time. Cries could be heard in the distance and then screeching from the narrow estuary they had crossed only minutes before.

Private Jordan went into the water to save himself from the men and found refuge when he was pulled into the ferryboat.

When the ferryboat landed Jordan on the other side in Ringabella he told the Artillerymen what had happened. In the darkness, they searched for Corporal Ashworth but found no trace of him and believed he had made his escape and would be at the barracks before them. The corporal didn't make it back to his barracks that night and so soldiers set out looking for him but didn't make it as far as Ringabella in the dark. A hat belonging to a corporal was found in Fountainstown on the beach and late that night was handed into Fort Camden.

Early on Monday morning Sergeant James Lamble of the Lancashire Regiment set out again towards Fountainstown with a few privates in search of the missing Corporal. Sometime around nine, a cry went out that something was spotted in the water about fifty yards from where the ferry landed. Men waded out and before long the body of a soldier was landed on the beach. It was the body of Corporal Ashworth and he bore all the signs of violence including several teeth missing. The Sergeant sent for the police. He was convinced that the row the night before led to Ashworth's death.

At about noon on Monday, the local police under Sergeant Carton made several arrests after receiving information about who had attacked Ashworth. Four local labourers were arrested, brothers Timothy and John Cronin, blacksmiths from Hoddersfield, Daniel Casey Knocknagore, Crosshaven and Jeremiah Murphy from Crosshaven. A few hours later that day, Michael Fitzgerald was also arrested on suspicion of being involved.

That evening all five were brought before magistrate Starkie in Crosshaven and charged with murder. They were remanded to Carrigaline Petty sessions on Tuesday after the inquest had concluded how Ashworth had died. The Corporal was only nineteen years old and had been in the service just a few years. He originally came from Bolton where his father was a police sergeant. He had been stationed in Camden only a few months.

Coroner Horgan opened the inquest at eight on Tuesday morning in Fort Camden. It was most unusual to start at this early hour, most began at midday allowing time for the Coroner to travel and a jury to be rounded up.

Fountainstown where the ferry crossed from Ringabella

Unusually a large jury of sixteen local men was sworn in that morning. From Myrtleville was William Daunt and farmer George Walton. From Crosshaven, William Noonan publican, Henry Lake Coal merchant, Thomas Batridge boat owner and John Dennis ships carpenter. Hotel owners from Crosshaven Michael Kennefick and Jeremiah O'Sullivan of the Railway Pier Hotel and farmers of Crosshaven Edmund Fitzgerald and John Driscoll. The remainder were Richard Busteed, Matthew Thomas, Samuel Fester, Timothy Lynch, Patrick Fishbourne and Charles Cooper.

A young boy Timothy Regan told how he spotted the body in the river on Monday morning a few hundred yards from the slip where the ferry lands.

Sergeant of the 1st Lancashire Fusiliers James Lamble said he was present when the body was seen and arranged for it to be got ashore. He recognised the body as Corporal Samuel Ashworth from his regiment. The sergeant saw two wounds at the back of the head and bleeding from the mouth. The face was very bruised and swollen especially around the eyes. Ashworth had run back towards the ferry to make his escape but didn't make it. He was knocked down on the beach.

Michael Crennell, the ferryman, was called to tell what he witnessed on Sunday.

He lived in Ringabella and for the last thirteen years ferried people across the river in his nineteen foot boat. That Sunday about four he took Corporal Ashworth with Private Jordan and three ladies to Ringabella.

About seven Michael said he took two red soldiers with three young ladies on board. There were four more men in the boat that he knew, Jeremiah Murphy, Daniel Casey and the Cronin brothers.

He landed them all at Fountainstown and returned to Ringabella. It was when he was coming back the next time he heard that there was a person in the water. He rowed as hard as he could and managed to reach Private Jordan and pull him out. For his own safety, he took Jordan to the Ringabella side where four artillerymen had gathered.

The ferryman believed the soldiers were sober that evening and had never met such well behaved soldiers in all his years' operating the ferry.

Matthew Regan told how he was on the ferry on Sunday night with James Ahern. He saw a Corporal on the beach after getting out of the ferry boat but said there wasn't a row, only a few loud words. He walked up to the road to where several men and women had gathered.

James Ahern, a friend of the last witness told a different story. James was a boatman living in Fountainstown. He recalled returning on the ferry and there being two red soldiers, Jeremiah Murphy, Matthew Regan, two Cronins, Dan Casey, the lynch sisters and Helena Murray. While walking up the beach he saw a man running after a soldier towards the water, but couldn't see who it was. He said his friend Matthew Regan was not drunk that night and had only three pints. He heard an argument on the beach but didn't see any fighting. He had heard Jeremiah Murphy in the boat talking about an earlier argument.

Helena Murray from Fountainstown admitted being in Desmond's public house on Sunday but denied being there with the soldiers. When asked was she drinking that afternoon she replied: "I paid for no drink". She eventually gave in saying she had one glass of porter and was talking to the soldiers.

Helena said she returned on the same ferry as the soldiers but left with James Ahern. While walking away up the beach she heard Corporal Ashworth say "if you want fighting I will give you plenty of it". She heard some screaming afterwards from the beach but didn't return to see who was doing it. On the boat, she heard someone say "it is not the blue soldiers we want but the red".

William Henry Allen a surgeon of the Army Medical Staff stationed at Camden Fort carried out an examination with the help of Dr Pearson. He said the two wounds at the back of the head were severe and the skull was fractured. He believed quite a lot of blood had been lost from these wounds. He described the face as swollen in the lips and over the left eye, which could have been the result of a blow from something blunt. During the post-mortem, he described finding the brain congested with blood and a clot on the left side. He said there was a bloody froth oozing out from the mouth. All other organs of the body were healthy, as he would expect for a man of Ashworth's age.

He concluded that death was due to blood on the brain caused by the wounds on the back of the head. Which were the result of violence inflicted by severe blows of a heavy object or kicks from a boot. Dr Pearson concluded with what the army doctor had said.

Coroner Horgan addressed the jury that day saying how sad a case it was. He asked them to find a verdict according to the medical evidence and to return an open verdict. He said this would allow the police to complete their investigation and the murder would be punished by the law. They found: That Samuel Ashworth was found dead at Fountainstown Strand on the 20th of October and that death was caused by extravasation of blood on the brain, resulting from violence inflicted by persons unknown.

Some said there had been a disagreement in Desmond's pub earlier that Sunday and that something occurred the Sunday before also. Other rumours spread that the attack was related to a young woman. The soldiers went to the pub and returned home with several young ladies that Sunday as we have already heard. There was often jealousy between the soldiers and the local young men. To the young women, the soldiers were a far more attractive prospect than the local men they were familiar with. It wasn't just the uniforms that attracted them though, the soldiers were unknown and seemed a novelty and they had a steady wage with chances of promotion. The local young men were labourers or worked for their father's. So it's perfectly plausible that there was tension between the soldiers and the local men about the women.

The day after the inquest it was heard that one of the first men arrested had turned and become an approver. This meant he was now giving information to the police to save himself.

At the next appearance in court, it was revealed who the approver was. One of the Cronin brothers admitted returning on the ferry that evening with two soldiers. He said it was his friends that turned on them but he didn't get involved. Instead, he tried to stop them. He helped Jordan from the water and tried to prevent him from getting a further beating but failed. Cronin said he saw what happened that evening in Fountainstown but didn't see what became of Corporal Ashworth after the beating. Later that night Jeremiah Murphy told him that he and Jeremiah Ahern threw the body into the sea. Soon after another arrest was made by the police, it was Jeremiah Ahern the son of a local farmer in Fountainstown.

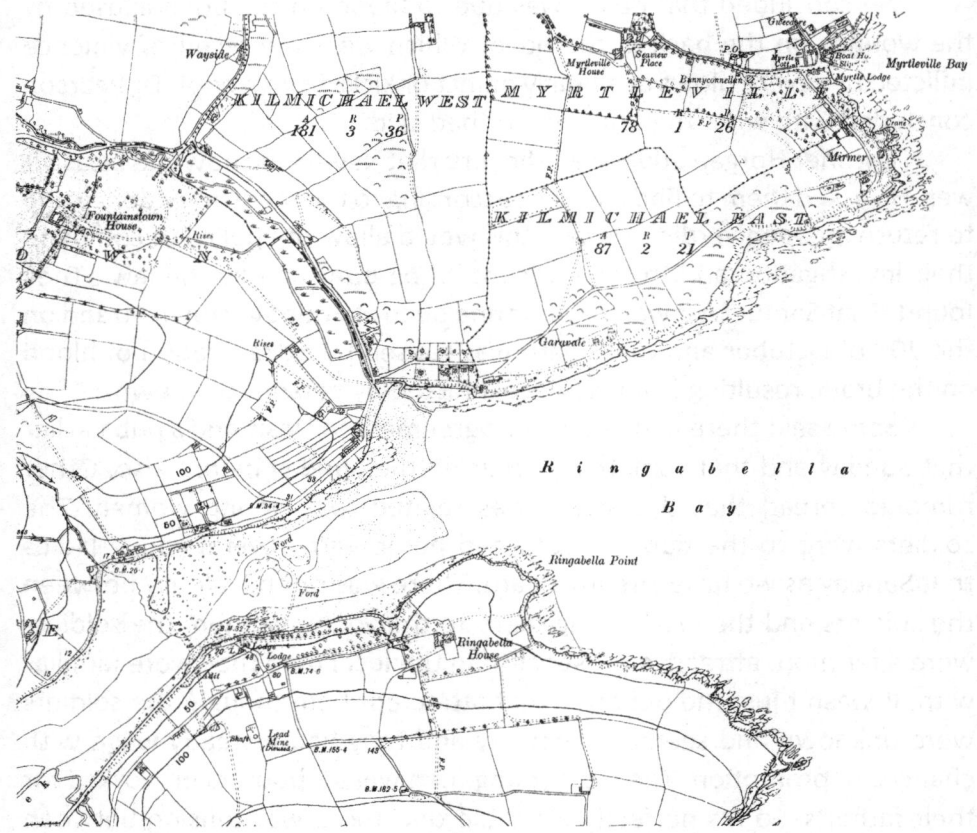

Map showing Ringabella Bay and the ferry crossing.

A few weeks later on the 30th of October, the case was heard again at the Tracton Petty Sessions. By now Timothy Cronin had been released from custody but his brother John had not. It was now four men charged with the murder of the Corporal. There was great local interest in the case and the small courtroom was packed. That day Murphy and Casey were represented by a Mr Blake, Ahern by Mr Healy, while John Cronin had employed Mr O'Connor.

That day in court Private Edward Jordan told again how he and Ashworth had been attacked. He could not identify any of those that carried out the attack but believed that all four or five of the men took turns kicking them. The only person he recognised was John Cronin who he pointed out. He said John helped him out of the water and later walked back to Crosshaven with him and the artillerymen.

Next, Matthew Regan told of being on the ferry boat also that evening. He left Desmond's pub about half six and walked to the ferry with James Ahern. Regan recalled seeing Jeremiah Murphy punch the corporal and Dan Casey strike the other soldier at the same time. He saw the Corporal ran away and witnessed John Cronin helping the private out of the water. At the inquest, he had denied even hearing a row that night saying it was only "high words".

He admitted to Blake (defence solicitor for Murphy & Casey) that at the inquest he told the opposite. Back then he had said he saw no row or anyone being hit that evening.

By far Timothy Cronin's statement was the most damning of all. He was one of the first arrested but now was swearing against Murphy and Casey while his brother was still one of the accused. Timothy said he saw it all, he was only four or five yards away when it all began on the beach. Jeremiah Murphy ran after the Corporal and knocked him down. When on the ground he said Murphy gave him several kicks while the Corporal begged for mercy. He heard the Corporal moaning but said the screeching was from the private who was struggling in the water.

Timothy and his brother helped the private from the water and told him he would be safe. But he said that while the private was in his brother's arms Dan Casey came up again and struck him a blow of his fist. It was then the private ran back into the water for a second time.

Timothy said the last time he saw the corporal on the beach he was about twenty yards from the water's edge. He didn't see what happened to him, but Jeremiah Murphy told him he and Ahern had driven the Corporal into the water. He couldn't account for the row with the soldiers and had not heard anything said on the ferryboat. He had been helping to row the boat that night while Murphy and the others were forward, the soldiers were at the aft end.

When Blake cross examined Timothy Cronin he tried his best to give the impression that Cronin had offered information to save himself. O'Connor who represented John Cronin objected repeatedly to Blake's questions. Blake persisted asking why he had given information, trying to get confirmation that he had been offered a deal by the police. Cronin eventually answered him saying he didn't want to go to the gallows an innocent man; he also wanted to save his brother who had also done nothing but help that night.

Sergeant of the Royal Artillery Joseph McGowan told the court it was about quarter to eight before he arrived in Fountainstown on the ferryboat that Sunday evening. Private Jordan returned with him after being pulled from the water by the ferryman. He met John Cronin on the beach and Cronin told him there had been a fight between the soldiers. Cronin even said that the Corporal had gotten beaten badly but had been last seen running across the fields. They left Fountainstown that night thinking that the Corporal would be at the barracks before them.

At this point, District Inspector Sommerville announced that there remained a good number of civilian witnesses to be called that day. Healy, the solicitor for Ahern, objected saying that most of the witnesses heard proved nothing for the prosecution.

Still it went on, Michael Fitzgerald, who at one point had been arrested under suspicion, was called but had seen nothing despite being on the strand that night.

Kate Fitzgerald was also there that night. She heard moaning and loud crying of "don't kill me I'm an Irishman" but didn't know who said it.

This time it was Dr Pearson who proved the medical evidence. As had been heard at the inquest the doctor described how badly beaten Corporal Ashworth had been especially on the face and head. He found an accumulation of blood in the skull and a clot in the left ventricle of the brain.

Pearson said once he and the Military Surgeon Allen completed the post-mortem, they both agreed that the Corporal had not died of drowning. He had been unconscious from the beating he received and death was due to the compression of blood on the brain.

Another soldier was called, Private James Scott who had also been to Desmond's public house. He recalled that Murphy, one of the Cronin's, and a man called Barry were in the pub. Scott said that Barry had a dog with him and Ashworth stood on the dog's paw. He claimed this led to an argument that resulted in Barry saying he would get him for it sometime. One of the accused, Jeremiah Murphy, said nothing at the time.

The district inspector alleged that the argument was the very motive that led to all this. The magistrates couldn't see the connection and disallowed the evidence saying it was irrelevant. Scott went on saying he was on sentry duty in Camden when Private Jordan returned that night.

Sergeant Carton told how the Cronin brothers were the first arrested on Monday. Later in the day he arrested Murphy and Casey and found marks like bloodstains on the sleeves of Casey's shirt. The shirt was produced in court and Mr Blake for the defence examined it. He produced a roar of laughter in the small courtroom when he claimed the stains were likely to be produced from picking blackberries.

The prosecution then rested and Mr Healy asked would his client Jeremiah Ahern be released. The magistrates agreed that there was no evidence against him. The same was asked for John Cronin and the magistrates agreed that both men should be discharged.

Mr Blake then tried the same thing for his client Dan Casey but was rejected. He was reminded that there was direct evidence against him. Blake persisted saying just one witness saw him punch Jordan this was hardly enough to keep him in jail. The solicitor even said his client could pay a substantial bail but they wouldn't hear of it. The remaining two men Jeremiah Murphy and Daniel Casey were returned for trial at the Winter Assizes, there was no question of bail. The pair were sent to Cork jail in the meantime.

On the 15th of December at the Cork Winter Assizes, Chief Justice Morris presided and 21 year old Jeremiah Murphy appeared. He stood charged with killing and murdering Samuel Ashworth. The case had become known as the "Crosshaven Murder" which was bad for Jeremiah Murphy's chance of survival. Daniel Casey was to be tried separately later that day.

Murphy most likely on the advice of his legal representatives, Mr Hennessy and Healy, pleaded not guilty. While the prosecution had Mr Atkinson, Mr Adams and crown solicitor Mr Gregg.

Atkinson began by first telling about young Samuel Ashworth. Only nineteen years old, in the service for two years and only in Camden with a few months. During this short time, he had been promoted to Corporal, Atkinson said this was a testament to his good character.

He went back to the 12th of October a week before Ashworth was killed. On that Sunday, Ashworth had also been to Desmond's public house in Ringabella. The prosecution now claimed that it was then Ashworth walked on Barry's dog and this led to the trouble a week later. He did admit though there may have been another motive behind the dispute.

Timothy Cronin told the court he was at the back of the crowd when Ashworth was first attacked. He saw Murphy pursue the soldier and knocked him down with a punch. He then kicked the soldier while on the ground and Cronin heard the soldier call out "oh mother, help me". Timothy claimed he told Murphy to stop, saying he would regret it in the morning but Murphy didn't listen.

He then heard the other soldier Jordan struggling in the water. His brother John went into the water to help him. Between them, they helped Jordan from the water and tried to protect him. He said Dan Casey came up and struck Jordan before he left again. Timothy admitted under cross examination that he was the first person arrested.

John Cronin was now also a witness for the crown since he was discharged.

He backed up what his brother had said entirely, saying he saw Murphy attacking Corporal Ashworth and Dan Casey beating Private Jordan.

Edward Jordan a private in the same battalion as the victim then gave his account. They left the pub about seven that evening and crossed on the ferry. After getting off at the Fountainstown side they had only gone a few yards when he saw a gang approaching. One he heard saying "that's him" and they were set upon.

John was kicked when on the ground but managed to somehow get up. He ran into the water and tried to swim back to Ringabella.

Half ways across he stopped due to exhaustion and decided the safest place was in the water. He thought he could stay until it was over by threading water. He said John Cronin came out to him and offered to help him ashore. Cronin promised to protect him but again when he landed in Fountainstown it started. This time three or four attacked him and one managed to get him with a stick.

Jordan ran back into the water again and swam for the other side. This time the ferry boat pulled him out and landed him on the other side.

He recalled while he was on the ground being kicked hearing his friend cry out but he could do nothing for him. Jordan made it back to the barracks that night with the help of other soldiers but he didn't see his friend alive again.

All the same, witnesses were called again but the Cronin brothers and Jordan were the primary evidence against Murphy. The doctors still maintained Ashworth had not died from drowning saying there was no water found in the lungs or chest.

When he got the chance, Hennessy for the defence, made the best attempt he could to save Jeremiah Murphy from the serious charge against him. He argued that the charge of murder was excessive saying the prosecution failed to prove any malice or premeditation. He summarised it as a sudden brawl where the deceased was struck down and ended up being taken out by the tide. What he was getting at was that nobody had actually seen Ashworth being thrown into the water that night. The defence fell down though when they had no evidence at all to call that day.

When Chief Justice Morris summed up, he admitted that the motive the prosecution suggested was difficult to understand. If it was the dog issue, why was it not Barry that sought revenge on the Corporal? He admitted that it could hardly be denied that Murphy's actions led to the death of the Corporal. He said now the question was for the jury to decide whether he was guilty of murder or manslaughter. Chief Justice Morris then gave the evidence for both but seemed to be leaning towards the lesser charge.

The jury listened to what he had to say and left the courtroom to deliberate. They were only gone a matter of minutes when the foreman returned with the verdict, guilty of manslaughter. Sentencing was put off until the end of the Assizes.

Daniel Casey was then brought forward to be tried for the same charge. Mr Atkinson addressed the court saying the crown no longer wished to proceed on the charge of murder against Daniel Casey. Mr Lawrence entered a plea of guilty of common assault on Private Jordan. He said there was no evidence that his client Daniel Casey attacked Ashworth, he only punched Jordan once. It was dealt with quickly and Daniel Casey's sentencing was also deferred until the end of the Assizes.

Jeremiah Murphy got ten years of penal servitude for manslaughter and Casey got one year from the 30th of October. Nobody had got to the bottom of the motive but who would kick a man so severely for accidentally walking on their dog. The real motive was most likely jealousy over the attention of a young woman. Corporal Ashworth, a young man in the prime of life who went out for a few drinks on a Sunday didn't deserve such a brutal end.

A Fatal Eviction
Knockskagh Clonakilty 1847

As Irish people, we are all aware of the history leading up to the famine and how landlords and middlemen overcharged the poor for tiny plots of land to live on. When the potato crop failed it was like a bubble that burst, as now the many in arrears never had a hope of paying. Some landlords were good to their tenants but many just turned them out onto the road with nowhere to go but the workhouse. Houses were often needlessly torn down just so they would not be reoccupied. The scene of such an eviction is clearly etched in our minds.

This story starts in the townland of Knockskagh about three miles north of Clonakilty. A tenant of the Earl of Shannon, John Northridge was three years in arrears of his rent and the landlord took proceedings against him. However Northridge wasn't your average poor tenant, he had spent a considerable amount of money improving the farm but things had gone against him. He had been hoping to secure a more permanent lease on the land but the landlord just wanted him out.

Several attempts had been made by the agent to carry out the eviction but John Northridge resisted. Unlike most evictions the agent, Mr Leslie had given him several chances to settle. He argued in May that the notice had been served to a labourer but his name was not on the writ of eviction. It went on until September when Mr Leslie with the bailiff and seventeen men went to Knockskagh and took procession of anything of worth. A quantity of corn, with several horses and carts, were taken. The party returned on Wednesday the 22nd of September to take possession of the house and finally evict Northridge who had no intention of giving it up. When eviction parties failed to gain access to a house easily, they would literally bring the entire house down. That day, Jeremiah O'Grady climbed onto the roof and began pulling the slates off to get in through the roof. A single shot was fired from within the house and O'Grady fell to an instant death. They had assumed that the house was empty, especially when they saw that John Northridge was not in the house. He had been seen walking away when the eviction notice was issued.

Mr Leslie left for Clonakilty where he informed the police and magistrates. He returned with an even bigger party of police, magistrates and military. They then proceeded to pull the roof from what was Northridge's house and went through with the eviction. They returned to Clonakilty with the body of Jeremiah Grady who was from the Courtmacsherry area.

The locals in Knockskagh did not have sympathy for Northridge being evicted but still, nobody came forward with information as to who was in the house. The inquest was held on Friday by Coroner Frances Baldwin from Bandon.

Mr Wright questioned the witnesses for the O'Grady family. Little could be done at the inquest but prove that the shot was fired from within the house as they had not yet identified who had fired it.

The verdict was "that some person to the said jurors unknown on the 22nd of September in the year aforesaid at Knockskagh in the county aforesaid in the house of a man named John Northridge, wilfully and feloniously discharged a certain gun loaded with powder slugs and shot, at the said Jeremiah Grady thereby causing a mortal wound on the right side of the head of which he, the said Jeremiah Grady then and there instantly died".

The landlord Richard Boyle the 4th Earl of Shannon offered a reward of £100 for information leading to the arrest of whoever fired the shot and the government put up the same amount.

The following day several magistrates held an inquiry into the matter, they had strong suspicions of John Northridge's involvement but there was little evidence against him. The hearing was forced to adjourn but John Northridge was arrested and taken into custody on the charge of aiding and abetting the murder of Jeremiah Grady. They knew that Northridge knew more and he was the only one to gain by preventing the eviction.

When the magistrates sat again, Northridge was committed to a trial and would spend at least a month or two in jail waiting for it.

There was some doubt as to whether the eviction notice Leslie the agent served that day was technically legal. It had been issued sometime before and Northridge had since retaken possession of the house. When Northridge walked away that day, he was by no means penniless on the side of the road. He had several other farms and was quite affluent compared to most. He was trying to protect his investment in the farm and make an arrangement for the rent arrears.

In November Colman O'Loughlan representing Northridge applied for bail for his client. He was in a position to put up a substantial bail. He contended that on the day of the eviction John Northridge was present and read the writ of execution before leaving.

Mr Bennett who appeared for the Attorney General had no desire to go into the details of the case or lack of them. He admitted that Northridge had given an affidavit denying any involvement and feared that might be enough to get him off. Chief Justice Blackburne also had no intention of going into the case, saying it was not about whether Northridge was guilty or not. He believed though that if Northridge got bail he was bound to abscond and refused the request. It was a fair assumption at the time considering how many were leaving the country to avoid starvation but Northridge's situation was very different to most.

The chief justice must have known quite well that there was not a shred of evidence against Northridge. Not only that, but the evidence of the agent Mr Leslie seeing him leave that day was in effect an alibi. They knew that Northridge knew more but no jury would convict him at a trial and there is no evidence he ever appeared at one.

Caught in the Crossfire
Kilbrittain 1868

The monthly fair held in the village of Kilbrittain was normally on the last week of the month. The November fair in the year 1868 was held on the 23rd and was said to be a quiet enough day. A few lingered in the public houses that night. About eleven or a few minutes after, two Policemen burst into Barrett's pub announcing that it should be cleared. The publican complied but a few were reluctant to go. One man at the counter in no rush to finish his drink asked the publican for a nights lodging so he would not have to go.

One of the policemen seemed agitated at the response or lack of it and this led to several altercations in the pub. It went on so long that a crowd gathered outside and tried to get in but the police prevented them. Word was sent to the barracks for backup and they managed to get through the crowd into the pub. They were still well outnumbered and the mob outside turned on them.

A constable pulled his sword and led the others out of the pub. Knowing they had lost the battle he tried to get back to the barracks. Outside the crowd seemed to also know their predicament and took advantage of the situation. The police were pasted with stones and one was hit in the head.

After making it back to the barracks a few constables got armed and set out for Dr Crowley's house. The mob on the street followed through the village heckling them and throwing stones. As they returned to the barracks by the bridge the crowd closed in on them from both sides. Two men the police had seen earlier in the pub were arrested and led away towards the barracks. The constables now had their loaded guns out and threatened to shoot at anyone who intervened. With the crowd still following along behind them to the barracks something happened and one of the prisoners was released. In the panic that ensued a single shot rang out followed by the flash from the gun. A man lay in the middle of the road on fire. It was followed quickly by orders and more shots were heard scattering much of the crowd.

It was Patrick Donovan who lay on the street and his mother along with others came to help him. The police no longer had any interest in their prisoners for the petty crimes; they were now responsible for much worse. A few made their feelings known to the policemen but they just walked away towards the barracks.

Donovan was helped off the road and they attempted to get him to limp towards the doctor but he couldn't stand even for a second. He was taken to Dr Patrick Crowley but only Mrs Crowley was home. She brought him in and did what she could for him. It was 2 am before the doctor returned and extracted the bullet from Donovan.

At seven the following morning Patrick Donovan died. He worked as a stable hand for Colonel Stawell of Kilbrittain Castle

On the 25th of November Coroner Somerville opened the inquest in of all places the barracks of Kilbrittain. Several magistrates were present, Colonel Alcock Stawell, W. Baldwin Sealy, Abraham Forster of Ballinspittle and resident magistrate Fitzgerald.

Bryan Galwey crown prosecutor was also there with local Sub Inspector of the police T Rodwell and county inspector Hill.

The jury was made up of local men, Hibernicus Scott - foreman, farmers David Walsh from Shanakill, James Ahern from Garranefeen and Patrick O'Hea from Ballynakeen. Also on the jury were Edward and William Moore, Robert and James Scott, Christopher Woods, John Cunningham, Thomas Busteed and Patrick Regan.

No sooner had they been sworn in when Fr Hurley addressed the coroner to complain. He said "I beg your pardon sir, there is one protestant more on the jury than the number of Catholics. As I think this is a case there may be party feeling in, I think the numbers ought to be equal. Both the coroner and Magistrate Fitzgerald thought there was no need, saying that the jury were respectable men who would not let such a thing hinder their view. Fr Hurley though insisted more than once that there should be six of each religion on the jury. When someone asked why there were not twelve jurors and the foreman it was agreed to swear in another. Denis Coghlan was sworn in.

Just as the jury settled when Robert Scott asked the coroner to be excused. He claimed to have been returning from Bandon several months before and was assaulted by the deceased. Scott said Donovan had struck his horse and then hit him but it was instigated by another person and he didn't blame him at all.

The coroner said surely an event like this would not now cloud his judgement and would not hear of him leaving the jury.

Before hearing any evidence the inquest proceeded to Kilbrittain castle to view the remains of Patrick Donovan. While there it was Rev Murphy who voiced his objections of how the inquest was being conducted. He argued that the jury should have been sworn in at the same place as and within sight of the body. Murphy also objected to the number of Protestants on the jury saying that only one in thirty in the area were protestant yet half the jury was.

Bryan Galwey then announced why he was present, to ensure the inquest was carried out correctly and he was sure the jury would act impartially. He then noted how the next of kin of the deceased were not legally represented at the inquest and suggested an adjournment until the matter was rectified. The coroner agreed to this and all that was heard that day was the formal identification of the body.

Jeremiah Coghlan a farmer from Ballymore was called for that reason. He testified to seeing the body. He said he knew Patrick Donovan for the last twenty five years. He also said Donovan was between thirty and thirty two years old and worked as a stable hand for Colonel Alcock Stawell.

They then adjourned until the following Tuesday. If anything this gave the police some time to get their story straight between them. They might have thought themselves above the law but couldn't control the outcome of the inquest nor sway the opinions of the jurors. Whatever verdict was found the coroner may be forced to act on it. A member of the police could be arrested on the strength of a coroner's warrant.

On the 1st of December, the Crown introduced Mr Wright crown solicitor at the inquest as legal advisor to the coroner. Bryan Galwey and crown solicitor Gillman now represented the police. Two Solicitors, Blake from Cork and O'Hea from Clonakilty now represented the Donovan's.

Wright explained he was only there to clear up legal questions should they arise. He made it clear that this was not a court of inquiry as there was neither a defendant nor plaintiff. He did say should evidence be heard against a particular person the jury should find accordingly and the coroner must act on it.

Mr O'Hea for the next of kin of Patrick Donovan told the coroner he believed that conflicting testimony could be heard from the witnesses. He suggested that all witnesses be removed from the room and examined one at a time.

With no other witnesses listening, Michael Ahern, a labourer from Harbour View was sworn in. He had come out of Connolly's pub that night about closing time and noticed a policeman running from Barrett's pub to the barracks and return just as fast.

He encountered several people who had come out of Barrett's and saw a few police approach from the barracks. He heard Constable Clifton say "now boys, there is a revolver with 6 balls in it, and the first of you whom I see throw a stone, will get the contents of that through his body".

When examined by Gillman, Ahern told of hearing lots of noise in Barrett's pub that night. There was a crowd both inside and outside but he saw no trouble. He refused to answer about stones being fired, but it was Mr Wright who warned him to answer truthfully or he could be committed. Hesitantly he admitted stones had been thrown at the police.

Local labourer Michael Burke was next heard. He was also thrown out of Connolly's pub that night. He heard something was going on in Barrett's. He went into the kitchen of Barrett's but was ordered out by a policeman.

Afterwards, he met Clifton at Fr. Murphy's gate, going towards the barracks with a prisoner, Dan Donovan. He asked Donovan what was going on and the constable threatened to shoot if he came any closer, warning him the gun was loaded. It was then they stopped and he said Dan Donovan was hit from behind with a stone. Burke said either the constable let him go or he struggled free and ran. Clifton went after him but stopped and fired a shot in the middle of the street.

Burke said he was still close, only a few yards away and saw the blaze from the gun in the darkness. Another shot was heard and then 2 more. These were fired by other policemen. The crowd that were there had scattered after the first shot. He heard Dan Donovan's mother cry out "Patrick is shot". Burke reckoned where he saw Donovan lying on the street was not more than a few yards from where Clifton had fired.

He went to Patrick, pulled him off the road and opening his shirt, found blood. He passed some comment to Clifton about what he had done, and how he should look after the man but the constable walked away.

When asked by O'Hea he was very clear, Clifton fired the first shot in the direction of where Donovan was found, Burke was only 2 yards from the Constable when he fired.

James Brown, a labourer from near Ballinspittle, claimed he heard a row going on, down by the bridge that night and he hid behind Fr. Murphy's wall. He thought he saw 2 policemen escorting Dan Donovan with Constable Clifton close behind. He saw Clifton fire a shot and said Donovan was not more than a yard from the gun. He heard Mrs Donovan crying her son was burnt, she ran to him and put out the fire at the back of his clothes. James swore to seeing the trouble between people and the police that night. He saw Patrick Donovan led away by two constables and then Clifton fired directly at him at close range.

When Denis Crowley, a letter carrier was called, he believed both Patrick and Dan Donovan were in the custody of the police that night. He thought Clifton stooped down and seconds later saw the flash from a gun, he then heard 5 more shots fired in the direction of the bridge.

The mother of the deceased man, Ellen Donovan was called. An interpreter was needed as the woman spoke only Irish. She said she was going home that night from Kilbrittain with her two sons when the police arrested them. She asked Constable Clifton to let them go and he could summon them in the morning as he knew where they lived.

She saw the police fire several shots that night but only identified Clifton as the man who shot her son. She heard Patrick say "Christ have mercy on me, bring me, Fr Simon".

When Galwey questioned her she did say she had only come to the village that night to fetch her two sons home. She pointed out Constable Clifton as the one who killed her son saying "if it was my son shot him, long ago he would be in gaol".

Farmer's son John Crowley from Glanduff near the village was sworn in. He witnessed the police coming out of Barrett's pub that night and saw the first shot fired by Clifton. Crowley was by the bridge and he saw both Dan and Patrick arrested and led away by Clifton. Dan, he thought wanted to get away but Clifton had his hand on his shoulder and said "you are my prisoner".

From across the bridge in Kilbrittain looking towards the village and the scene of the shooting.

By Fr Murphy's he heard Dan complain as if he had been hit and the police scattered as Clifton cried out "fire fire". Crowley described what he saw next when he heard the shot and it was as if the blaze left Clifton's hand and set fire to Patrick who fell.

Patrick's mother was calling out and then she quenched the flames on her son's clothes.

The inquest was then adjourned until the following Thursday.

At this point, it must have been clear to the police how it was going. There was plenty of direct evidence against Constable Clifton and the system would do everything to clear him. Mrs Donovan was right if her son had shot a policeman he would be locked up with no one to defend him.

When the inquest was resumed on Thursday it was held in Barrett's pub where all the trouble began. James Barrett publican was the first witness called that day and he recalled the night of the 22nd after the fair. Constable Clifton entered his pub about eleven and requested that it be cleared and he agreed to do it. He said that Clifton didn't seem to be as steady as he normally was but didn't know why that was.

James told those in the pub to leave and then saw Constable Clifton struggling with someone in the kitchen. Patrick Donovan was talking to Constable Clifton when more police arrived. Next, he saw Clifton grab a hold of Dan Donovan and with another policeman threw him on the ground. A third policeman arrived and one of them was knocking Dan's head against the ground while he called out "police don't kill me". Clifton then asked him to go to the barracks for more men and he went out the back way.

When he returned the police were still there and he tried to keep the peace between them and those who had not left the pub. He saw Clifton had his sword out and ordered the others "men be at them".

James Crowley who worked in the pub said that they asked everyone to leave and they were going without any trouble. No one was drinking at the time except Patrick Donovan who had a pint of porter on the counter in front of him. Donovan agreed to leave but only after finishing his pint but then he asked the publican could he have lodging for the night and stay altogether. Barrett agreed he could stay and another man John Caverley said he would also stay. Both Caverley and Donovan then went in behind the counter but Constable Clifton grabbed hold of Caverley and pulled him out.

Caverley was dragged into the hall by Clifton and all the other customers were thrown out except Donovan. Crowley recalled locking the door and Barrett was sent out the back way to fetch more police from the barracks. Dan Donovan managed to get in the back entrance to the pub and challenged the police in the kitchen. Crowley said the police set upon him, knocked him to the ground and assaulted Dan. He told the inquest that it went on for about fifteen minutes, he was not in the room all the time but heard someone call out that the Donovan's had been killed by the police. Then the door was opened and the crowd outside piled into the pub.

John O'Brien, when sworn in, told of earlier that day when the fair was on in the village. He saw Patrick Donovan standing about with his hands in his pockets when Constable Clifton came up the street. He stopped and pointing his stick at Patrick said "Donovan if I catch you here for the evening, I will have your life". O'Brien under cross examination explained that he had not come forward with this until Fr Hurley had asked from the altar for people to tell what they knew. He knew that the inquest had been held the week before but did not go.

When Dan Donovan was sworn in that day he said that while in Connolly's pub that night he heard his brother was in bother with the police in Barrett's.

Mr Blake asked that the revolver Clifton had used that night be produced. A policeman produced it but warned that it was loaded with six balls in it. Blake couldn't understand this and questioned why had the gun been altered as it was a piece of evidence. Mr Galwey would not answer this only saying that the Constable would need to be questioned.

The questioning of Dan resumed and he told how he got into Barrett's pub by the back way only to be assaulted by Clifton and another Constable. He had done nothing to provoke them only ask that his brother be let go and summoned in the morning. Dan told of being thrown on the ground, kicked and dragged about. They also banged his head against the floor and he saw them doing the same to his brother. All the time he was trying to get away from them to open the door and let the crowd outside in.

When the door did open and people pushed their way in he didn't know what happened but there was trouble with the police. Dan said he and his brother left the pub as quick as they could and headed for home with his mother. On the way home the police arrested him and his brother leading them to the barrack with a revolver pointed at them. He recalled meeting Burke and was struck then from behind so hard it nearly knocked him down; he thought it was one of the police but then they let him go.

Dan told how he was not a few yards from Constable Clifton when he fired the shot at Patrick. He saw the flame from the gun as he pointed it straight at his brother.

Patrick Donovan's waistcoat was then produced and it was plain to see the bullet hole. Dan identified the waistcoat as belonging to his brother and the burn marks on it were also pointed out.

Dr Patrick Crowley told how it was two o clock in the morning before he treated Patrick Donovan. He found a gunshot near the liver and cut into the wound to extract the bullet which was lodged two inches from the spine. The bullet had since been given to County Inspector Hill but the doctor could not say how far the shot was fired from. He had also found a sharp straight wound on the right side of the forehead which could be caused by something sharp such as a sword.

Crowley then told of the post mortem he had carried out with Dr Jagoe and Dr Belcher. They concluded that Donovan died from shock and internal haemorrhage due to the gunshot wound and both doctors gave corroborating evidence.

Dr Jagoe was questioned by Mr Gillman as he had examined Constable Clifton on the 25th. He had a cut over the right eye, an inch and a half in length which could have been caused by a sharp stone. The doctor also observed a black eye and said that he could still not certify Clifton as being fit or out of danger. Constable Warnock suffered a similar wound but on the right temple. Warnock also had a bruise on the back of the head from something blunter. Constable Hennessy also had a cut on the right side of his head similar to the others. Constable Carroll had several bruises on his forehead, arm and shoulder which he was complaining of paining him.

When questioned by Mr Blake, County Inspector Hill admitted the bullet produced, which was extracted from Patrick Donovan, was from a revolver and of the same type the police used. Hill told of arriving in Kilbrittain four hours after the shooting but did not ask for any of the guns used. He confirmed that both Carroll and Clifton had fired two shots from each of their revolvers and then admitted to examining the revolvers.

As he was not in custody and not a suspect despite the evidence, Constable James Clifton was questioned. Clifton gave a very different version of events that night. He admitted to going into Barrett's pub at ten past eleven, most in the pub left immediately but he said a few remained still demanding drink. The constable caught John Caverley by the shoulder to gently push him out but claimed he was struck by a fist. He also claimed two men that night completely refused to leave the pub, John Caverley and Patrick Donovan. With everyone else gone the door was closed.

Clifton said he persuaded the publican to go to the barracks for more policemen and he left out the back. He also claimed that while Barrett was gone Patrick Donovan assaulted Constable Carroll several times. He made no mention of Dan Donovan getting into the pub at all. Then the crowd burst in and they were overpowered entirely, Clifton said it took a few minutes to battle his way out of the pub and he was kicked and beaten. As they left the pub stones were thrown at them and Constable Warnock was struck on the head. He then realised that only three had got out and Constable Hennessy was still inside. With their swords, they got back inside and helped Hennessy out of the pub.

When the four got back to the barracks, both Hennessy and Warnock were injured and asked for the doctor. Clifton justified arming himself and the four others going to Dr Crowley's that night. He warned the crowd several times to stop throwing stones or he would shoot.

Returning from the doctor's house Clifton arrested Patrick Donovan first, then Dan. He was struck several times by stones and turned to the crowd saying "we will be obliged to fire in our own defence unless the stone throwing is stopped". With this warning, the stone throwing intensified and Clifton claimed two shots were fired at the crowd. He said this dispersed the crowd for a while and he made some progress towards the barracks.

When the stone throwing resumed, it came from several directions, his prisoner was struck and he was forced to release him when he was struck himself on the forehead. He made no direct reference to the shot he fired only saying "we then had to fire on the people in the direction of the crowd". He denied completely meeting Patrick Donovan earlier that day and threatening him. Clifton then directly denied the allegations against him saying "it is not true that on the evening while the deceased was in the custody of the police, one at each side of him, and I behind him I fired a revolver in his back".

Then Blake cross examined the Constable with very direct questions:
"This is a very sad affair Mr Clifton? It is indeed and I am very sorry for it.
Who shot Donovan? I can't tell.
You won't say who shot Donovan? I cannot.
Who fired the first two shots? I fired one of them.
Why did you not say that at first when you were asked the question? The question was not put to me. I was sworn to tell the whole truth, but I did not consider it necessary to tell that I had fired one of the shots myself.
Did you conceal part of the truth when you did not tell who fired the first shots?
I am telling the fact now.
Did you conceal part of the truth when you did not tell who fired the first shots?

Yes because I was not asked, I did not do so advisedly.

And you can't say who shot Donovan? No.

Was it Constable Clifton? No, it was not, this is I could not say that.

It may have been Constable Clifton? It may."

He still denied to Mr Blake that either of the first two shots fired struck Patrick Donovan. Clifton now said that when he fired the first shot he had his hand on Dan Donovan and turned around towards the bridge to fire. He claimed he could not have hit Patrick as he was to his left side and the positions were the same when he fired again at the crowd.

The inquest was adjourned until the following Tuesday. When it did resume that Tuesday Mr Julian now represented Constable Walsh from Upton and Constable Carroll from Bandon.

Carroll was the first witness and was questioned by his solicitor Mr Julian. As you would expect Carroll's version was very similar to the one Clifton had given. He also said two men refused to leave the pub and Caverley struck Clifton with his fist. He went to his colleague's assistance but claimed Patrick Donovan struck him. Carroll also claimed it was he and not Donovan who was flung onto the ground and held there for a few minutes. While on the floor he was kicked and jumped upon but he didn't see Donovan ill treated. He had arrested Donovan in the pub for assault but was forced to release him when the crowd rushed in. He described how they struggled to get back to the barracks that night and how they were all struck by stones.

On the shooting Carroll also said that when the first two shots were fired Patrick Donovan was still in custody and was not hit. Constable Kennedy fired one but he didn't know who fired the other. He said it was about eight minutes later when the next shots were fired and it was then he fired a shot. Carroll denied that any of the shots were fired directly at Patrick Donovan. Blake asked again was Donovan shot while in custody but Carroll denied this also It was three or four minutes after the first shots that Donovan was released and the same time until Donovan was shot.

Under Cross examination by Blake, the constable admitted to having Patrick Donovan on the floor of the pub but denied banging his head against the floor.

The remainder of the constables, Kennedy, Warnock, Walsh and Walker were all examined but gave the same story. None had seen Clifton fire directly at Donovan. John Caverley was not called to corroborate what had happened in the pub that night.

Blake made his speech for the next of kin asking the jury to return a verdict of murder against Constable Clifton. He compared the conflicting evidence that had been heard saying why would the people all have told the same story if it was not true. The police on the other hand were trained and accustomed to questioning. Blake suggested that Donovan was going home quietly with his mother when arrested by Clifton and dragged towards the barracks. He noted how all the constables claimed no orders were given to fire yet several people testified to hearing "fire fire".

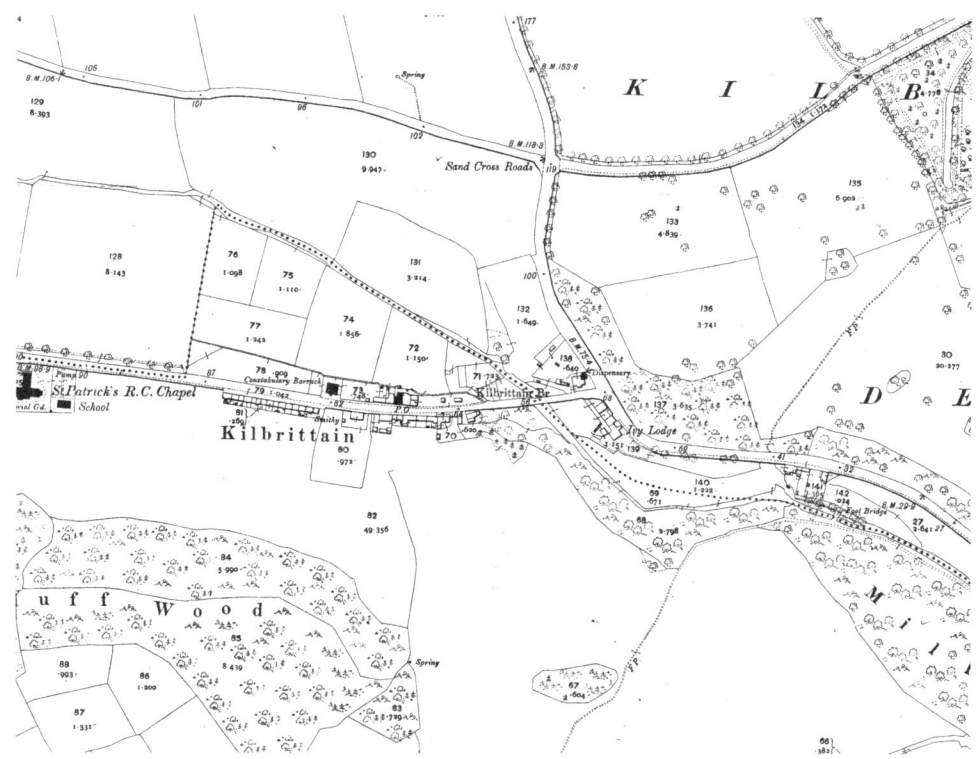

Map showing the village of Kilbrittain

When all the evidence had been heard that day Mr Galwey addressed the inquest saying even if the Donovan's were illegally arrested the people had no right to interfere. Legally he said if a constable were killed that night the charge would be murder but the death of one of the attackers was a justifiable homicide. He believed it was a clear case where the police were justified in using their guns as their own lives were in danger.

It was not the coroner who summed up the evidence but the legal advisor Mr Wright, a crown solicitor. It was late when he finished, almost seven in the evening before the jury left. Three hours later they returned with no verdict as they could not decide and as such the inquest failed. Don't forget it was the police who summoned the jury of the inquest. The police and the Crown thought they had the whole thing wrapped up but for the common people who gave another story.

It was now their word against that of the law, all the police right up to the County Inspector wanted the whole affair covered up. The very fact that none of the constables enquired of Patrick Donovan that night showed their contempt.

Rumours immediately spread that the Donovan family would take a case against Constable Clifton. As no verdict was reached it was their only option to try to get justice with the whole of the legal system against them. Blake made the application but it was not heard at the petty sessions until February the following year.

On the 9th of February at Ballinspittle Petty Sessions, Blake applied again before the magistrates for information to be heard against Constable Clifton on the charge of murder. Mr Julian on behalf of Clifton was against the application. Blake felt it was not necessary to go over all the facts again as the magistrates were all present at the inquest and heard it there.

There was also a perjury case against James Brown who had given evidence at the inquest. Mr Julian did not object to hearing information against Clifton but objected to Brown's testimony being heard. The statements given at the inquest were read out and each witness swore again to the information, all except James Brown.

Julian called sub constable Kennedy who had not been heard at the inquest. He was not at Barrett's pub that night and began by saying how Warnock and Hennessy were injured when they returned to the barracks. Kennedy armed himself and set out for the doctors with Clifton and the others. He recalled a mob still outside Barrett's and seven or eight people followed them to the doctors. There was no trouble or stones thrown until they were at the bridge returning from Dr Crowley's.

After arresting the Donovan's the stones were coming in all directions at such a rate that they were forced to release the prisoners. Kennedy also maintained that it was two or three minutes after this when the first shot was fired. Then two more shots were fired, one he fired himself. He denied Donovan was shot by Clifton while in custody.

When examined by Blake the constable claimed it was an hour and a half later that night before any of the police heard a man was shot by the bridge. Blake went further asking "then I take it from you, you did not consider it your duty or worth your while to go out to see whether any of the people were injured?" But Kennedy did not answer. When Blake asked again the constable this time replied that it was not their duty.

Then he said it was Constable Carroll who told him to fire that night. He did not take aim but said "tis one of the rules of the constabulary they must take aim when they fire". But Kennedy still maintained he did not aim nor did he feel it was his duty to do so. On the question of who first gave the order to fire he was unsure but thought he heard Clifton give the order.

"Did he not on your oath, fire himself before giving orders to anyone?
I am not certain. He may have been 3 or 4 yards before me.
Did he fire or did he not before giving the orders to the others?
It was before, I am not certain.
What were you going to say when you said 'it was before' just now?
I can't exactly say."

Then Kennedy went back to the same story, that Donovan was released at least 2 or 3 minutes before any shot was fired. He said 6 shots were fired in total, 2 by Clifton.

Daniel Donovan was then called. He was questioned by Mr Julian. He asked why they delayed so long in issuing the summons against the constable. Donovan couldn't explain it. Julian then asked who was behind the case and paying their expenses. Donovan insisted it was him and his mother taking the case against the constable. Fr. Murphy had raised a sum of money by subscription and they used this to pay Mr Blake.

It was revealed by Blake that a proposal had been put to the Donovan's by the police, to drop the case and forgive Clifton, but they refused. Julian denied any knowledge of this. Blake then made some comments about how the crown had defended the police at the inquest. One of the magistrates Mr Fitzgerald insisted that it was nothing to do with the crown now but for the magistrates to decide.

When Mr Julian made his long speech he asked for the case to be dropped. He said Clifton was only doing his duty that night. He made no direct reference to the facts of the case though. Julian was known for defending the police, 5 years later in a similar case in Kinsale, he quoted the law. The police must fire on a ringleader in a riot. But Donovan was no ringleader, he was in their custody.

One of the magistrates quoted a case where the defendant's evidence contradicts completely that of the complainant it must be sent before a jury. It took the magistrates an hour and a half to decide but they managed to agree that Clifton should be sent for trial at the assizes before a jury.

The perjury case against James Brown then was called. Coroner Somerville produced a testimony Brown had given at the inquest but failed to recognise him. Head constable Jones who was at the inquest recognised Brown and swore to that effect.

Edward Butler swore that James Brown worked for him and was at his farm all day on the 23rd of November. Another labourer of Butlers John Hayes gave the same evidence. Brown had worked all day at the farm near Ballinspittle five miles from Kilbrittain. He went to bed between 9 and 10 that evening. Swiftly a warrant was issued for Browns arrest and he was sent for trial on the charge of perjury.

Why had Brown bothered to give such information, when there were so many others that had? It wasn't as if the case needed him to do it, or that he was encouraged to do so. It did show though that the crown had looked into each and every witness at the inquest and failed to find anything against the other witnesses.

At the Cork Spring Assizes the following year James Clifton was charged with the manslaughter of Patrick Donovan before Justice O'Brien. It was a most unusual position as the crown was now prosecuting one of their own. Normally the police in such cases prevented it from getting so far but this time the evidence was too strong. They had managed to get the charge reduced to manslaughter and Clifton was safe from the hangman.

For the crown prosecution was Mr Coffee and Mr Waters both Queen's Counsel, with Mr Nelligan and Mr O'Hea. Clifton was defended by Mr Heron also Queens Counsel and Mr Fitzgibbon.

It was Mr Coffee who opened the case for the prosecution by stating the facts of what had occurred after the fair in Kilbrittain on the 23rd of November. He did say an altercation broke out in the pub where the police were treated badly but the police ill treated the people also.

Coffee told the jury it was up to them to decide from what they heard whether Clifton fired the fatal shot or not. If they decided he fired the shot they must ask was it done in the course of duty or did Clifton cross that line and do it out of revenge and malice.

The evidence was much the same as the inquest, Daniel Donovan, his mother, Michael Ahern, Michael Burke and John Crowley all said the first shot hit Patrick. It was fired by Clifton at close range while Patrick was still in custody.

Constable Carroll, Kennedy and Walsh all then gave an almost identical account, that Donovan was not hit by the first shots fired. Kennedy even claimed that he was unaware at the time a man had been shot and did not see Mrs Donovan there that night. While Walsh did not see Clifton fire a shot at all.

Mr Heron made a speech that was so long for the defence of Clifton, that the case had to be adjourned till the following day. He argued that a Constable with twenty three years experience and training would not do such a thing. His theory, which was not supported by evidence, was that Patrick Donovan struggled free of the police and joined his friends throwing stones. He suggested Patrick was shot while in the crowd. It seemed a little late to suggest this, as the evidence of the other constables did not support this at all.

It was Mr Green who then spoke for the prosecution and said there was no reason for the police to arm themselves that night. He went on to say that the second arrest of Donovan was illegal and he had a right to struggle free. Green fell short though and did not go further and say that what Clifton had done amounted to murder. The furthest he would go was to suggest it was "utter recklessness of human life". The crown was never going to prosecute a policeman with their usual vigour, Green it seemed was just going through the motions.

Justice O'Brien summing up pointed out the obvious fact that the evidence each side was completely opposed. He left it to the jury which side was to be believed, but he did ask if Constable Clifton's life was in danger when he fired.

The jury only deliberated for a very short time before returning a verdict of not guilty and Clifton was discharged. It was the easier verdict to find. What would have happened if they found a guilty verdict? Would Constable Clifton have been hung for murder? The crown would never have allowed this to happen.

Burnt Alive
Cappa Bandon 1847

Everyone knows what happened in the year 1847 in this country. So many people died of starvation that the poor were hastily buried in unmarked graves. In November of that year, the hurried burial of a child in Farranthomas graveyard, west of Bandon, aroused suspicions.

On Tuesday 30th November the police went to Sullivan's house in Cappa about four miles west of Bandon and asked for the father of the child but he was nowhere to be found. From there they went to the graveyard and exhumed the child's body. What they found was shocking and confirmed that something terrible had occurred. The child's body was identifiable but badly burned.

The police continued their search for the child's father, Robert Sullivan in the local area. His wife had died several months before and they had six children. As well as the children three servants also lived in Sullivan's. With the information, the servants provided, the police began to piece together the terrible events that had led to the death of young John Sullivan.

Robert Sullivan had returned home on Saturday night after drinking in Bandon during the day. Later that night something happened in the house and John Sullivan who was only 4 or 5, was badly burned. He died on Monday morning and there had been no trace of his father since Sunday morning.

An inquest was held on Wednesday in Bandon Courthouse by Coroner Franklin Baldwin. There was not much evidence produced that day as Robert Sullivan had still not been located.

John Sullivan's body was identified by his uncle, also John, but he had no further information as he lived two miles from his brother's house. It was he who had arranged the funeral for his nephew on Monday.

Dr Samuel Wood gave medical evidence and the body was shown to the jury. The doctor described the extensive burns to the child's back and noted how the hands and face were not harmed. He concluded that young John Sullivan suffered prolonged exposure to fire. Woods reckoned the child was big and strong enough to pull himself away from it so he believed he had been restrained.

The inquest was adjourned till Friday the 3rd of December for the police to make further inquiries and obtain more witnesses. The coroner warned the jurors that they faced fines of £100 for failing to attend the inquest.

More witnesses were produced when the inquest sat that Friday. It was heard that Robert Sullivan was drinking in Bandon the Saturday before till late. He was not so drunk though as he managed to drive home from town with his horse and cart.

Sullivan went to bed that night but later got up again looking for little Johnny. He was seen trying to shove the child's head into a pot of water but it wouldn't fit.

One of Sullivan's labourers Timothy O'Leary told how he was asleep that night when another servant John Rashleigh woke him. In the kitchen, he saw young John Sullivan on the fire and his father not far away. He thought Robert Sullivan was drunk and calling his young son names. Once the child was got from the fire Robert stared at him for some time before saying "if he is not burnt between the legs he may recover". It was Timothy's sister Catherine who put the child to bed that night.

John Rashleigh said he was in bed on Saturday night when Robert returned home. John recalled getting up to let his master and daughter Sally into the house. They both sat at the fire and Sally asked him to wake young Johnny to give him something to eat. Afterwards, everyone in the house went to bed but Rashleigh got up again when his master called him for a light.

He went to his master's bedroom with the light and heard him say "are you my Johnny". The father then stuck his child's head into a pot of water that was near the bed. Rashleigh said he took the child from him and tried to dry him off and asked Robert what he was doing. Robert then grabbed the child from him and pulled him into the kitchen still saying to the child that he wasn't his Johnny at all.

When Rashleigh got to the kitchen the child was on the fire and his father was holding him there. The child was desperately struggling and cried out "oh dada oh dada" while his father still maintained he was not his. Rashleigh told the inquest he made no attempt to save little Johnny as Robert had a bill hook and threatened him with it. Instead, he called Timothy O'Leary and fled to the nearest house for help.

When he returned to the house with the neighbours, Robert asked him to get some oil to rub on the burns before taking him to bed.

On Sunday morning Robert left the house and that was the last time he had seen him. Johnny survived until Monday morning and Rashleigh said the neighbours told him he should inform the police which he did.

The coroner had heard enough that day and was confident the jury could reach a verdict without too much trouble. They found that death was a result of wilful murder caused by the father of the child, Robert Sullivan.

It's easy to imagine that there was no chance of finding a man on the run back in famine times. Communication was much slower and the means of identifying him was nowhere near like it is today. It was for this reason that Head Constable Wright set out from Bandon to retrace the steps a desperate man would take fleeing justice.

On the 6th of December Head Constable Wright from Bandon arrested Sullivan on board a ship in Liverpool. Sullivan had bought passage on the ship 'Constitution' which was due to leave in a few days. He was in a hurry to disappear and had paid 12 shillings extra to change to the 'Cambridge' which was due to leave sooner. It was due to bad weather the 'Cambridge' couldn't sail and allowed the head constable to catch up with him.

Once arrested, Sullivan admitted his terrible deed and expressed his regret. He told the police it was as a result of drink he had done it and now deserved to be executed for it.

Sullivan's actions on Saturday night were clearly that of a mad man but would a mad man flee the country? A mad man would have run off aimlessly about the locality until found but Robert had devised a plan. He decided to do what so many others were doing at the time and leave the country, never to be seen again. It was an obvious thing to do; he wouldn't arouse any suspicion as so many were fleeing the famine.

Sullivan was brought back to Ireland and spent the next few months in jail waiting for the Spring Assizes. It seems the verdict of the inquest was enough to send him for trial and there is no record of a magisterial investigation being held.

When it came to the Cork Spring Assizes that year it was never a question of whether Sullivan had done it or not. Mr Bennett opening the case for the prosecution asked was Sullivan sane when he had carried it out? Did he understand at the time what he had done or was it only afterwards when he realised? The charge against him was murder, by putting his child in the fire he sustained such injuries that resulted in death.

The servant present that night John Rashleigh was still one of the key witnesses. He now gave a more detailed account than the inquest despite it being months later. Rashleigh believed Robert had drink taken that night when he returned from Bandon. At first, he said the father played with Johnny but before going to bed he heard him asking "are you my son Johnny in the name of the father".

About an hour later his master called him to the bedroom, he was still asking the same question to the child. After trying to shove the child's head into a pot of water John saw him grab a billhook then pull the child into the kitchen saying "you are not my child at all you are a sheffraun".

He heard the screams and entering the kitchen he heard Robert shout "I'll roast you and toast you in the name of the father". In panic and in fear of his own life John ran out of the house to get help. It was those he called who went into the house and struggled to get the child from the fire.

At this point, Robert went to bed and Rashleigh and the others did what they could with the severe burns. The following morning about nine he saw Robert leave without saying a word and he didn't see him again until he was in custody in Bandon Bridewell.

Rashleigh explained why he hadn't gone for a doctor that night saying, Robert's brother and family were present and they didn't mention it. He had not seen his master doing anything unusual before that night but under cross examination admitted that he often heard him talking to himself in the fields.

Another servant present that night was Catherine Leary. She heard someone say to Robert "you would not have burned your child if you had the lord to guide you" but he replied, "it was in the name of the lord I did it because I thought he was a sheffraun". She didn't believe that her master was drunk at all that night.

Mr O'Hea for the defence did the only thing he could for his client, plead he was suffering from insanity at the time. Obviously, he didn't mention Sullivan was sane enough afterwards to flee the country knowing he would suffer a deadly punishment. O'Hea asked for an acquittal saying Sullivan's conscience was deficient when he killed his child. Still, the defence called no evidence at all to prove that Sullivan was insane.

The judge summed the evidence up and explained the options which the jury may decide upon. He described how a person may suffer from delusions and commit crimes unconscious of consequences at the time. The same person may later become perfectly aware of what they had done.

Often juries spent hours deliberating and couldn't reach a decision. That day the jury accepted the judge's advice and didn't even leave the courtroom. There and then in the jury box, they all agreed and found a verdict of not guilty on grounds of insanity. The judge sentenced Sullivan to be held in custody at the pleasure of the Lord Lieutenant, which in effect was for the remainder of his life.

A Brother's Revenge

Willowhill Minane Bridge Carrigaline 1843

Mrs Buckley was a pregnant mother of two children in her thirties. Her husband had several brothers. One of them, Thomas, lived in the same house as them until recently. The relationship between them was strained and Mrs Buckley was quite aware it was like a powder keg, all it needed was the spark.

About nine am on Tuesday the 6th of June her twelve year old came running in saying their cock was fighting with his uncle. The boy was heard calling "Oh mother he'll kill the cock". Mrs Buckley knew this would only make Thomas worse as the cock had belonged to his mother who had died sometime before. She remained in the house but shouted to her son "come in or he will serve you the same way".

She was right Thomas made a go for his nephew but he made his escape into the house. It was no escape at all for Thomas made his way into the house and went to the bedroom he normally slept in. Shortly afterwards he returned to the kitchen armed with a graffaun.

Mrs Buckley was boiling a pot of potatoes over the fire for breakfast. Thomas sat at the kitchen table but inside he was raging. When the woman of the house stooped over at the fire checking the breakfast Thomas took the opportunity. He lashed out with the graffaun and the pregnant woman didn't stand a chance. He landed six blows at least to her head and face in a matter of seconds.

Mrs Buckley lay there helplessly. At least Thomas didn't turn on the child also. Instead, Thomas ran from the house and fled across the fields.

It must have been the young fella that ran for help as his mother lay in a pool of blood by the fireside. It was over two miles to the police in Ballyfeard and a doctor was also notified.

When Dr McDermott from Ballyfeard arrived at Buckley's he knew immediately there was little he could do for the woman. She was still alive but suffering greatly and he knew it was just a matter of time. He found her was skull fractured behind the ear and her face was so badly cut one of her cheeks was almost cut from her face.

Willowhill near where the murder occurred

Police in Ballyfeard pursued Thomas in the direction of Crosshaven. Constables Pigott and Coughlan tracked him through the plantations at Hoddersfield until they met at the Owenabue. The constables found a coat and shoes on O'Grady's pier near Crosshaven. They came to the conclusion that Thomas Buckley had swum across the river and made his escape. Soon afterwards a few fishermen came on something floating in the river and it was the body of Thomas Buckley. In his short few minutes in the water, he had drowned.

Back at Willowhill Thomas' sister in law was still barely alive. It was the following morning that she succumbed to her head injuries and passed away.

The Buckley brothers owned a family boat of which they all had a share. They were employed in transporting sand and there had been a dispute about the proceeds. Thomas claimed that his share had been withheld from him and for some reason he swore vengeance on his brother. For several nights before the tragedy, Thomas did not sleep in the house. Instead, he slept in the hay in the yard and had cut the tail from his brother's pig. It turned out that Thomas was not only a brother in law to the woman he had killed, they were also cousins.

Get off my Head
Lissarourke Newcestown 1916

In 1916 as some were plotting and planning a rising, the vast majority were going about their business as normal. In February of that year in the remote townland of Lissarourke, a young married farmer lay dead. The inquest found: "that the deceased died at Lissarourke on 16th of February 1916 and we say death was due to meningitis arising from fracture of the base of the skull caused by direct violence at Lissarourke on the night of the second inst".

Timothy O'Regan went to the fair in Bandon on the 2nd of February and failed to make it home. It was his wife Margaret who found him not far from home after making it all the way from Bandon. He was lying in his own blood on the side of the road and unable to tell what had happened to him.

She brought him home and sent one of the servants for Dr Smyth. By Saturday the 5th Timothy's condition improved a little and he came around. He managed to speak but could not tell what had happened to him. Every day his wife asked but Timothy recalled nothing, saying he would remember in a few days. For days Timothy complained desperately about the terrible pains he was suffering in his head. Then the doctor noticed the symptoms of meningitis which back then he could do nothing about. Steadily Timothy's condition worsened day after day until he died on the 16th of February.

A few days before one of their servants who had been to the fair with Timothy on the 2nd disappeared from the farm without telling anyone he was leaving. The family knew nothing of how Timothy came to be thrown on the road on the way home.

Timothy went to the fair with a cow that was in calf to sell. He had sent his servant Peter Daly off to Bandon early with the cow. A while later O'Regan set out in his pony and trap to complete the sale of the cow.

In the afternoon he met his neighbour John Ryan, both of them had failed to sell their cows. Between them, they decided to send Daly home with the two cows, while Ryan joined the farmer in the pony and trap. Peter Daly left first and was joined along the way by a man called McSweeney.

Timothy O'Regan heading towards the laneway leading to his house, image by Claire O'Donovan.

The pony and trap with the two farmers caught up and overtook the cows being driven along the road. In Newcestown, O'Regan and Ryan stopped for a drink at Richard O'Sullivan's pub. Peter Daly and McSweeney were invited in for a drink with the farmers. Before he did join them Daly drove the cows on the road a little, towards home.

After a drink or so O'Regan reminded his servant of his duties saying "Peter go and look after the cow".

A little later the pony and trap came on Daly again, now they were much closer to home, at the gate to Ryan's boreen. The farmers no longer needed the pony and trap, so Daly was instructed to take it home. O'Regan said he had to go to Ryan's to retrieve a lamp he had left there earlier.

Daly arrived home about seven that evening asking the woman of the house had the cow arrived home. She had not seen the cow but gave Daly his supper.

Afterwards, she told Daly to go out and look for her husband. He left with her instructions but returned not long after. He said O'Regan was fine and sober wherever he was.

She was not satisfied with this at all and demanded he saddle the pony and head to Newcestown to look for Timothy. Daly refused to go and she grew worried that something was amiss. Margaret O'Regan then set out herself along the road that night looking for her husband. Not far from the entrance to her own boreen she came on her husband lying face down on the road moaning.

He may have had several drinks on the way home but his injuries were not consistent with falling. An inquest was organised quickly because there was some suspicion around his injuries which resulted in his death.

That very day Coroner Richard Neville arrived at Lissarourke and opened the inquest in O'Regan's house. Thomas Tweedy county inspector, Hugh Greer District Inspector, Sergeant Sheehan Kinneigh and Constable Lawless Mount Pleasant were all present for the police. The jury comprised of all local men, the foreman was Timothy Lordan a farmer from Lissarourke. Several other farmers from Lissarourke were John Callaghan, Jeremiah Scannell, Jeremiah Mahony and labourer James Good. From the nearby townland, Belrose Upper farmers William Horgan, James Holland, Jeremiah and John Ryan and William Hurley. Jeremiah and Patrick Corcoran farmers from Bengour West and John Murray, Labourer Rushfield.

The remains were formally identified by Margaret O'Regan when she said: "I am the widow of deceased; I recognise his body lying in the adjoining room". She then recalled the 2nd of February saying Daly returned home between seven and eight that night. She asked "where is the boss" and he replied "Ryan's".

After supper, she sent Daly to Ryan's and he returned thirty minutes later saying the boss had left Ryan's with John Cullinane. She ordered Daly out again to Cullinane's this time, he returned saying Timothy had left there with Denis Cullinane and Patrick Lordan. Daly also told he had checked Tim Aherne's and Tim Lordan's but there was no sign of him.

She said it was between eight and nine that she set out with a servant girl. At first, she went to all the houses Daly had but failed to find him. She returned to the entrance to her boreen and met John and Julia Cullinane there.

She headed west along the road with them and found her husband about 160 yards from the gate. He was lying on the left side of the road unconscious and bleeding. Between them, they brought Timothy home and sent word for Dr Smyth.

With no actual witnesses to call that had seen what occurred to Timothy that night all that remained was to call the doctor.

Dr Thomas Smyth said it was after midnight when he arrived at O'Regan's. Timothy was then lying in bed semi unconscious. His clothes were covered in mud and drenched in blood. He found several wounds on his head describing one as "torn, jagged wound about an inch and a quarter long over the right temple". There was another similar wound on the crown of the head and a puncture wound on the other side.

The left side of the jaw also bore the signs of trauma; four teeth were missing from the upper jaw with another hanging out. Dr Smyth said he realised that the first night Timothy was suffering from concussion but it took longer to find the fracture on the base of the skull. At first, he observed blood coming from the ears but a day later it changed to a clear liquid.

When he visited O'Regan on the second day, more bruises were visible and two black eyes had formed. This condition is now better known as racoon eyes and signifies severe head injury and a fracture of the base of the skull. Dr Smyth said that on Saturday the 5th O'Regan improved and was able to speak. He remained like this for five or six days but then his condition quickly deteriorated.

Smyth explained that the wounds were quite severe and he was sure the violence was inflicted by a blunt instrument such as a stick. The doctor could see no possible way Timothy's injuries were self-inflicted by falling about the road.

The doctor told of asking O'Regan if he recalled seeing Peter Daly that night and Timothy said he had near his gate. He then asked Timothy "did he do anything to you" but all he could say was "I do not know. I will know in a few days when I get my senses".

He asked again the Thursday before did he see Daly that night and got the same answer, that he did at his own gate. This time the doctor asked what did Daly say and Timothy replied that Daly said: "the cow did not come back".

And that was how the jury came to the verdict they did. Nobody had seen what had occurred so they were heavily dependent on the medical evidence.

The obvious explanation was that O'Regan met Peter Daly on the way home that night and was annoyed that the cow had not come back.

Daly's disappearance simply implicated him in the events that followed that night. For several days, there was no sign of Peter Daly and so the police began searching for him.

Timothy was the eldest of his eight siblings and the only one to remain at home and inherit the family farm. Seven years before Timothy had married Margaret Daly, a farmers daughter from Lahanaght near Drimoleague. Timothy's parents Peter and Mary were still alive when he married, and he was the last of the nine children to remain at home. Timothy O'Regan was just thirty nine years old when he died.

Not much was known about the suspect Peter Daly. He was 19 years old and had only been working there since July of the year before. He was originally from somewhere between Bantry and Kilcrohane. His mother was supposed to be Kate Donovan living in Pound Street, Bantry. Daly had been hired for 12 months and was to be paid £12 for the years work.

After the inquest on Friday the 18th of February, the funeral took place at Newcestown church.

The inquest was merely concerned with how Timothy O'Regan died and made no mention of by whom. Suspicion naturally fell on Peter Daly who was still missing. The police had begun to search for him, sending out a description all over Cork and further afield. His non appearance alone said a lot. If he was innocent he had nothing to fear and would have given evidence at the inquest.

Several locals were questioned by the Police, who had seen Timothy that night. It was confirmed that the last time he had been seen alive and well was when he walked towards his own gate that night. Yet he had been found further to the west, past his gate.

It took several days for any further breakthrough in the case. On Thursday the 24th of February the police made an arrest in Coosane north of Ballydehob. They found a labourer working for farmer John Skuce, who had been there for just over a week. The young lad said his name was O'Regan but the police arrested him. They suspected it was Peter Daly who had been missing since the 10th.

The suspect was taken to Skibbereen and then by the 2:50 train to Ballineen. That evening there was a special sitting of the court in Ballineen and Peter Daly was formally charged with the murder of Timothy O'Regan.

No actual evidence was produced that day but a remand of eight days was granted. Afterwards, the police took Daly on the train to Cork where he was sent to the County Gaol.

It was at a special sitting of Ballineen Court on Saturday the 4th of March that evidence was heard, before resident magistrate A.G.W Harrell. District Inspector Hugh Greer led the prosecution in the absence of crown solicitor Mr Sherlock.

It was the brother in law of the accused that spoke first saying the defence had engaged Jonas Travers Wolfe of Skibbereen but that he would not arrive until eleven.

Greer then iterated how serious a case it was and said only a few witnesses would be called that day.

First called was Denis Cullinane who introduced himself as living in Killanear and working for Mr Lordan as a butter buyer. He recalled meeting Timothy O'Regan in his father's house on the night of the 2nd. He reckoned it was about quarter past seven but he couldn't be sure. He left with Timothy about ten minutes afterwards, heading for Mr Lordan's house. Along the way, they met Patrick Lordan on horseback.

They stopped at the entrance to Lordan's which was a little short of O'Regan's gate and they parted company. He said Timothy was walking towards his gate with a lantern as they left. Denis said he and Patrick then took the lane to Lordan's at about 7:45.

Greer asked about O'Regan's condition that night, "perfectly sober, with no sign of drink on him" was the reply. The questioning then moved on to the accused Peter Daly, Denis said he saw him in Lordan's about nine asking for Timothy O'Regan. The next time he saw Daly was about half ten, this time looking for a horse to send for the doctor.

Patrick Lordan gave the same account as Denis had of the events on the 2nd. He said before parting company with O'Regan that night the three men chatted at the entrance to his boreen. They left Timothy heading for his own boreen entrance which was only about 30 or 40 yards away. He also said that Timothy was sober that night.

He believed it was about nine when Daly came looking for O'Regan. They told him he was not there but not to worry as he was fine wherever he was. They told him he had been sober earlier. But Daly disagreed with them saying "he was not so in Newcestown earlier". He also told of Daly returning at 10:30 looking for a horse to fetch the doctor. Patrick said his brother Dan offered to go for the doctor instead as he had a motorbike.

Newcestown publican, Richard O'Sullivan was called as a witness. He had also been to the fair in Bandon on the 2nd. He arrived home about four, had his dinner and went into the pub afterwards. In there at the time was his servant John McSweeney, Peter Daly, Timothy O'Regan and John Ryan from Kilaneer. Sullivan said John Ryan stood him a drink and he took it. The publican bought a round of drink for the four men, after this he heard Timothy tell his servant Daly to go look after the cow, which he did. The publican believed both Ryan and O'Regan were sober when they left.

Richard told how he was aware that Timothy had a cow to sell at the fair but failed to do so. The next morning he saw O'Regan's cow outside the pub in Newcestown and he told his servant John McSweeney to do something about it.

District Inspector Greer announced that he wished to call no more witnesses that day. He had another witness lined up but he was sick and failed to attend. He proposed to adjourn for a further eight days.

Jonas Wolfe who had declined to cross examine any witnesses that day enquired would one more day in court do but Greer said no it would take at least three more days. The district inspector seemed keen to get the help of Mr Sherlock for the next day in court. The following Friday was suggested but Greer rejected it saying Mr Sherlock was in Bandon dealing with a bigamy case that day. Daly was sent back to gaol for another eight days and the prosecution needed to come up with something better the next time.

Hearing that Mr Sherlock was going to Bandon for a bigamy case, I was intrigued. It was completely unrelated to the murder case except that Mr Sherlock was involved. Turns out John William Brodie, a Lance Corporal in the Royal Field Artillery stationed in Bandon married a local woman Hannah McCarthy.

Hannah aged 20, who lived in Cavendish Quay in Bandon, must have known little of his past when they married. Brodie was a protestant and shockingly back then he converted in the months before marriage, so clearly it was planned. His real trouble was he was still married to his first wife Edith Phillips in Frindsbury Kent since 1911 and they had three children.

Lance Corporal Brodie pleaded guilty to the charge of bigamy for when he married Hannah in Ballymodan Church on the 1st January 1916. He had been wounded at the Western Front the year before and returned with head injuries and being struck by shrapnel. He was also said to have been suffering shellshock afterwards.

How he came to get caught was most likely when the army was discharging him as an invalid, unfit for duty. His army paperwork would have recorded his first wife and children. Brodie got six months of hard labour for his crime at the Summer Assizes but ended up back in the army again and was sent to Turkey the following year.

And…back to the murder case.

Peter Daly was brought before Ballineen petty sessions again on the 16th of March. As Mr Sherlock had not been present the previous day he felt it his duty to say a few words as if he was opening the case. He admitted that the evidence to be heard was mostly circumstantial but later a dying declaration would be revealed.

One fact he pointed out was that Mrs O'Regan sent Peter Daly out looking for Timothy about 7:45. He asked was it a coincidence that Cullinane saw O'Regan heading towards his laneway at the same time. It was in the next half hour he said: "Timothy Regan was done to death on the road, knocked on the road and injuries inflicted on him which resulted in his death". With this, Sherlock concluded by saying he was sure that the case should go forward for a trial at the next Assizes.

Margaret O'Regan gave a more concise account that day of the events leading up to finding her husband lying at the roadside. She mentioned how after giving Daly his supper she was not yet concerned for her husband. She told Daly her husband would be annoyed that the cow had not returned and asked him to go and tell him. She was then worried the cow might calf on the road and the calf might die.

She sent him out twice that night looking for Timothy and each time Daly was reluctant to go. She went out herself, with another servant Minne Brien and Daly; they first went to Cullinane's, then to Ryan's. The three of them then returned to the entrance to her own boreen, where Timothy had last been seen. Margaret said she remained there with Daly and sent Minne to check the house to see had he returned in the meantime.

She then suggested to Daly to saddle the pony to go to Newcestown thinking Timothy must have gone back there. She proposed herself and

Minne would go west the road and check Lordan's again. She said Daly objected to going to Newcestown saying he would go west with Minnie and check Lordan's. Daly told her to go home but she didn't go, hearing footsteps on the road from the east. It was John and Julia Cullinane asking had Timothy been found. It was then she heard moaning coming from along the road to the west. She described the terrible scene she found that night "his head was towards the fence. He was on his face and hands in a most awful condition. He was all blood, his face and his coat. There was a pool of blood under him and more of it back of him and the cap rested on his head. The lamp was at the back of him on the road, the glass of it broken and it was not lighting".

The questioning continued until Sherlock asked did Timothy say anything. Margaret said, "well he could not explain anything right until the following Saturday".

She was asked what he said but Jonas Wolfe objected to that being heard. There were some exchanges between Sherlock and Wolfe concerning what could be heard. Sherlock again said that later in the case a dying declaration would be proved. It was explained to Margaret what she had to exclude, she was told: "don't say anything your husband said unless it was in the presence of Daly".

Sherlock changed tack asking:
Had your husband any money on him going to the fair? Yes, £8 or £9.
Was that found on him? Yes.
Did Daly remain working on the farm? He did.
Until when? 11th of February.
What happened on the 11th? My husband asked did the cow return.

Sherlock continued asking several times what happened that Daly left the farm despite Wolfe objecting. Margaret said there were wages due to Daly when he left and Wolfe disagreed with this. He asked about a missing overcoat and Wolfe seemed surprised saying "is there a charge of larceny against him? If the police had any compassion on him they would give him an overcoat and not leave him there all day in danger of getting cold". Sherlock was having none of it though and told him "there is a charge of larceny of an overcoat but it is a separate charge".

When Jonas Wolfe got the chance he asked Margaret had John and Julia Cullinane not walked right past her husband on the road that night.

But they had not as they had come from their house in Kilaneer which was in the other direction.

Dr Smyth again gave the medical evidence, which was as of yet the only evidence that Timothy O'Regan was beaten that night. The doctor did tell of Saturday the 5th when O'Regan regained consciousness and was able to speak for a while. He asked O'Regan did he know what happened that night but Timothy said: "I must have got a very bad beating, I have a very bad pain in my head, I think I'll die". The doctor said Timothy's condition improved enough by the 10th that he managed to walk to another room. In the days after, meningitis set in which the doctor concluded resulted in death.

The next witness was John Lordan from Laaravoolta the townland to the south, a cousin of Patrick Lordan. He recalled walking up Lordan's lane to his uncle's house when he heard a moaning sound. He came from the direction in which he had seen a light at the bend in the road. He stopped in the lane for a second but heard no more and carried on to Timothy Lordan's house.

Later he said Peter Daly arrived looking for Timothy O'Regan. It was Peter Daly that said he had met O'Regan at the old lane and he was sober and fine then.

Julia Cullinane gave an account that agreed with that of Mrs O'Regan. She went out with her brother John and met Mrs O'Regan at the gate. Her brother John also backed up her testimony but added that he went to Lordan's with Daly to send word for the doctor. Along the way he said to Daly "I don't think he will do at all", to which Daly replied, "do you think so".

A sister of Mrs O'Regan, Mary Anne Daly (no relation to the accused) told of being in O'Regan's house on the 2nd of February. Her evidence matched that of her sister. She did tell that on that night Daly was asked to help and take off his master's boots and leggings but he refused.

The following day she brought Daly into the room where Timothy was lying. She said he couldn't bear to look at him or the wounds. Mary Anne remarked that while the woman cared for the man of the house, Peter Daly never enquired how he was.

When asked about the night of the 10th Mary Anne said she was in the room upstairs with Timothy and his brother Con. She described Timothy as raving and he called out for Peter Daly to get off his head.

The most damning evidence against the accused that day came from an unlikely source that had not been mentioned in the search at all that night. It was sixteen year old Andrew O'Rourke who also worked at O'Regan's and shared a bed with Daly. Andrew began telling of the night of the 10th of February saying he was in bed about ten or eleven. Daly asked him had the O'Regan's suspicions on him but Andrew said no. But it was clear Daly felt they had as he told Andrew "they are only waiting until Tim Regan gets alright to swear on me".

Later they heard Tim O'Regan shouting in bed saying "Peter Daly get off my head". Hearing this Daly asked him "did you hear that". Daly also told him that the police were waiting outside the gate every night.

They then heard Jim Daly and Con O'Regan come downstairs and go to lock the door. Daly grew worried and said to Andrew "They're going out for the police to arrest me". Daly believed he was going to get a beating and told Andrew he should clear off and enlist in the army. Daly said, "someone was going to jail over this and it is I". That night he asked Andrew "will you call me at four in the morning" but he never did. Andrew said he woke up at eight the following morning and Daly was gone.

District Inspector Greer was next to question when Wolfe asked would he finish that day. Greer said it would take at least two more days. Hearing this Wolfe claimed that the prosecution was trying to drag the case out and keep Peter Daly in jail until July. He said it was possible to have Daly tried the following week at the Spring Assizes. Wolfe then asked about the dying declaration and Sherlock said this would be proved by district inspector Greer.

Wolfe asked why the dying declaration was not produced at the inquest when the County Inspector was present. He maintained that it was most unusual for evidence to be withheld until the special court. Wolfe asked that the county inspector be present at the next sitting and asked for the dispositions of the inquest to be produced. Mr Sherlock refused this request and it was now Wolfe who was trying to delay hearing the dying declaration till another day and asking for the county inspector. Finally, they agreed to adjourn and remand Daly for eight days.

The court sat again in Ballineen on Thursday the 27th of April. There had been several remands at the Cork police office. Always a bad sign for the prosecution, it meant they were struggling to come up with the evidence. Daly stood charged that he "feloniously and maliciously killed and slain Timothy P O'Regan of Lissarourke". Resident magistrate Harrell led the magistrates with George Sherlock and District Inspector Hugh Greer representing the Crown prosecution. Well known solicitor Jonas Travers Wolfe from Skibbereen was there to make the case for the defence.

It began that day with District Inspector Greer as the first witness, questioned by his colleague Mr Sherlock.

"Do you recollect 12th February? Yes

Did you visit the house of Tim O'Regan? I did.

What Hour? 10.30 am.

Did anyone accompany you? Yes.

Who? Sergeant Sheehan.

Did you both go into the room where Tim was lying? Yes, upstairs.

Was anybody else present? Yes, Mrs O'Regan.

Did you in the presence of the dying man direct your sergeant to put some questions to the dying man?"

It was here that Wolfe objected, his tactic was to prevent this being heard at all. Sherlock was frustrated with this, remarking how the dying declaration was essential. Wolfe quipped back "Mr Greer is not dying, he does not look it" but this just frustrated Sherlock even more.

Sherlock tried coming around it, he asked, did the sergeant ask O'Regan something. Wolfe continued with his objection and it was upheld.

Sherlock began again, asking Greer, in consequence of a statement made to the sergeant was the following question put to the dying man. But again Wolfe objected saying "I object there is nobody dying at all" and Sherlock quickly fired in "but he is dead".

The exchanges went on between Mr Wolfe & Mr Sherlock. Wolfe continuously objected, preventing the prosecution from going further. His point was that O'Regan did not know he was dying on the 11th.

Eventually, Wolfe referenced cases showing that a dying declaration could only be made 'in extremis' where the person knew they were dying and gave up all hope of recovery. Wolfe was told the case was to proceed and he must object in writing.

It was decided to clear the court and the statement Greer gave was heard in camera. The press & public were allowed in again to hear the testimony of John McSweeney. All he had to say was relating to bringing the cows from the fair to Newcestown and the drink that was drunk there.

The brother of the deceased Cornelius O'Regan who was a farm labourer living in Bengour West was called next. He went to his brother's house on the 4th of February having heard what happened. Con described seeing his brother in bed all bandaged up and barely recognisable. He said his face was bruised and badly swollen.

He asked Daly about going to the fair and Daly said he left Tim at Ryan's that night. Constable O'Sullivan said when he first saw Daly in Skuce's farmhouse he asked "Peter what brought you here?" and he got the reply "I do not know". When he placed Daly under arrest he cautioned him but all Daly said was "I did not do it".

Sergeant Sheehan of Kinneigh was called as he had initiated the investigation. First, he told of going to see Timothy O'Regan lying in bed. All he managed to say was "I asked him..." when Wolfe objected.

Then he tried again saying how on the 8th of February he searched O'Regan's for Peter Daly. He left for John Ryan's house & eventually when returning found Peter Daly in the loft of the outhouse. He managed to question Daly that day and even got a statement from him. Wolfe objected on the grounds Daly had not been cautioned or arrested at that point. The statement was allowed and Wolfe's objection was noted.

The statement read:

"On the 2nd of February 1916, I accompanied my master Tim O'Regan to Bandon Fair with a cow and about 2:45 pm he sent me home before him with the cow and another cow belonging to John Ryan, Killaneer. My master overtook me at Newcestown and John Ryan was with him and a woman who I did not know. We had a few drinks in the public house of Richard O'Sullivan and came on for home together. At Killaneer Cross John Ryan missed his car lamp, Ryan said he would go back to Newcestown to look for the lamp and my master was preventing him. My master then told me to come home with the horse and cart and I did. I reached home at about 7:30 pm. I had supper then and after supper came into the stall and looked at the cattle and then walked up the road as far as John Ryan's. I met no one on the road. I went into John Ryan's; I could not give the time I went in there. I did not delay five minutes. I came back home again, I don't know the time but it was only five minutes when I went out again looking for my master who did not turn up. I went to Cullinane's of Killaneer and he was not there. I asked was Tim Regan there and they told me he was gone home. I came back then and went to Lordan's of Lissarourke and asked was Tim Regan there. They told me he was not. Myself and Jim Aherne went as far as Thade Lordan's inquiring for my master and Denis Cullinane told me he was gone home, that he parted company with him at Lordan's gate. When I came back Mrs Regan and the servant girl Minne Brien were gone out looking for him. I waited until they came back and when they came in I told them I could not find him. The three of us then went looking for him and went up the Kilaneer road again and when passing Cullinane's cottage I went in to see if they had any account of him. I could not tell the time it was then. They told me he did not come in and asked me did I try Lordan's, I said I did. I then went to John Ryan's again. Mrs Regan and her servant were with me. They were gone to bed, we came back again and when we came to the end of the lane nearing the house, Minne Brien went in to see did he come and he was not inside. I then told Mrs Regan to come in and that myself and Minne Brien would look for him. We then heard John Cullinane and his sister coming up the road and we waited for them. We went up the road then looking for my master and heard a moan. We all stood and listened and went up another bit and John Cullinane saw something black on the side of the road. I then saw it before the women. We went towards it and found Timothy Regan there lying on the roadside. He was not out on the road. On the track of the wheels, there was blood about a foot outside him. I and Cullinane took him up. He was not able to stand or speak and we brought him home. He was all covered over with blood and Daniel Lordan went for Dr Smyth of Enniskeane".

After the statement was read out Sergeant Sheehan said that Peter Daly told him he could write but refused to sign the statement and instead he put his mark on it. Jonas Wolfe declined to cross examine the sergeant in court that day.

Wolfe claimed there could not be a prima facie case against his client. He said based on what he had heard it should not go before a jury referring to the evidence as "absurd". Wolfe referred to Mr Sherlock's earlier statement that the evidence was circumstantial, saying there was as much against one of the witnesses as his client. He didn't go any further and point the finger at anyone but said one particular witness was more suspicious than Peter Daly.

The magistrate, however, believed there was a prima facie case against Peter Daly and returned it for trial at the next assizes. Their opinion was that such cases should be held in camera where the magistrate could state his reasons.

Peter Daly left Ballineen on the 4 O'clock train. He was taken back to Cork Gaol where he would remain until the Summer Assizes which was months away.

Jonas Wolfe was wrong when he said Peter Daly would suffer in jail until the summer, it was much longer. The case did not come before an Assize court until the 12th of December. Peter Daly pleaded not guilty before Justice Pim; the charge was still of wilful murder.

The prosecution came well prepared, now they had Mr P Fleming, King's Counsel, James Reardon and Anthony Carroll, crown solicitor. There was no sign of Jonas Wolfe after all the hard work on Daly's behalf. Now the defence was represented by Joseph O'Connor and Mr F Wynne.

When Fleming opened the case it became clear that nothing new would be heard in court. The evidence would once again be mostly circumstantial in nature. They relied heavily on what the young boy O'Rourke had heard Daly say in bed before running away.

Fleming asked why Daly had assumed the name Tim Regan and gave his address as Crookston while on the run. He asked the jury to listen to the evidence which he said pointed to the fact Peter Daly inflicted injuries on Timothy O'Regan which led to his death.

The same witnesses were heard all over again, some for a third time. Their recollections could not have been as clear now as at the inquest or magisterial investigation.

In court, it was all heard once more, Mrs O'Regan and the frantic search for her husband that night. The spot of blood she had seen on Peter Daly's face and how on one occasion that night he was gone for half an hour.

So many of the neighbours saying Tim O'Regan was sober that night. He was last seen 30 yards from the entrance gate to his house, with a lantern lighting.

It was cleared up that day why no mention had been made of young O'Rourke in the search. He had only come to work at O'Regan's on the 4th of February.

Andrew was questioned again about the night Tim O'Regan was shouting in bed on the 10th of February. He denied to Daly hearing what Timothy had said but heard "Peter Daly come off my head". Daly had said to him "did you hear that, will I go out and put on my clothes". A while later Daly became more agitated saying "the three lads are going to beat me, now let them all come, here's a fellow won't fall first". Andrew told the court how Daly talked of running away and enlisting saying "I suppose three years won't save me from gaol, it would be good to enlist now. I hope I'll meet you coming out of gaol and we will have a jolly smoke".

Andrew was questioned further; he told how the day before Daly had been cleaning his clothes and shoes. Under cross examination by O'Connor, the servant revealed that O'Regan could be heard raving for several nights before the 10th but on those occasions, he could not be understood.

Margaret O'Regan was questioned again as she had been several times before. We had already heard her asking Daly "where is the boss". Giving Daly his supper and then sending him out again to look for her husband. When he returned he claimed "the boss" had gone to Cullinane's.

Now Margaret said she then asked Daly why he didn't go to Cullinane's. The servant sat himself down in the kitchen claiming he was tired and had a headache. Margaret then told him either he would go back out or she would. We know he did leave again, this time returning with the information Timothy had left Cullinane's.

Reardon now asked the widow had she noticed anything unusual about Daly that night. It was then she revealed she had seen a spot of blood on Daly's face after he returned from Ryan's after being out for half an hour.

Reardon enquired did Daly notice the spot of blood. Margaret said:" there was a looking glass in the window and he turned towards it and wiped it off with his hand".

Then she described finding her husband at the roadside that night and how he died on the 16th of February.

She said it was the 11th of February when Peter Daly left suddenly. Up till then, he had never asked at all about how her husband was. He disappeared early one morning leaving behind his clothes and without collecting wages due to him.

What was heard in court that day was the prosecution and their professor in Dublin had failed to find blood on any of the clothes belonging to Peter Daly.

When the prosecution rested their case Justice Pim commented on how remarkable it was that no blood was found on Peter Daly's clothes. The judge said after helping Tim O'Regan home there should have been some signs of blood on him. The speck of blood Mrs O'Regan referred to was seen before Timothy was found.

O'Connor then made the case for the defence, saying how there was no evidence at all to connect Peter Daly with the death. He relied heavily on the fact no blood was found on Daly's clothes. O'Connor then went further where Wolfe had not gone before and pointed the finger at someone else. He suggested that John Lordan was as suspicious as the accused and could be placed close to the scene of the crime. This was ridiculous as John Lordan need never have given evidence and no one would have known he passed by at that time. All he did was pass up Lordan's laneway on the way to his uncles. O'Connor claimed the only evidence against Peter Daly was the fact he ran away.

Finally, Justice Pim summed up the evidence and made his own opinion known. He could see how there was enough suspicion against Peter Daly to get to where the case was. But he said that was all there was against Daly, suspicion. The judge said he was not going to sum up all of the evidence and took full responsibility for it. Instead, he gave his opinion bluntly that there was no real substantial proof against Daly for a jury to find him guilty.

The jury when they did retire had little option and returned fifteen minutes later with a verdict of not guilty. Justice Pim then ordered Peter Daly to be discharged remarking that the suspicions on him were not justified.

As far as the law was concerned there was not enough evidence to prove him guilty. For the O'Regan's there would be no closure. Someone had attacked Timothy so close to home that night and the motive remained a mystery.

It seems strange but back then the accused could not be questioned in court. In this case, if Daly had been questioned he may have incriminated himself and would have had to explain his every move that night.

The Price of Jealousy
Horsehead Lodge Passage West 1896

A little outside the village of Passage West one Saturday in October, Minnie Foley went to the village shop with her elderly parents. Later she returned alone to the lodge house of Horsehead where they lived. A few feet from the lodge gate, a figure sprang out of the darkness and made a grab for her. He had something shiny in his hand but she didn't quite see what it was in the moonlight.

She knew it was her brother in law and ran towards the gate which was slightly open. Quick thinking she slammed the gate shut in his face and was safe from him for a moment. She screamed loudly with fright when he got close and called to her sister in the house to unlock the door and let her in. The door to the lodge was already open though and looking in she knew instantly that her attacker had been already. There on the floor right in front of her was her sister Ellen covered in blood. Her throat was severely cut and the blood was everywhere. On top of her was her youngest child who had suffered a similar fate.

Minnie turned and fled the house and ran to Mrs Flynn in the big house, Horsehead. A few of the women there got the courage to venture down to the lodge. They found there was nothing that could be done and ran back in horror fearing for their own lives.

Before word got out that night a man walked to the police barracks in Passage West. He strolled into the day room threw a razor up onto the table and said "I have killed my wife and two children; they are lying dead at the lodge". The two constables were in disbelief and called the Sergeant who asked was it true.

Edward Foley with his hands stained in blood confirmed it was true after repeated questions. The sergeant duly arrested him put him in a cell and headed for the murder scene. When the Sergeant went to the door of the lodge just as Minnie had, he knew that Foley had told no lie. Just inside the door were Ellen Foley and her six month old baby Cornelius across her knees, both with their throats slit and blood everywhere. Upstairs in a tiny bedroom of the lodge, two year old Thomas was found in bed. He had not escaped his father's razor. Lying on his back he had been murdered in his sleep.

On Sunday morning in the barracks when he awoke Foley was calm, ate his breakfast and smoked his pipe contently. The night before when he turned himself in, Foley appeared highly excited but had no drink taken.

Also on Sunday, County Inspector Gamble with District Inspector Byrne and resident magistrate Mr Horne arrived from Cobh. Edward Foley was charged in court and remanded in custody until a special sitting of the court the following Wednesday. When charged that day all he said was "it is true, it is only too true".

In the afternoon it took a large escort of police to take him to the train station and on to Cork Gaol. The crowd gathered and showed their hatred for Foley by booing, hissing and repeated attempts to kick or hit him. A cousin of Ellen's managed to break through the Police and strike Foley's head in disgust at what he had done.

The Inquest was held on the 19th by Coroner Horgan in Daniel Murphy's pub in Passage. A jury of local men was sworn in with George A Patterson as foreman. It was made up of publicans James O'Mahony, Main Street, Thomas O'Mahony, Railway Street and John Edgell Strand Street and Thomas Williams shoemaker, Main Street. More were Henry John Philpott Lindsay a landlord, Patrick Callaghan, John Murphy Agent from Strand Street and William O'Leary. Also John McDonnell a shopkeeper Ferrypoint, Maurice Ahern seafarer Fair Hill, Daniel Mahony tailor Lucia Place, Daniel Butler Insurance Agent from The Glen and James Brady.

District inspector Byrne from Cobh led the examination of the witnesses for the Crown. Ellen's mother, Julia Foley appeared very much shaken but composed herself just enough to tell the inquest in a low voice how she had left home at half seven on Saturday evening. She had put Tom to bed upstairs first, left Ellen in the kitchen with the baby and reminded her to lock the door as she left.

Dr Arthur O'Keeffe described how on Sunday morning he went to the lodge and found the bodies unmoved since the night before. Ellen, he said, "was lying on her back, her hair was loose and soaked in blood on the floor". He then went into the injuries he found. Her throat had been cut to the spinal cord, all the blood vessels and the windpipe had been severed. He also found two slashes on the right cheek but otherwise, there were no other injuries or signs of struggle on the body. The doctor stated the obvious to everyone, death was instantaneous and inflicted by a sharp instrument such as the bloody razor.

*Depiction of the lodge at Horsehead,
with thanks to Irish Newspaper Archives and Evening Echo.*

Then the baby, the doctor said it was found in a position that little Cornelius had just rolled out of his mother's arms. As regards the injuries, it was the same as his mother. O'Keeffe then told of going upstairs in the house and finding little Thomas lying on his back in the bed. He found no signs of a struggle at all suggesting he suffered the same fate as his family while he lay sleeping. His throat has also been cut in the same manner but more to the left hand side.

The only other witness that day was Constable Courtney who told how Foley arrived into the barracks on Saturday night and gave himself up. Courtney recalled how Foley's hands were covered in blood and he threw a bloody razor onto the table saying "there's the razor". One of the questions posed to the constable was "did you ask him why he did it". Courtney recalled Foley telling him that the children did not belong to him.

Courtney also described the scene he found that evening in the lodge house. Aside from the razor Foley had given in at the barracks, Courtney found a bloodstained cleaver in the lodge.

The Coroner only very briefly spoke to the jury saying he had no doubt they could easily reach a verdict. The jury in a short time agreed to a verdict: That the said deceased were found dead at Pembroke on the 17th instant and that death resulted from haemorrhage from a wound in the throat, inflicted with a razor by Edward Foley on the said date.

Later that day the funeral took place and such a sad scene had never been seen in Passage. The coffins were shouldered to the old graveyard and followed by a large cortege. Baby Cornelius was placed in the coffin with his mother and Thomas was in another little coffin. The church bell tolled as they made their way to the graveyard that afternoon. Fr Christopher Murphy who had married the couple three years before had the sad task of carrying out the funeral service.

From the evidence produced at the inquest and Foley's confession, there could be no doubt that he did it. What the police and everyone outside the family initially struggled to grasp was the motive, why had he snapped and done such a thing.

A few years before Cornelius Foley and his wife Julia with their two daughters moved to the lodge at Horsehead. They had been living at Glenbrook and moving to the lodge also secured work from Mr Flynn at the big house. Cornelius acted as lodge keeper and gardener at Horsehead while his wife found work in the house. The eldest of the two daughters Ellen married Edward Foley in January of 1893. It was not love at first sight by any means; the match was an arranged one and forced upon the couple. Edward was from Green Street in Cork where his father Timothy was a boilermaker.

Edward got work as a ticket collector on the steamer boats of the Cork Blackrock and Passage Railway Company and maybe that was how he came to be in Passage West. Before getting married Ellen had been in service in a house in Monkstown and would have been forced to give up that position. Edward was then 35 years old and she was 12 years younger than him.

The newlyweds moved into a cottage across the road in Toureen, only a few hundred yards from her parents. Ellen was the dutiful wife and did everything for her husband; she would often be seen at the pier, giving him meals while he worked on the steamers. Their marriage was not a happy one no matter what Ellen did for him her husband was suspicious of her. His jealousy drove him to repeatedly accuse her of being unfaithful to him without foundation.

Another depiction of the gate and lodge at Horsehead, with thanks to Irish Newspaper Archives and Evening Echo.

When their first child Thomas was born it did nothing to improve Edward's behaviour. Instead, he denied being the father and refused to attend the christening but nobody took heed of him. Ellen suffered from her husband's abusive behaviour but now had the baby to look after.

When the second child Cornelius was born in May of 1896 the situation grew worse, Edward neglected his job and instead followed his wife about suspiciously. His repeated failure to turn up for work ended up in his dismissal from the job. With even more time on his hand's matters spiralled out of control. Ellen then had to work harder to support the family while her idle husband was consumed with jealously. His ill treatment of her ended in the police visiting the cottage several times but still, Ellen remained with him against the advice of many people.

In October Ellen eventually was forced to leave him and move back into the lodge at Horsehead. She now had her family to help look after the children while she worked but still returned daily with meals for her husband. Edward went to Cork and got a job as a labourer with the Cork Gas Company. It only lasted a few days, when he returned to Passage he was completely consumed in jealousy of his wife and followed her every move. His behaviour became threatening and Ellen's family were living in fear of him and continually watching their backs.

On Wednesday morning Foley was brought back to Passage on the train and attracted attention wherever he went with the police. By the time he got to the courthouse, a crowd had gathered. The police were on hand to prevent trouble. The public were not allowed inside but Foley was brought to the courthouse an hour before time and it took several constables to keep the crowd at bay. About eleven the magistrates, Captain Byam Roberts, Eyre Powell and Dr Beamish turned up. Sergeant Mostyn then arrived and announced that evidence would be heard in the barracks where Resident Magistrate Horne was already waiting. Foley was then escorted to the barracks and the crowd followed closely behind.

Eventually, the evidence against Foley was heard in the day room of the barracks where he had made his confession the Saturday before. First Dr O'Keeffe repeated the gruesome evidence that he had given at the inquest.

Julia Foley, mother and grandmother of the deceased was so weak she had to be helped into the room. Resident Magistrate Horne comforted her saying "we'll give you as little trouble as we can, for we're all sorry for you". She spoke quietly as she described the miserable life her daughter had since getting married to Edward Foley. Julia told how the couple were married three years and lived at Toureen Terrace.

One of the magistrates Dr Beamish intervened and explained that they had lived in Toureen but it was not Toureen Terrace. He wished to make it clear as it would be bad for the people living in Toureen Terrace.

Julia was reluctant to repeat the terrible things Foley said to his wife but told that he often threatened to kill her. Julia described her son-in-law that he "bore the worst character of any man ever reared in the county of Cork". She explained that it was not the first time Ellen had left her husband and moved back to the lodge. It had happened many times before and after a few days they would make up and Ellen would move back with the children until the next time. Julia told that when Ellen arrived at her house the week before with the children she had a black eye. She also admitted she had supported her daughter since she was married, not just when Edward was not working. When he was working on the boats, he rarely gave money to Ellen and instead spent it on drink. Julia also told that their grandson Thomas had been living in the lodge for the last few months.

What was the gateway to Horsehead with the lodge just inside.

When she finished her testimony, Foley was allowed to cross examine her. This was only because he had no legal representation. Resident Magistrate Horne asked him:"Now Edward Foley you heard what your mother-in-law said, have you anything to say", "no sir" he replied. It was enough to send the old woman into a panic when she heard his voice and called out "let me see the murderer now". A few policemen quickly blocked her view of him and she signed her statement before being led out of the room.

When Minnie Foley was helped into the court to give evidence she was trembling. At the witness box, she became frantic looking about the room crying "where is he, where is he". She was so terrified at the thought of seeing Edward. It was obvious Minnie could not testify when she almost fainted.

Another witness was to be brought in but there was a delay of a few minutes and Minnie was brought back in. This time she composed herself enough to begin and explain how she lived in Horsehead house where she was in service for Mr Flynn. Minnie managed to get her evidence out but she was distracted and her eyes searched the room looking for him. She then had to retell how she had escaped her brother in law that night only to find her sister lying in a pool of blood.

Minnie told that her sister had a mark on her face a few days before and said Foley had done it. Earlier that Saturday she saw him at Horsehead looking for his wife with a stick in his hand. Minnie admitted that her sister was afraid of her husband that day and came to her crying.

When her evidence was given Foley was asked again had he something to ask her but he declined again with "no sir". It was enough just hearing those two works to send Minnie into hysterics, she was heard crying "I see him" as she was being led out. Foley just stood there hiding his head in his hands.

Sergeant Patrick Mostyn gave evidence of arresting Foley and the confession he had given in the barracks. He also described the bloody scene at the lodge that night. After inspecting the lodge he returned to the barracks and cautioned Foley before formally arresting him. The Sergeant said that when he gave the usual caution Foley said "all right I am prepared to die. No one will be laughing at me on the quay now again. I was the laughing stock of the country. She may blame her mother. She would not leave her live with me, she may blame Mrs Duggan and her father and mother for her death. Is she dead? They may blame themselves".

Then the Sergeant described the lock on the door of the lodge and how he found it easy to force in when locked. He also admitted to knowing Edward Foley before that Saturday and how a complaint was made that he was assaulting his wife about a year before.

At the end of the evidence, it was Mr Byrne who suggested remanding Foley for a further eight days to see if anything else cropped up. While it was being discussed in court whether he should be remanded, it was Foley who interrupted them saying "gentlemen, I would prefer the case to close, I am pleading guilty". Magistrate Horne warned him not to say anymore but also told him he could not just ignore his statement. Foley though just repeated it with "sir, I am pleading guilty". Now Horne explained the law telling Foley that since he was cautioned in the barracks that night any statement he made could be used in evidence against him but all Foley said to that was "it is immaterial to me sir".

Horne again cautioned Foley who then said, "I have nothing at all to say, sir, I have no mercy to expect from anyone, I hope God will pardon me for the crime I have committed and may God pardon the man who supplied me with the weapon to kill her, I have no more to say, sir."

Resident Horne was left with no other option but to comply with Foley's request and close the case sending him for trial. It left everyone but Foley a little uneasy, Horne and the other magistrates knew what Foley's fate was.

When it came to a trial often judges didn't like it when the accused pleaded guilty. You would think not having to not hear all the gruesome evidence was an advantage but some judges were uneasy sending a man to the gallows having not heard the evidence against them.

For Edward Foley, there was no other option but to plead guilty. At the Munster Winter Assizes on a Friday in December that is what he did. Justice Madden asked "do you know the effect of pleading guilty to the charge of murder", the reply was "yes my lord". A man's life was at stake so he asked again "are you fully aware of the consequences" and the reply was the same. It was then repeated for each charge of murder and Foley pleaded guilty to each.

Foley's ability to plead was then discussed by Mr Ronan for the crown. He handed a document from the gaol doctor to the judge but it was not read out to the court. Ronan then suggested further inquiry into Foley's mental state was required saying "we are informed the man was perfectly sane, we will have the gaol doctor present in the morning". Justice Madden agreed and added, "I think sentencing should immediately follow".

The following morning Mr Ronan addressed the court saying further inquiries into Foley's mental state had been made. No doctor was called but Mr Ronan told the court that the crown was still of the same opinion, Foley was fit to plead.

The clerk of the court Mr Standish O'Grady read out the indictments against Foley, to which he replied firmly each time "guilty sir". Justice Madden then asked why the sentence of death should not be passed on him. Foley had little to say but managed "my lord I will only say a few words, I beg to state in the presence of you my lord that I am sorry for the crime I have committed, I will say no more my lord". Then Justice Madden explained to him that several doctors had deemed him fit to plead so the judge was obliged to accept it and the consequences saying "for you Edward Foley there is in this world no hope".

The judge put on the black cap and proceeded to sentence:

"The sentence and judgement of the court is and I do hereby adjudge and order that you Edward Foley be taken from the bar of this court where you now stand to the place from whence you came, her majesty's prison in the county of Cork and that you be kept there until Saturday the 9th day of January, which be in the year of our lord 1897 and that you be taken on that day to the common place of execution within the walls of the prison in which you shall be confined, and that you be then and there hanged by the neck until you are dead and that your body be buried within the precincts of the prison in which you shall have been then confined and may God have mercy on your soul."

Foley was said to have remained cool while the judge was sentencing him but then began to shake. Before he had the chance to become more emotional he was removed from the court.

For the first few days after his sentence of doom, Foley seemed indifferent to it; he slept well in jail and took his meals. But this changed as the days wore on; he struggled to sleep, turned to religion and expressed his regret for what he had done. Maybe it was only then that he realised the position he was in and refused to see any visitors in the jail.

Despite the terrible crime Edward Foley had carried out, in mid December there was a petition sent to the Lord Lieutenant for a reprieve from the death sentence. Foley had given himself up and admitted it right from the start. By doing this and pleading guilty he was denied a trial and verdict. It was now argued that if he had a trial, the jury may have recommended him to mercy. An anonymous letter to the Cork Examiner suggested that Foley was driven to believing his wife was unfaithful by continual pestering by his co-workers. They said that over time this led to his mental state and temporary insanity which overtook him. Even Foley had admitted to the police that he was often mocked and jeered at work concerning his wife and children. When arrested, he had told the police "they won't be laughing at me on the quays anymore now".

In jail, Edward Foley was now quietly resigned to the fate that awaited him and told of his regret at every opportunity.

It was Monday the 21st of December when Foley was informed that he had gotten a reprieve from the sentence of death. His reaction to the news was indifference; maybe at that point, he was resigned to die and it seemed better than years of regret. Now instead of the hangman, he faced penal servitude for the remainder of his life. On New Year's Eve Foley was transferred to Mountjoy, it had to be done quietly for fear of a demonstration on the streets or at the train station. News reporters got wind of it and watched his every move on the train to Dublin. There was nothing to report though, Foley's mood was quiet and once at Mountjoy, he would end his days there.

Cornelius Foley, his wife Julia and his daughter moved out of the lodge at Horsehead to live nearer Douglas and Julia died the following year.

Brien's Betrayal
Newcestown 1828

On the 4th of May Hanora Brien, a fifty year old housewife was found dead at her home near the village of Newcestown. Her body bore all the signs of a struggle and marks of strangulation could be seen on her throat. Her arms were badly bruised from her desperate attempts to get away from whoever had their hand to her throat.

The police under Mr Watkins searched the area and they found her husband James Brien acting suspiciously, trying to escape. James had spent years in the militia as a soldier but had worked as a labourer for the last number of years.

An inquest was held by Coroner James O'Brien who was helped by local magistrate Maskelyne Alcock from Roughgrove. They had no actual evidence against her husband, just a suspected motive. The inquest viewed the body and could see the marks of fingers on her neck. They heard that Honora Brien had died of strangulation.

After several hours of hearing the evidence, the jury found a verdict of wilful murder against James Brien. A coroners warrant was issued against him on the charge which was enough back then to have him sent for trial on the capital charge. The only motive for him killing his wife was a rumour that he was involved with another woman who had money. She had lent him money on several occasions which he had used to buy pigs and he wanted to marry her.

With a coroners warrant there was no need for a magisterial investigation and James Brien was sent to jail to await his fate. There were never more executions than in the 1820s, one didn't have to commit murder to be hung. Many convicted of lesser crimes were sentenced to death. Murderers were denied a Christian burial. So if evidence was found against James Brien there was no doubt that he would be dead by the end of the summer.

On the third day of the Cork Spring Assizes in August, James Brien was brought before Baron Pennefather. The crown lacking actual evidence against Brien had decided to reduce the charge to that of manslaughter and he duly pleaded guilty to the reduced charge. At the start of the Assizes that year Pennefather had commented that the number of serious cases before him was less than normal, just seven murder and eight rape cases.

Newcestown as it is in more recent times.

But one case at the Assizes did stand out and completely overshadowed an ordinary wife murder. Captain William Stewart of the ship Mary Russell was on trial for killing seven of his crewmen in a frenzied attack aboard the ship while en route from the West Indies to Cork. The great Daniel O'Connell was to defend the captain but failed to make it.

So the Newcestown murder disappeared and was completely forgotten about soon after. It was a particularly unusual case in that at no point was any evidence given against the accused whatsoever. Or put another way everyone knew he did it but no one could prove it.

A Brother's Plight
Kinsale 1838

Ireland in the 1830s offered little in the way of prospects for an ordinary young man. With a population of eight million people and the vast majority living directly off the land something had to give and it would in the next few years. Until then every generation did very little different than the one before, it was a struggle to survive.

One option of survival was to join the British Army or Navy, it must have seemed like an exciting life and an opportunity to see the world. In September of 1838 two young lads, John Allen and Florence Mahony set out to Kinsale intending to enlist in the 36th regiment. But once there they changed their minds and decided against taking the Queen's shilling.

On the way home the pair met John's older brother William who had been sent to look for him. Now that he had caught him before enlisting they decided to turn again towards Kinsale. None of them had seen the town before and felt as they had come this far they might as well.

Maybe they enjoyed the town a bit much as they stayed till after dark. Now in the darkness they probably regretted not going home sooner. The lads had only made it out of the town near Camphill when they met two local men on the road.

One of the men was leading a horse and as they passed the horse slipped on a rock. Quickly he turned to John Allen and in the darkness accused him of interfering with the horse. John denied the charge against him as did his friends but soon he found himself knocked down on the road by the owner of the horse.

John got up and attempted to retaliate but the man got the upper hand and knocked him again. This time lying on the road he received several kicks before he got himself up.

Meanwhile, the other man with the horse became excited and called out Murder. At the same time, he grabbed a stone and lashed out flinging it at William Allen who up to then had only been a bystander. William got a blow to the head and fell to the ground helplessly.

Six or seven more locals arrived intent on trouble and turned on Mahony. One of the men with the horse realised what they had done, talked them down and they all left, most likely knowing they had gone too far.

John rushed to his brother's side, after all, if he had not run off to Kinsale they would not be here. William was in no fit state to walk home to the city and instead they found lodging nearby. But even the following morning there was no hope of setting out for home with William's condition. John and Florence must have been racked with guilt looking at William thrown there helplessly and they could do nothing for him. They reported the attack to the police and Head Constable Condon helped them out by looking into the matter.

By Saturday William's condition had worsened and they were forced to take him to the local hospital. William succumbed to his dreadful head injury and died in the hospital. By now Head Constable Condon was in pursuit of the men who attacked Allen. On Sunday morning Condon tracked down the suspects who were local men living very close by where it had occurred. Cornelius Keohane and Laurence Flynn were arrested pending the verdict of the inquest.

The following morning the inquest was held with the suspects present. Both men were identified as being involved. John Allen and Florence Mahony recognised them in front of a big crowd in the court.

The inquest heard that it was Flynn who had first attacked John Allen but Keohane carried out the attack with the stone. The jury had no trouble reaching a verdict that William Allen died as a result of a blow of a stone to the right side of his head inflicted by Cornelius Keohane who was aided and abetted by Laurence Flynn. Back then with such a verdict, a coroner's warrant could be issued which was enough to send the men to trial at the next Assizes in Cork on the capital charge.

After the inquest, the Sovereign of Kinsale who led the town Corporation agreed to cover the expenses for the funeral. It was only then that the two friends who had set out looking for adventure could return home with the body and dreadful news.

There is no record that either Flynn or Keohane were ever brought to trial which is unusual as there was such evidence against them. Even if the charges against them were reduced to manslaughter they would have faced a life of penal servitude or transportation.

Left for Dead
Tullyland Bandon 1930

Just outside Bandon in the townland of Tullyland an unusual package was found at the side of the road. Inside a black bag wrapped in a cloth and a white pillow was the body of a newborn baby girl. Detective Sergeant Peter Kenny from Bandon was called but it was dark for hours before he arrived that night. He began an investigation to track down who had left it there. In the baby's hand was a few blades of grass and a label in the package had the words "Connolly Kinsale".

The Gardaí knew that they were most likely looking for a young unmarried woman who had recently given birth. Dr Denis Hennessy was called to the barracks in Bandon and the following morning carried out a post mortem. At the inquest, the doctor told how he believed the baby had been born alive but could not tell how long after it had died.

Later that day after making a few inquiries the guards headed towards Ballinspittle. In the townland of Kilkerran, they went to the house of Daniel O'Driscoll and found his twenty year old daughter unwell in bed. Mary O'Driscoll said she was sick in bed for a few days but had managed to get up that day for a while. She was cautioned by the sergeant but denied having giving birth. As sick as she was Mary got out of bed at the guards request and got dressed. It was then that Sergeant Kenny found a letter under the mattress to a local man, Tadhg Hunt. As the guards were reading the letter, Mary gave in. She made a statement and admitted to giving birth.

Now that everything was known, a doctor could be called for Mary and she could get the medical attention she needed. The following morning Dr McCarthy arrived at the house and found her condition so bad he recommended she go to hospital. Later detective Kenny arranged for her to be taken to Kinsale Hospital.

In the early hours of the morning, the guards went to Hunt's farm in Ballyhandle and found twenty eight year old Tadhg Hunt in bed. He was cautioned by the Sergeant but denied all knowledge of the baby found at the side of the road. On the way back to the barracks, Hunt realised that Mary had made a statement so he also gave in and admitted knowledge of the baby.

On the 7th of November, the case came before Judge Crotty at the Bandon District Court. Tadhg was called by his full name Timothy Hunt and charged with conspiring with Mary O'Driscoll that they wilfully, feloniously and with malice aforethought murdered an unnamed female baby born to Mary O'Driscoll.

Thomas Healy State Solicitor led the case for the prosecution while Hunt was represented by Mr Neville and Mary O'Driscoll who was not present was represented by P.J O Driscoll.

Inspector Deeney stated that both accused should be charged together and asked for a remand of 14 days to complete their inquires.

A month later the case had not moved on a bit. Again at the Bandon District Court Detective Sergeant Kenny asked for a remand saying he still had more inquiries to make and needed more time. Healy agreed with a remand saying how Mary was still nowhere near fit enough to appear in court.

Neville made it clear in court that he believed the murder charge against his client was not justified. He asked for bail for Hunt saying his father was a large farmer and a substantial sum could be put up. Healy, who had some sympathy, asked when he had ever seen such a serious case where an accused got bail. Neville replied that there was no hope of ever securing a murder conviction, but Healy was not backing down. Eventually, justice Crotty refused bail and Hunt was remanded till a later date.

It was the Friday before Christmas when the pair were actually charged in court and evidence was heard. The state charged them "That on November 4th 1930 the said Mary O'Driscoll and Timothy Hunt did at Kilkerran conspire to murder an unnamed female infant, born to the said Mary O'Driscoll, and at the same time and place they did, wilfully and feloniously and with malice aforethought kill and murder the said infant".

Dr McCarthy told how on the morning of the 7th of November he was called to O'Driscoll's house. He found Mary in bed and very weak so he recommended she be taken to hospital. While he treated her, she admitted to him that she had given birth to a baby the Tuesday before.

The townland of Tullyland somewhere near to where the wrapped up body was found

Dr Denis Hennessy, the medical officer in Bandon, told how he was called to the Garda Barracks in South Main Street on the 5th of November. There he saw the dead body of a female baby in a black bag. It was the following morning he carried out the post mortem where he concluded that the baby was healthy and had been born alive. He said the death was caused simply by exposure as he found no signs of violence of the body. He also said that lack of care and attention, as well as malnutrition, contributed to the death.

Detective Kenny from Bandon gave the Garda evidence of finding the black bag in Tullyland and about questioning Mary O'Driscoll. It was he who had found the letter under the mattress and he produced it in court. Mr Neville for the defence objected to the letter being used as evidence but it was dismissed. Kenny told how when he found it he read out a few lines of it and as a result, Mary gave a statement. Later in Kinsale Hospital, he showed her the black bag and she made another statement "I see the bag produced now and it is the bag in which I put my baby and left it in the field for Tadhg Hunt to take away".

He then went on to the arrest of Timothy Hunt and how he at first denied any knowledge of a baby. Kenny said it was after arresting Hunt on the way to the barracks he stopped the car at a crossroads near O'Driscoll's. Hunt asked had he seen Mary already and what had she said.

Kenny told him she had already given a statement admitting to having a baby and leaving it in a field. It was then Hunt also gave in and admitted his part in it, being cautioned before making a statement. Both defence solicitors objected to this statement being allowed, saying that it was not voluntarily given and on the grounds of how it was obtained from him. The judge noted the objections but allowed the statement to be allowed as evidence.

Inspector Deeney who accompanied Kenny when both defendants gave statements was then questioned but revealed little that had not already been heard. Under cross examination, he was asked how sick and incapable was Mary O'Driscoll when she made a statement but he didn't answer. Neville asked several questions, was Hunt threatened or intimidated in any way to give a statement but he denied it. He recalled Detective McKenna writing down the statement at the side of the road but couldn't explain why the first two lines had been left blank. He did say that the fountain pen ran out while McKenna was writing and the statement had to be finished by pencil.

Detective McKenna gave a similar account of being present when the bag was found and when both defendants gave statements. Neville questioned him in detail about taking the statement from Hunt. McKenna admitted that over two hours after the statement being taken he added two lines to the start of it in the presence of Hunt and both of them again signed it. He contended that the statement was not altered or added to in any way, he only added a title or heading to it. McKenna explained that they had not taken a statement in Hunt's house due to his father Armiger being ill at the time. When asked again by Neville about the first statement Hunt had given, McKenna explained the circumstances of how it came about. He claimed they stopped at the crossroads to meet several more of the Gardaí. All four in the car got out and it was Detective Kenny who walked up the road with the accused. When they returned Hunt had agreed to make a statement which was taken from him at the crossroads and signed there and then.

When Justice Crotty heard the evidence against them, he reduced the charge to manslaughter and returned them for trial in the Circuit Court in the New Year. Bail was set at £400 and two sureties of £200 for Hunt and £400 for Mary.

Another month later at the Cork Criminal Circuit Court, Justice Kenny presided over the case. The defendants were charged with manslaughter and conspiring to kill a baby. Now answering the charge and pleading guilty was Timothy and Mary Hunt. Once the evidence was heard their legal counsel pleaded for leniency saying how they were since married. They had married in Ballinspittle church only a week before. Due to the circumstances and hearing that they were now married Justice Kenny took a lenient view of it and he bound the defendants to the peace for twelve months.

What was it in the thirties and decades afterwards that drove those unmarried and pregnant to do such drastic things? At the time almost three quarters of men in Ireland between 25 and 34 were single. Many marriages were arranged, and some were forced to cover up a potential scandal. No matter how common or natural it is, getting pregnant outside of marriage was seen as a scandal. It was probably well known back then how bad the maternity institutions were and how badly the women were treated there. Society itself was very much to blame for scandalising young women. The government gave the church free rein to deal with them as they saw fit. Families feared that knock on the door and the shame of their daughter being taken away to an institution. As bad and all as the institutions were it will never be known how many didn't get taken away and covered up the birth of their baby.

This was just fourteen years since the 1916 proclamation promised to cherish all the children of the nation equally. Although they were referring to all the people of the country it still applies. With the martyrs of the rising dead, these ideals fell by the wayside and even with independence, the inequality continued in different ways.

Unfortunately, it was many decades later before society came to terms with it and no longer relied on the church that profiteered from the plight of young women. Strangely contraception was only banned in 1935 but would not have been available before that anyway. It was 1980 before the law changed and contraception was legalised and another 39 years before abortion was legalised in 2019. Whether you agree with abortion or not it seems better than what a woman felt forced to do in the thirties leaving babies to die at the side of the road.

Kiely's Killed
Nohoval 1885

A Sunday evening in the little village of Nohoval, the pubs are busy and some had been there for most of the day. It's coming to the end of the only day off in the week for many back then. On the street outside with the first signs of spring, men are gathered in groups chatting and watching those coming and going.

After some scuffle near Quinn's pub, a young man Jeremiah Kiely comes staggering up the road. The few standing by the church wall know him and quickly realise it's not a beating he has gotten. Kiely's hands are grasping his stomach in pain, he has been stabbed twice.

Someone ran down the village and came upon Maurice Quinn still standing there on the road. Quinn said he was only sorry he didn't kill him. He is asked why he has done such a thing but makes no reply. Maurice Quinn was then held there until the police arrived on the scene and then handed over. It was not going to be a whodunit as the sergeant was told "this is the prisoner, the man who committed the deed". All the while Quinn said nothing and made no attempt to deny it.

The police quickly marched him off to the nearest barrack in Ballyfeard about two miles away. Many in the village were confused about the reason for the whole affair. It seems Maurice Quinn had a falling out with his uncle James. Jeremiah Kiely had no part in this but intervened in an attempt to make peace between uncle and nephew. Maurice was intending to get his uncle with the knife and managed it, but he also got Jeremiah. Jeremiah had come out of it much worse off than anyone else.

There was only one problem, if he didn't intend to stab Kiely why had he stabbed him twice? It's hard enough to stick a knife in someone once but twice surely was no accident.

Back then doctors could do little to prevent infection in a stomach wound. There were no antibiotics and any operation only risked further infection. Dr Morgan could do little but attend to Kiely and hope for an improvement.

On Tuesday the 3rd of March Jeremiah Kiely died after suffering since Sunday evening. The man who had stabbed him was Maurice Quinn a twenty two year old fisherman from Kinure near Oysterhaven.

The inquest was held by coroner Horgan on the 5th of March. Dr Morgan told of the injuries he had found, a wound in the small intestine and another in the bladder. He said these corresponded to the stab wounds and resulted in Kiely's death. The jury accepted the coroner's suggestion and returned an obvious verdict that Jeremiah Kiely had died from the stab wounds he had received in Nohoval that Sunday.

Maurice Quinn was not present at the inquest but the following day he was escorted to the Tracton Petty sessions by armed police. He was charged with maliciously stabbing Jeremiah Kiely who had died as a result and also with inflicting injuries on James Quinn, also by stabbing.

Unusually it was Fr James O'Keeffe parish priest who spoke first. He condemned the violence in his parish and said drinking on Sunday was to blame for it all.

Solicitor O'Hea instead of trying to prevent the case from going to trial began by asking for the opposite. It seems like he had already given in when he asked, if it was to go to trial could the hearing be completed that day. His client he said was poor and could not suffer a remand, he wanted no delay and hoped it would be heard at the Spring Assizes later that month.

James Quinn, uncle of the accused, who had been stabbed was not in court that day but a statement he had given was read out.

O'Hea reserved his defence that day and was saving it for the Assizes. The magistrates from what was heard concluded that there was a prima facie case to answer. They then did what O'Hea wanted and duly returned the case for trial at the upcoming Assizes.

On the 27th of March at the Spring Assizes, Maurice Quinn was charged with murder before Justice Andrews. Considering Kiely had been stabbed on the 1st of March and died on the 3rd it was very quick to come before a jury, but with the case being so straight forward the prosecution was sure of a conviction.

However, Maurice Quinn pleaded not guilty and was defended by barrister Tim Healy who was also an M.P. Mr O'Hea the solicitor who had represented him before was also present. Mr Green King's Counsel led the case for the Crown prosecution.

Opening the case Green stated that this was no ordinary pub brawl gone wrong. He said Quinn wilfully and deliberately carried it out, what he said at the time proved this. The crown claimed there was a history between the men and were sure the jury would return a verdict of guilty against him.

The barracks near Ballyfeard where Quinn was brought to.

So sure was the prosecution that they had no actual witness that saw what happened. Or maybe nobody was willing to come forward and testify against Quinn.

Daniel McCarthy told the court that he knew both the deceased and the accused men. On the first of March, he was talking to John O'Neill by the church wall when Kiely approached. He knew something was wrong and Kiely showed him the stab wounds in his stomach.

He went towards the village with O'Neill and came upon Maurice Quinn outside Quinn's pub. He knew Quinn had done it and grabbed him by the collar saying he should be ashamed of himself for what he had done. He said Maurice made an attempt to break away but O'Neill helped detain him. They asked what it was all about and Quinn told them of a falling out three years before. The Sergeant arrived not long after and they handed him over.

When cross examined the first question he was asked was "did you see any blow struck" and he answered "no not at all" but Kiely had told them it was Quinn. Not only had he not seen Quinn attack Kiely but he had not seen a knife in Quinn's hand.

John O'Neill gave a very similar account to what McCarthy had. He thought it was about half five that Sunday evening he was standing by the church gate when it all kicked off.

He recalled helping McCarthy but said a crowd had gathered outside the pub. O'Neill said the reason he got involved was one of the crowd called out that Quinn might stab McCarthy. He asked Quinn that evening what it was all about but didn't understand it at the time. Up until then, he had not known of any dispute between them.

Sergeant O'Sullivan told of arresting Quinn in the village of Nohoval. He was in the barracks in Ballyfeard when he got a report of the stabbing two miles away. The sergeant set out for Nohoval with two constables and found Quinn detained by McCarthy. Back in the barrack, he cautioned Quinn about making a statement and then examined his clothes.

He was then cross examined by Healy, the sergeant said a person told him the knife had been burned in Quinn's pub but did not reveal who told him. He was also told that the knife had been burned by Patrick Quinn but he was not being charged as an accomplice. He made it clear he did not want the jury to think it was Maurice who destroyed the knife.

Healy asked "would it not occur to you, as an experienced police officer, that the person who would destroy evidence of crime would be the guilty party? Sergeant Sullivan said "generally so" but then told that the accused and Patrick Quinn were cousins.

The sergeant had never known Maurice Quinn to be in any trouble before that day and said Quinn was a candidate for joining the R.I.C. It had been mentioned that drink was the source of the trouble but the Sergeant reckoned there was no sign of drink on any that day.

Patrick Quinn, first cousin of the accused, the man who was alleged to have hidden the knife was called and questioned by Mr Moriarty. He made no attempt to hide his part, Patrick said he heard a noise outside Murphy's pub that evening and went out to see Maurice with a knife in his hand. He took it from him broke the blade from the handle and threw it into the fire in Quinn's pub.

He then went outside with Daniel Dempsey and saw Kiely against the wall in the yard of Murphy's pub. Patrick saw that Kiely had been stabbed but let Dempsey with him and went home.

When Healy questioned him for the defence he revealed that after taking the knife he saw James Quinn and his son hit Maurice. He said they turned on Maurice without the knife and knocked him down but Patrick helped him up. Patrick also claimed that earlier in the evening he heard Jeremiah Kiely challenging someone calling for the "best man in Oysterhaven".

Constable Ryan who had taken Quinn to the barracks that evening was produced. He told that in the barracks Maurice asked to have James Quinn brought to him saying he would forgive him. At the time Ryan didn't know who he was referring to and was told by Maurice that he was the other man he stabbed. Ryan said that Maurice seemed confused about how Kiely was stabbed and told how Kiely was not involved but tried to make peace between them.

Maurice also told the police that he was not drunk at all as he had only shared four and a half gallons between five people. (For those of us too young for the imperial system it was thirty six pints of porter shared between five of them).

In the barracks Sunday evening Quinn was worried and asked Ryan would Kiely die and would he hang for it saying "I suppose I will be transported for it anyway". Quinn wasn't aware that transportation had ceased decades before instead so he faced years of hard labour or execution. The defence declined to cross examine Constable Ryan.

Dr Morgan described the post mortem he had carried out on Kiely and that he had died as a direct result of the stab wounds he had received.

Jeremiah Kiely's dying declaration was proved by the justice of the peace Mr Henry Whitney from Nohoval. All he needed to read from it was "Maurice Quinn had a knife in his hand and stabbed me with it twice in the belly". For a dying declaration to be legal the accused man needed to also be present and allowed to pose questions to the dying man. It was heard that Quinn had been present but said nothing, nor asked a question to Kiely.

With that, the prosecution closed its case confident in securing a conviction.

Denis Collins was called by the defence and gave Healy a slightly different account of what had already been heard. He claimed to hear Kiely challenge the accused that evening with "I'll fight you, I'll fight you" and then hit Quinn a few times with his fist. He saw Patrick take the knife away but didn't see Maurice do anything to Kiely.

Timothy Healy did what he was well known for and gave a very eloquent speech for Quinn. Healy claimed there was no conclusive evidence produced by the crown to show it was Maurice Quinn who stabbed Kiely. He concluded by asking the jury to acquit Quinn on the charge against him.

Justice Andrews summing up told the jury that if they believed Quinn had stabbed him they could not acquit him. However, if they thought it was not premeditated they may decide to find a verdict of manslaughter.

The jury took almost three quarters of an hour and returned with the verdict guilty of manslaughter. Quinn's sentencing was deferred to the end of the Assizes and he was sent back to prison.

It was Saturday morning when Quinn was brought before Justice Andrews for sentencing. The judge addressed Quinn saying despite him being indicted for murder the jury took the more lenient view of manslaughter. He had read some reports of Kiely's previous good character but found the attack to be most severe. For that reason and that a man's life was lost Andrews said it was his duty to not go easy on him. Quinn was given ten years of penal servitude and was transferred to Mountjoy Prison to serve out the remainder of his years in prison.

The Ballinhassig Massacre
Ballinhassig 1845

In the year 1845, a feud between two factions in Ballinhassig and Ballygarvan was common knowledge. Everyone knew that it would come to a head in a fight at the fair in Ballinhassig

Back then a country fair wasn't just when farmers came to sell their produce or livestock and purchase necessities. It was much more than that, traders and amusements of all sorts set up their tents in the fair green. Farm labourers often had the day off to come to town and meet up with friends and relations; it was the greatest social outing of the year. There was a dark side to fairs, lots of drink was consumed which led to trouble breaking out. At one time in Ireland, a third of all murders occurred when returning home after a fair.

This trouble was different though as it was planned and known about for weeks and the police or local magistrates had every opportunity to prevent it.

At the fair that day the police numbered 18, led by sub-inspector Kelly from Kinsale. They patrolled the village but there was not the slightest sign of trouble.

About eight that night most of the fairgoers had left for home and the tents of the fair were being taken down. A man came riding on a horse shouting and beating it with his hat. A crowd armed with sticks gathered about him anticipating what would happen next. On the horse was Thomas Sullivan better known as his nickname the Ranter. He was said to be the leader of one faction. He was getting revenge for his brother and challenged a man called Neill. Quickly a crowd gathered about them and there were men on each side ready to fight. How much fighting went on that day or how long it lasted is not clear but soon enough Inspector Kelly and his police posse were on the scene.

The crowd protested to the Ranter being taken into custody and several of his friends promised to take him directly home away from the fight instead. Nothing would do Kelly but to arrest the Ranter in front of a big crowd who began to turn on the police.

Kelly insisted that he would have to be taken into custody and appear before a magistrate.

Some of the local magistrates William Meade, John Molony and John Biggs had been at the fair during the day but they had retired to Molony's Ballinaboy house which was not far away. Some said that the magistrates could see what was going on but chose not to intervene.

Several attempts were made to rescue the Ranter from his captors but the police were having none of it. With the crowd pressing in on them the police made for the dispensary in the middle of the village which was used as a temporary barrack for the fair. It was here they held the Ranter. Once inside several of the police re-emerged put their backs to the wall and fixed their bayonets ready for trouble. All the time the crowd pressed in against the police but there was not much trouble until a few stones were thrown from the back of the crowd. Several others had gone around to the other side of the dispensary and were attempting to gain access by the roof. No doubt stones were thrown but the police knew they would be.

No attempt was made by the police to stop those on the roof, instead, they turned on the crowd on the street. There was no warning at all given by the police nor was the Riot Act readout which should have been. Suddenly shots rang out with two or three police emerging from the dispensary before running back in to reload, more fired at the same time from the window. The volleys of shots continued even when the unarmed crowd fled. This resulted in many of those hit being struck defencelessly from behind while trying to flee. In the midst of the chaos, the Ranter managed to escape the dispensary and survived being shot.

With the crowd dispersed, Kelly and his constables emerged from the dispensary and charged through the chaos with their bayonets to the barracks. At one point on the hill, the police turned around and fired a few more shots for no reason at all killing one more on the spot.

When they got back to the barracks only one Constable, Dawson had sustained any injuries. Back in the village, it resembled a war zone with bodies everywhere. Some just lay where they fell while others were helped out of the village by their friends and relations. It would have been easier to get help if all those wounded remained in the village but they most likely feared being shot at again and so desperately wanted the safety of their own homes. Desperate families could be seen fleeing the village that night in all directions carrying their loved ones.

Word spread quickly throughout the countryside of what had occurred. That night a huge body of police arrived under sub-inspector Walker but their presence was not welcome. Several local priests also turned up and did what they could, administering the last rites to several in the village. Dr Tresilian did what he could for the injured in the village but many of those wounded fled from Ballinhassig.

Later that night the weather turned with torrential rain, but still Dr Evers set out for Ballinhassig hearing of the tragedy. By that time those injured were scattered far and wide as many had been taken to their homes all over the locality. He went from house to house working under the light of a candle. He worked through the night but found many had already succumbed to their injuries. In all the houses visited that night women and children wept for their loved ones.

Depiction of the shooting that appeared in the papers at the time, image courtesy of the National Library of Ireland.

One of the first he came on that night was Jeremiah Coughlan a small farmer from Skehanagh. His body was lifeless, having been shot in the back and the bullet passing right through his lungs.

Moving on the doctor found John Walsh a young man from Carrigaline in a house in the village. He had been shot in the leg and the bone had been shattered to pieces. Despite the bone splinters sticking out the doctor managed to bandage him up and he was most grateful. Evers suggested he be taken to hospital for amputation for any hope of survival.

Map of Ballinhassig Village showing where the shooting occurred, image courtesy of the National Library of Ireland

In Adamstown, he found Maurice Corcoran at home in bed with his wife and four children at his bedside. A bullet wound between the ribs had gone right through the chest. Maurice was vomiting blood and the doctor knew he was dying and could do nothing.

The doctor then went on to John Desmond's house where he found him in a similar position in bed. He had two gunshot wounds, one in the hip and was suffering terrible pain. Dr Evers had to work quickly and extracted one of the balls and dressed the wounds. He had little hope for Desmond who had only married months before.

Moving on to Ballinphelic the doctor treated Richard Barrett a farmer's son who had been shot in the hand.

In Liskillea he found Jeremiah Conway shot in the right shoulder blade but the bullet exited through the armpit. He suffered terrible blood loss and was weak. Doctor Evers had little hope for him surviving at all but sent him to the hospital anyway.

Not far away at Rerour was another young man named John Walsh who also got shot between the ribs with the bullet passing right through the chest and exiting at the armpit.

Then the doctor came to the house of Julia whose maiden name was Holland but had recently married O'Callaghan. She had been shot at the Bridge after the police had left the dispensary. Her injuries were similar to others, shot from behind and the bullet lacerated the lungs causing internal bleeding. She was said to have been fired upon by Constable Dawson while she had a child in her arms.

Another depiction showing the shooting from the dispensary, image courtesy of the National Library of Ireland.

Returning to the village the doctor met Michael Donnelly an old man who had been shot in the right arm and suffered so much blood loss that he was weak. He was lucky that the bone was intact and for once Evers was confident he would recover with care and attention.

How the doctor managed to find and attend to so many that night was a feat in itself but there were many others the doctor did not manage to visit. Most had been removed to their own houses and were scattered in all directions. Cornelius Forde from Ballynavohee was shot dead on the spot having been hit in the chest. Charles McCarthy from Ballyheada was shot dead at the door of his cousin's house in the village, he left a wife and four children behind.

By the following morning there was hardly a soul to be seen out in the village, by then there was seven dead and twenty two more seriously wounded. Dr Harris had also arrived the night before but spent his time attending to Constable Dawson who had been injured after the firing had ceased. Of all the seriously wounded there were so many stories of lucky escapes and the death count could have been so much higher. One old woman had been grazed on the nose by a bullet and with another shot only sustained a minor injury to the forehead.

As bad as it was it could have been much worse. In total thirty two shots were fired in the village and two more while the police retreated. Each policeman was armed with twenty shots but none fired more than four. Most likely the police would have fired more but the unarmed crowd had cleared.

The condemnation of the police behaviour that night was instant and widespread amongst the poor ordinary people. Many blamed the local magistrates for knowing trouble was brewing at the fair and not being in attendance to direct the police. One gentleman John O'Brien from the Western Road in Cork who had witnessed some of the action spoke out. He had been dining with Mr Keller who owned the Mills and was returning home in his horse and gig when trouble first broke out. He directed several people away as he heard the firing but was sure it was blanks being fired at the time. He met the police charging back to their barracks afterwards and noted that Inspector Kelly seemed very excited. O'Brien told him then that there was no need for what he had done, all he needed to do was to speak civilly to the crowd and they would have complied.

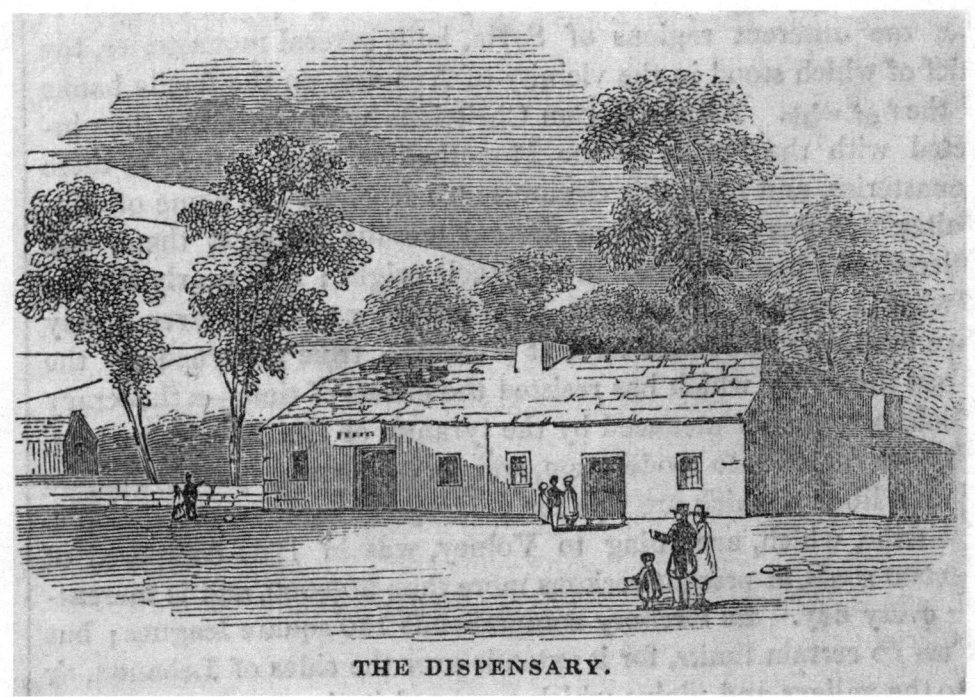

THE DISPENSARY.

The Dispensary in Ballinhassig, image courtesy of the National Library of Ireland

The following morning several magistrates poured into the village one armed with a band of dragoons but it was all too late. Only medical help was needed now for the poor misfortunes suffering badly and not getting the constant care that Dawson had. The police were afraid and it took a large posse of them under sub-inspector Green to escort Dawson to hospital in Cork.

On Wednesday Coroner Franklin Baldwin arrived and set about, with the help of several local magistrates, empanelling a jury for the inquest. Normally an inquest jury consisted of respectable men from the locality such as shopkeepers, publicans, farmers and the like but this time was different. It was made up of the gentry from all over the area, as far away as Kinsale.

On Thursday morning when the inquest opened the coroner wished to have all twenty three names on the panel called for the jury. Daniel Lombard from Mount Mary Ballinhassig was to be the foreman. Several of those called tried to get out of it giving medical and all sorts of excuses but the coroner was having none of it. Benjamin Roberts from Annaghmore

House near Innishannon made every excuse he could. He even claimed he had never seen a dead body before and that his hearing was very bad. He was asked in a very low voice how long his hearing was bad and answered five or six years, only to be told he could hear well enough.

You could not blame those trying to get out of jury duty in this case as their first task that morning was to set out to view the bodies. The coroner called the list of names of the seven who were dead, Jeremiah Coughlan of Skehanagh, Charles McCarthy Ballyheada, Cornelius Forde from Ballynavohee and Tim Kerigan Ballyclonaghy. Three from Adamstown were Julia O'Callaghan better known as her maiden name Holland, Maurice Corcoran and John Desmond.

The coroner with several magistrates and the twenty three jurors set out to view the bodies. With so many dead it took hours travelling the countryside and it was six that evening before they returned to Ballinhassig. All those on the jury were bound over by £100 to appear the following morning.

When the inquest sat Friday morning in the loft of the Mills, one magistrate told of the miserable day before viewing the bodies. The weather had been the same as Thursday night with terrible rain all day. He described the pitiful scene at each house, the crowd of jurors magistrates, priests and doctors had to coax the grieving relations out so they could do what they needed. At one house a wife refused to leave her husband's side and had to be removed forcibly to let the doctors do their job, in another house a woman fainted. In each and every house they met women and children crying for their loved ones and never before had such a dreadful sight been seen. Even the Coroner agreed that he had also never witnessed such scenes.

From the get go that morning, the proceedings seemed very different to a normal inquest. For a start the jury members were not what you would normally have, also every magistrate in the district was present. Then several legal representatives approached the coroner. A Mr Walsh answered for the friends and relations of the deceased. Another, Mr Scannell wouldn't say who he represented but Walsh accused him of being there for the police.

Eventually, police inspector Percy agreed to release a list of police who had been armed in Ballinhassig that night. List of names of the police: Constable John Dunn, Sub Constables Michael Brennan and

Thomas Corcoran from Ballymartle Station. Constable William Hannan, Sub Constable William Coughlan, John O'Farrell and Thomas Walsh from Ballyfeard Station. From the Carrigaline Station, Constable Richard Piggott, Sub Constables Patrick Carroll and Patrick Sullivan. From Wilton police station was Sub Constables Anthony Ryan, Andrew Douglas and John Daly. Douglas police Station Sub Constable John Ryan and Robert Agar. From Ballinhassig was acting constable Denis Dawson and Kinsale Station Sub Constable Richard Hickson. Also present was Sub Constables Timothy Fogarty, Daniel Willis and James Donaldson.

The first witness Dr Evers was questioned by Mr Walsh and he described in detail the injuries he had found on the bodies he examined. All had died from gunshot wounds and all but one of the bodies had been shot in the back or side.

Scannell's interest in the case became obvious when he was permitted to cross examine the witnesses. He tried to get the doctor to say a man could be turned sideways when making an attack and subsequently get shot.

John Keller said he examined the dispensary at ten that night after the shooting. He found no signs of stones being thrown at it and every bottle on the shelves was intact.

Dr Wall told how he had examined the body of Julia Callaghan with Dr Tresilian. She had her back turned when shot, as the ball entered near the spine, passed through her lung and exited at the collar bone.

Again when Scannell got the chance he tried to make out she was stopping to get a missile when shot, throwing a stone or standing next to someone who was. Even when it was mentioned that Julia had a child in her arms at the time he still maintained she must have been up to no good.

Mr John O'Brien gave similar testimony as to the account he had given in the papers. He like many believed the police were firing blanks that night until he saw for himself the damage that was done.

The inquest began to get messy and very sidetracked when several more men claimed to be legally representing other parties. They claimed to have a right to get involved without stating who they stood for and insisted on examining witnesses. A juror spoke plainly through all the legal arguments saying "Mr Coroner we want evidence, not speeches" and eventually the proceedings moved on.

When it came to the direct evidence, Mr Walsh addressed the inquest and asked that the police and their inspector be produced as it was against them. The inquest was now shaping up to be more like a magisterial investigation than an inquest. Many knew well the likelihood of the law investigating police conduct, was slim so the inquest was the best chance. Walsh suggested adjourning until Monday to have the police present but the coroner insisted they carry on.

Edward Duggan was called and he explained that he lived in the fourth house from the cross, opposite the dispensary. He had been to the fair and it was as quiet as he had ever seen. Returning home he brought out a stool to his door and sat there as it was a summers evening. He saw a man dragged into the dispensary by the police and the crowd following closely behind. He said the police tried to keep them back with their bayonets but then went into the dispensary. Within seconds he heard the first volley of shots fired. Peering out he saw a man down on the street, in all he saw the police fire out of the dispensary three times. Then a few of them came out together, fired and went back in to load while others went out and fired.

On Saturday morning at the inquest, all the police involved except Dawson were produced. Mr Scannell made it clear that no shots were fired that evening until Kelly gave the orders to do so. He had no objection to questions being asked in the presence of the police as long as they would not be directly questioned.

Then Walsh asked, "if the seven persons whose bodies were viewed by the jury and whose death they met to enquire into came by their deaths in consequence of gunshot wounds fired by that party?"

This led to a long debate but Scannell was adamant they were a police force who were armed and acted under orders of their superior. Eventually, Walsh cleverly asked did those orders to fire cover all the shots fired that evening. Scannell admitted to not knowing the particulars of the case but said the superior officer felt it was "justified and necessary". Walsh pretty much repeated his question but the reply he got now was "the officer in charge cannot tell what took place in a particular place and if anything took place it is hard to call him to be responsible". Walsh kept up the pressure asking was any order given to cease firing and received the reply "certainly not".

Patrick Hurley from Ballyhooleen described to the inquest how he came to the fair in Ballinhassig just for a look around as so many others had. He heard the shots and saw the police firing in all directions from the dispensary. At the time he was standing in the middle of the crossroads and heard Julia O'Callaghan fall near him. He helped carry her away to a stream and put water on her face thinking she had only fainted but later realised she was dead.

Hurley said he knew Tom the Ranter and his brother Jerry, but not very well and could not tell one of the brothers from the other. He was asked did he see the Ranter riding a horse about at the fair and beating it with his hat but Hurley said it was Ted Goulding that was on the horse.

The inquest went on for days hearing the same evidence from many witnesses. Over the course of those days, four more died of their gunshot wounds sustained at the fair. They were John Hourihan, John Walsh, Tom Delea and Patrick Sullivan.

At the inquest several of the relations of the dead gave evidence. Even Charles Callaghan from Ballymartle was called. He told of being separated from his wife when he jumped over a wall into an orchard. When the firing ceased he found a crowd standing around the body of his wife and their three month old baby.

Several of the local magistrates were called but knew little in the way of details. Some had been to the fair during the day but had left by evening. All denied hearing the rumours that there would be trouble at the fair.

When it came to the defence of the police Mr Scannell called Sub Constable Richard Hickson. He had been at the fair that evening. This caused a sensation in court as well as several objections, but Scannell explained that Hickson had not carried a gun that night; he was an orderly for Kelly. This was why his name was not on the list of police supplied to the inquest.

He recalled a man on a horse, beating it with his hat. The man seemed cross and had many people with him. Hickson said "he appeared inclined to fight" the crowd had sticks and were shouting. When the man on the horse was arrested the mob pushed in around them and tried to prevent him from being taken away. He heard the people cry out "bualadh peelers" and reckoned there was two or three hundred present. The mob pushed in so close around the police, that it made it difficult to take the prisoner to the dispensary. Once there the stones rained down on them and several times Kelly implored them to back off. He heard the order to fix bayonets given but this made no effect on the angry crowd. When the orders were given to prime and load the guns the mob was still only feet away and were sure they would not be fired upon. According to Hickson with the window and door driven in by stones the police asked Kelly could they fire but he asked them to wait a while. Even the Ranter himself went to the window and beckoned the crowd to move on but he got struck by a stone.

They asked again to fire and this time Kelly gave in but asked that they fire steadily and not all at once. Two or three fired first and it was then that some of the crowd made a hole in the roof. Hickson said he only heard one more shot, four or five minutes later. A juror asked did they go outside to fire but he denied this saying the shots were fired from the windows or doorway.

Cross examined by Mr Walsh, Hickson swore that he was telling the truth. Walsh asked how long was it from the time they loaded until the first shot. He reckoned it was about five to ten minutes. Hickson also told that the men had asked Kelly three times could they fire. When asked the names of the men that fired that day he refused to tell.

Several more witnesses were called for the police; one was a local farmer Thomas Hornibrook. Another was thirteen year old Michael Hourigan who had only come to Ballinhassig with the police from Wilton. His father was the sergeant in there but was not at the fair.

Young Michael said the police were beaten into the dispensary by an angry mob armed with sticks who were throwing stones at them. From about thirty feet away he saw the police fix their bayonets but failed to drive the mob back.

Another big farmer James Warner from Castlewhite was called by Scannell. He admitted to seeing a fight and hearing shots fired. Warner would not commit to answering any questions directly, he also wouldn't estimate the size of the crowd or how long the fight went on. No matter how many questions were put to him the farmer maintained the same stance. He even refused to say that people were shot after hearing the shots and seeing them on the ground. From what he said it seems he walked out of the village passed people on the ground and did nothing to help anyone.

Even Scannell became frustrated and called him a "stupid devil" for repeatedly refusing to answer.

Denis Falvey told of being at the fair but left to dine at Mr Keller's. He left with John O'Brien about half seven and they encountered the crowd outside the dispensary where the police were trying to hold them back with bayonets. He saw a big stick thrown from the back of the crowd at the police but couldn't say if it struck anyone. It landed near the police chief and he thought Kelly seemed excited afterwards. He said the stones were thrown by fifteen or sixteen year old boys at the back of the crowd. They were not thrown by those at the front that the police were pushing back.

When the shots were fired he saw the crowd disperse and the boys went to the gable end of the dispensary to avoid the shots. It was then stones were thrown onto the roof of the dispensary. Falvey's evidence made a lot more sense than the witness before him. He recalled seeing Charles McCarthy shot in the back while running away and tried helping him into a house before leaving. He described the police leaving the dispensary as very disorderly. Falvey then went back to Mr Keller's.

Falvey swore that he had answered as honestly and fairly as he could. To Mr Scannell, he said, "I think the police got great cause to defend themselves and that for a while they showed great forbearance in the beginning." He couldn't describe the people at the front of the crowd as peaceable, they were shouting and pushing in on the police but he didn't see them throwing any stones. It was about two or three minutes he believed between the police going into the dispensary and the first shots fired. He reckoned the crowd gathered in the village was about a hundred people.

Scannell tried to get him to admit to making several statements. He denied several but admitting to saying "the police were justified in defending themselves but not in killing them".

Several jurors also posed questions. Falvey's assessment of the situation seemed very fair and balanced. He did think Charles McCarthy was wantonly shot while trying to escape and that the police were not justified in firing as much as they had. He had heard what he thought was twelve or fourteen shots fired that day.

When the local magistrate John Molony was called he admitted to being at home that night dining with Meade and Biggs, the other magistrates. He denied knowing there was going to be trouble at the fair but said he had been there earlier but not as a magistrate, he was there to deal in cattle. According to Molony the first he heard of trouble that night was about nine when Cornelius Keller came running to his house. He set out for the village at once with the other magistrates and found a wounded man just outside his own gate by the bridge.

After several days of hearing evidence and much legal argument, the inquest came to a close. Back then inquests were normally held the morning after death and were wrapped up in a matter of hours. A suspect could be named in the verdict and a coroner had the power to issue a warrant to have them arrested. In this case, though, the inquest seemed much more like a magisterial investigation with legal arguments from both sides.

From the 23 jurors, only nine decided upon a verdict of wilful murder. The remaining fourteen found for justifiable homicide which exonerated the police behaviour completely. Obviously, the police were satisfied with the verdict and were now confident there would be no further legal action. In some quarters there was an outcry and a call to have the police unarmed in future as was the case in England.

Neither the public nor the press agreed with the verdict and termed it the Ballinhassig Massacre. It wasn't the first or last in Ireland, in Cork, the Gortroe Massacre of 1832 was still clear in people's memory.

Within days a petition was signed by many notable people in Cork and sent to Mayor Richard Dowden, it read:

"To the right worshipful Richard Dowden Mayor, we the undersigned inhabitants of the City of Cork request you will call a public meeting to express to Her Majesty's government our opinion that an investigation before the coroner at Ballinhassig on the bodies of seven persons killed there by the Police force does not sufficiently satisfy the justice of the case. It being fully ascertained that there had been no provocation given to the police sufficient to justify an indiscriminate firing on the people. Likewise to express a hope that the use of firearms may be in future denied to the police force in Ireland as it is in England."

It was in turn sent to the Chief Secretary for Ireland Thomas Freemantle, and asked for the police conduct to be further investigated. It was never going to happen though for the government was always going to protect the police.

The reply from Mr Lucas the under Secretary in mid August firmly showed the English governments feelings towards the poor Irish people. It read "sees no grounds for any measure upon the part of the Executive Government in reference to the subject matter of that memorial".

The regulations of the police concerning firing at the public were:

397 *Wherever the necessity of firing should unfortunately arise, it ought to be at the leaders of a riot or the assailants of the police and if possible with effect. Firing over the heads of mobs engaged in an illegal pursuit must not be allowed, as a harmless fire, instead of intimidating would give confidence to the daring and the guilty.*

398 *Whenever police acting under the orders of a high or sub sheriff, magistrate or coroner, shall receive directions to fire, they must not upon any account fire, excepting by regular word of command from the senior constabulary officer or constable present, and the officer or constable must not give the word of command to fire unless distinctly required so to do by the high or sub sheriff, magistrate or coroner, under whose authority he may be acting. In cases where there shall be no magistrates or sheriff present and the police may be obliged to fire in their own defence, they will not do so without the express order of the officer, head or constable in charge who is just as responsible for such order as if he actually fired himself, and in all cases, the officer or other person in command must exercise the utmost forbearance consistent with the safety of his party before he shall give the order to fire and must in every instance exercise a humane discretion as to the extent of such firing.*

The police could argue that they had followed their rules but Sub Inspector Kelly did not seem as responsible for giving the orders as he should. Had he exercised the utmost forbearance? He hardly showed humane discretion when people running away were shot. The police rules state they must fire at the ringleaders, but men running away or a woman with a child in her arms don't seem too much like ringleaders.

There was a huge sense of unrest in the area for some time after and it showed itself in several ways. The local protestant schoolmaster Thomas Hornibrook had given evidence at the inquest for the police. Such was the ill feeling in the area Hornibrook found himself getting constant abuse everywhere he went. Once a mob became so angry that the police had to be called to break it up but luckily it did not result in any shot fired.

Another local protestant farmer James Tait from Myrtle Hill had also given evidence for the police at the inquest. Several threats were made to Tait after the inquest and early on Friday morning in late July, several of his outbuildings were set ablaze. He lost two cows and the sheds in the fire that was believed to be malicious.

Ballinhassig in more recent times.

In August that year, an unusual case came before the magistrates at Carrigaline Petty sessions. The Ranter's father in law took a case against him for the assault of his daughter. It was alleged that the Ranter's wife blamed him for being the cause of all the killings in Ballinhassig. She was especially upset after hearing that a relation of hers had been shot there. Reacting to this the Ranter was said to have assaulted his wife badly who was heavily pregnant at the time. After the kicking and beating she reputedly received, the poor woman gave birth prematurely to twins who didn't survive. Her health was still precarious and not out of danger.

Some maintained that the Ranter terrorised the district and still had the support of a large faction.

A relief fund had been set up for the family of the dead and the survivors who were maimed and wounded. It revealed a little about the families of those affected by the tragedy. Julia Callaghan was married to Charlie Callaghan and left behind a very young child, only a few months old. She was a first cousin of Maurice Corcoran, a married labourer. Maurice left a wife and four young children.

Jeremiah Coughlan, known to his family as Darby was from Skehanagh. He was a labourer and married with one child and another on the way. Timothy Kerrigan was a farmer who went to the fair to sell three sheep. He was married with one young child. Cornelius Forde was a twenty four year old single labourer who still lived at home with his parents.

Some of those badly wounded who also received sums from the fund were Richard Barrett from Fivemilebridge, John Forde a tailor who had been shot in his right thigh, Michael Deasy from Ballyheada was shot in his left arm, Michael Donnelly shot in the right arm, Michael Sullivan from Cork City had his leg fractured in two places, Jeremiah Conway and Cornelius Collins. John Walsh from Kilmoney had his leg amputated to save him.

By September Daniel O'Connell sent a letter from Derrynane with twenty guineas for the relief fund. He had kept himself abreast of the proceedings and deplored what had occurred referring to it as slaughter. Not only was O'Connell an M.P and known as the Liberator, but he was also the best barrister in Ireland at the time and could argue any case. He was by far the best legal mind in Ireland and to have him onside meant something.

But O'Connell's letter was not full of advice, for, in this case, he saw no chance of justice being served for those shot in Ballinhassig. He could not see how the inquest found the verdict they had but because of it, he believed further legal proceedings were prevented. O'Connell advised nothing be done as an indictment for murder or even manslaughter would never be obtained, except by presenting it to a Grand Jury. It was unusual for O'Connell to be so pessimistic.

What began as a fight between two factions quickly turned into one against the police. It is easy to say that if there was no trouble at the fair the police would have shot nobody. It is just as easy to say the police should not have fired on an unarmed crowd no matter how angry they were. Of all the evidence given at the inquest, Denis Falvey seems to have given the most balanced view. He had no hatred of the police and thought they had done well to not fire at first. It was then it all went wrong and as Falvey also mentioned the police were not justified firing indiscriminately or wantonly into the crowd at people trying to flee. Their own rules were to fire at the ring leaders and Falvey was right on another count that a leader with a cool head could have done so much more to control the crowd. Kelly should have been made responsible, he let them fire and then failed to order a cease fire when it got out of control.

It wasn't just the shooting though it was the way they seemed to march out of the village with no concern for anyone but themselves. There was never a shred of sympathy for those lying dead or wounded all around them. That was how poor ordinary people were treated at the time. The population of the country was eight million and the vast majority were living in destitution. The law certainly benefited the well off to control the poor. Had eleven of the gentry been shot it would have been very different.

A Greedy Landlord
Barna Innishannon 1838

On the 10th of September, Mr Gash with his agent James Butler, his son also James Butler and Matthew Butler went to collect a debt from Michael Ford in Barna just outside Innishannon. Ford had a few acres of land rented, but also let out several labourers' cottages just below Barna Cross and where the N71 now runs.

That day in September though it was not an eviction party that went to Barna as there was no bailiff present. It seems what Gash wanted that day was to seize something belonging to Ford as payment. There is even a word for what they did that day, distrain meaning to seize property to obtain money for rent. It was a word that was in common use back then.

The men rounded up several sheep, a horse and began driving them from the farm. Michael Ford knew that without a horse the game was up for him and he would not be able to keep the farm. It was the beginning of the end that would see him evicted and penniless on the side of the road.

Ford ran out to try to stop the men. Several times he offered to pay what was due but they did not seem interested in money. He did everything he could to prevent them from taking what was his but was clearly outnumbered. James Butler senior was armed with a stick. Ford wrestled it from him and snapped it across his knee. In doing so though he fell to the ground where the Butler's set upon him. First James Butler Senior delivered a few kicks and then his son gave it to him with a stone.

The Butler's came away from the struggle with some injuries but it was Michael Ford who suffered the most. The following day he died from head injuries he had suffered in the struggle to save his livelihood.

If anything this showed up the problems with the rent system in Ireland, so many suffered. Mr Thomas Frewen held an estate of several thousand acres and was renting portions of it to Thomas Gash, such as the townland of Barna. Gash then let out farms of several acres to farmers. Each of these farmers such as Ford sublet up to five or six tiny plots to labourers.

In Ireland, we have been quick to vilify the landlords. The rents paid by the labourers with their tiny plots were very high. It was the farmers and middlemen that did this overcharging or rack renting as it was known.

The inquest was held in Innishannon by coroner Francis Baldwin on Wednesday 12th of September. It took nine hours that day before the jury reached a verdict.

Several witnesses were produced who had observed the fracas. It was heard that Michael Ford offered to pay the outstanding rent on several occasions but was ignored. Ford's hand was said to be in his pocket at the time so they had not actually seen if he had the money or not. It was also heard that the sum of rent outstanding to Mr Gash was only 4s 10d.

Dr Samuel Orr described the injuries he had found on the body of Michael Ford. On the head were several bruises and under one the skull was badly fractured. He concluded that death resulted in that fracture which would have been caused by a large blunt object such as a stone.

Ford made a dying declaration and that was read out. He had implicated James Butler father and son more than the others. The verdict they reached was "that deceased came by his death in consequence of wounds inflicted by James Butler Senior and James Butler Jun, aided and assisted by Matthew Butler and Mr Gash".

It was a verdict that clearly implicated them but didn't go so far as to call it murder. Nonetheless, a case was made against James Butler Senior and he was returned to trial for killing Ford. The following year James Butler was charged with killing Michael Ford at the Cork Spring Assizes. Justice Baron Richards presided.

Evidence was given by a young boy James Clifford, who described how Ford struggled that day in September. He saw Ford breaking the stick and then got kicked in the side several times by the accused. He heard James Butler Junior warn any man who intervened that he would knock out his brains with the stone he had. As the livestock were driven away Ford was again attacked and knocked into the dyke by the younger Butler who warned he would do the same to anyone else. Young Clifford also added that he had seen Mr Gash strike Ford several times on the chest also.

Local man John Conroy also gave evidence. He witnessed Mr Gash tripping Ford in the struggle and then warning him to leave or he would break every bone in his body. Ford, he said still went after them several times offering to pay saying "here Mr Gash is your rent, let them stay with me". Conroy said he saw the younger Butler first strike Ford on the chest with a stone and then on the head. He then heard the young man boasting that he had finished Ford.

Barna Cross near Innishannon close to where Ford lived.

Ellen Ford married to the son of the deceased was then called. She told how on the Saturday before the occurrence Mr Gash came to the farm. He found Ford in a field and asked him why he dared to be there after not paying his rent. Ellen explained that her father in law offered to pay his March rent which was 4s 10d but Mr Gash refused and tried to deny him the use of the land. Gash demanded something for security against the Michaelmas rent which was not due for another three weeks at the end of September. Ellen also recalled how Gash became threatening towards her father in law that Saturday. She heard her father in law say he had security in two horses, five sheep and two acres of potatoes that were almost ready to be dug.

Mr Freeman representing the accused argued that it was Ford who acted illegally resisting his goods being seized for rent due. He went further saying that even if the seizing was unfair Ford should have not physically resisted and instead taken legal action. He referred to Mr Gash as respectable in society and said Ford struck the first blow.

Justice Richards summing up called the whole affair most unfortunate, especially considering the small sum of money involved. He said distraining livestock when an offer of rent was made was unjustified and a most illegal practice. He admitted that while Ford resisting was not legal the force used that day was completely unnecessary.

Mr Freeman then approached the bench and made a last minute attempt of arguing the application of the law on the case but the judge was having none of it.

In a short time, the jury returned a verdict of guilty of manslaughter and also noted that unnecessary violence was used that day. The judge then addressed James Butler telling him he believed that the jury had been merciful to him with their finding.

He did excuse his behaviour a little saying "you appear to have been acting under the control and direction of a respectable family". Then he asked directly "why was not this Mr Gash produced?" Freeman argued that Gash could not be produced as he was once indicted. The judge sarcastically replied, "I am glad to hear that, as it removes feelings obvious to be entertained from my mind". A solicitor for the prosecution Mr Bennett intervened saying the charges against Mr Gash had since been dropped by the crown.

The judge replied saying several times that Mr Gash could and should have been produced. He called his behaviour most reprehensible and cowardly. Now the judge told the court that the evidence produced had to be considered for sentencing as Mr Gash had declined the opportunity to give his version. James Butler senior's sentence was deferred until the end of the Assizes and a case against Mr Gash was called a few days later but nothing came of it.

Baron Richards seemed like a man who would have dealt with Mr Gash had he been charged with a crime. Most likely Gash used his influence to keep himself out of the dock and was willing to let his agent James Butler take the blame. It's strange considering the evidence that the younger James Butler was not charged. Evidence stated that he had struck Ford on the head and even boasted about it. Baron Richard's was right though that none of the Butler's would have been there that day nor would they have been so violent except for the encouragement of Mr Gash. At the end of the Assizes, there was no mention of the sentence James Butler received but it is hard to see him escaping a few years of hard labour.

As if the rent system wasn't bad enough, the small farmer had no hope at all with such sharp practices as Gash was employing. In this case, he had no interest in the rent due but must have seen Ford as means to a quick buck. If Gash had succeeded in getting away with the livestock it was worth much more than the rent due. Then when Ford was unable to pay the Michaelmas due to losing his horse, Gash would evict and have possession of the two acres of potatoes. Gash seems like a man who wanted to extract every last penny from his tenants and still maintain his respectability in society.

Do Not Hesitate to Shoot!
Timoleague 1889

One September Saturday in Timoleague crowds gathered from all around the district. The shops were shut as a mark of respect and police had been drafted into the village expecting trouble. The police remained in the barracks though for the sight of them on the streets might be the spark to set it off.

Daniel Donoghue was only twenty three, unmarried and had lived with his widowed mother. Up to 3000 people lined the streets and the route to the graveyard, all deeply shocked by the circumstances surrounding the death of this young man.

It would be Monday before the inquest was held and the details heard but everyone knew basically what had occurred. The Tuesday evening before there had been some trouble with the police in Timoleague. The result of which, Daniel Donoghue was shot by Constable Cullinane who was rumoured to have drink taken. Another rumour going about was that the two constables had been suspended and the Sergeant of Timoleague had also been removed for letting them on duty that night. But by the end of the week when Daniel died, the police claimed a riot had occurred on Tuesday. Many blamed the government and particularly Chief Secretary for Ireland, Arthur Balfour, for the police attitude towards the Irish. Others quoted the famous telegram Captain Plunkett had sent to Youghal only the year before "don't hesitate to shoot"

It was most unusual for a body to be released for the funeral before the inquest. Inquests were quick affairs with a jury of twelve local men sworn in, the body viewed and post-mortem carried out before burial. The inquest could have been held on Saturday but was delayed. It was agreed by Cronin the resident magistrate with Fr Murphy and Dr Magner that the funeral could take place on Saturday but the coffin when placed in the ground was not to be covered. This was because once the inquest jury were sworn in; they were required to view the body before evidence was heard.

By noon on Monday when the inquest was to sit, it became obvious why it was delayed. The coroner arrived to hold the inquest and there was nobody present but Dr Garde. The police were going about the countryside trying to put together a jury that they choose. Local shopkeepers, publicans and respectable men from Timoleague were ignored for people the police chose to bring the verdict they required.

It was three in the afternoon before the inquest finally began. No sooner had the twelve men of the jury answered to their names when Mr Shinkwin representing the next of kin of the deceased objected. He asked the coroner why the jury was only twelve men, saying such cases should have the full twenty three. Both men then accused each other of being mistaken with Somerville quipping he must then be mistaken for twenty years. Shinkwin was adamant that if ever a case needed the full complement of jurors this was it. While Somerville argued that twelve was sufficient to find a verdict.

The twelve jurors produced were Benjamin Daunt, James Morgan, and Michael Calnan. From Courtmacsherry was the foreman Jasper Travers a Shipwright, John Jermyn shopkeeper, Thomas Heard farmer from Butlerstown and Benjamin Lovell farmer from Abbeymahon. The five others were Denis Driscoll Senior, Denis Driscoll Junior, Patrick McCarthy, Patrick Donovan and Michael T McCarthy.

Already it was clear that the inquest was going to be protracted. Shinkwin argued that seven of the jurors were protestant and shared little in politics or religion with the deceased. The remaining five he admitted were Catholics but of lower intelligence than their neighbours. He claimed it was nothing short of the police trying to pack a jury to achieve the desired verdict. He seemed prepared and quoted *Jervis on Coroners* at which Somerville began to give in but was then worried where he would get more jurors at such short notice. One of the Jurors Benjamin Daunt took exception to what Shinkwin had said about them.

Shinkwin wasn't backing down and announced that three of the jurors could hardly speak English. It was local parish priest Fr Murphy who backed him up asking why the jury was made up of men from several miles away when any number of intelligent men live locally. He said the five Catholic men on the jury had no understanding of what was required of them. Shinkwin then announced that Patrick Donovan lived four miles from Timoleague and was selected because his brother was a policeman. It was also heard that Michael T McCarthy was illiterate and he was removed from the jury.

It took all afternoon for more jurors to turn up. There was Thomas White from Ballinascarthy, John Woods and William John Parker, a publican from Courtmacsherry.

Shinkwin still objected to the fourteen jurors and by now the Protestants had taken his methods as personally insulting to them. At last, the coroner insisted they go and they all left the courtroom. A wagonette was found to take the jury to Ballintemple graveyard five miles away.

When they returned that evening it was half six and the day was gone. Not a shred of evidence had yet been heard but District Inspector Purcell asked for an adjournment until the 17th.

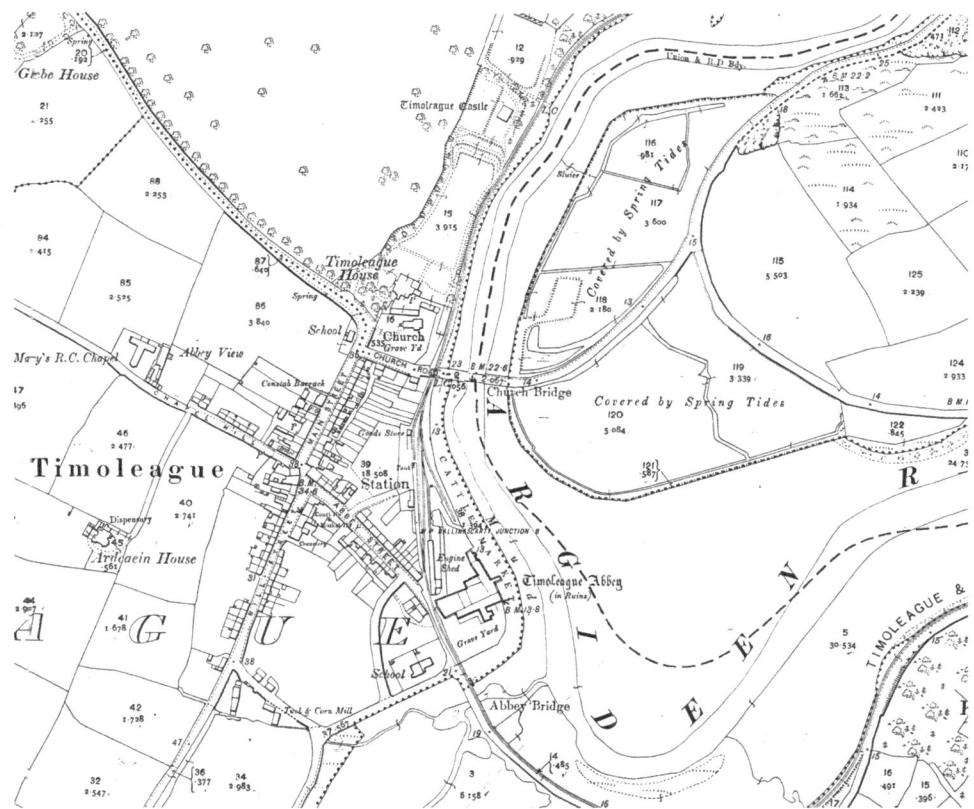

Map showing Timoleague at the time of the shooting

Before the inquest sat again news had spread far and wide and everyone knew what to expect from the inquest. One report referred to the jury as mostly conservatives with a few Catholics that could barely speak English. The Chief Secretary of Ireland Arthur Balfour would do nothing but back the police. The Lord Chief Justice of Ireland was himself known as Peter the Packer. Many already compared the case to similar ones in Midleton and Youghal a year or so before (see *Murder Most Local, Historic Murders of East Cork*). There were strong suspicions that in this case the police were drunk that night in Timoleague and everyone wondered how they could possibly cover this up.

On Tuesday the 17th the inquest sat again and now a Mr Robert Gregg was present having been sent by the Attorney General to represent the crown. Mr Wynne also announced he was there for the police.

Shinkwin began by objecting to County Inspector Hojel, District Inspector Jones and Resident Magistrate Cronin sitting on the bench alongside the coroner. He said the coroner should sit alone and not be interfered with by them. For what it was worth they got up and sat with everyone else.

Mr Shinkwin announced that he had not been given the name of a single witness to be heard that day. The Coroner and Mr Wynne were also not aware of who was to be called. Shinkwin asked had the Crown witnesses to call; he said that if a civilian was the suspect they would have many. Eventually, the witnesses for both sides were identified and asked to leave the room; they were then called in one by one.

It must have come as a shock to many when the first witness was Constable Cullinane the very man who had fired the shot. He was questioned first by Mr Wynne. He said he went to patrol in Timoleague that night with Constable Thomas Burns. They left the barrack at nine and came upon a scuffle outside Eugene McCarthy's at quarter past ten. Cullinane said he clearly saw Daniel Dempsey assaulting Jeremiah Donovan hitting him twice with his fist.

The police stepped in and arrested labourer Dempsey, who he said was drunk. Cullinane told the inquest how they were leading Daniel away when his brother Patrick intervened grabbing the prisoner by the collar to free him. He claimed Patrick struck him with a bottle on the forehead so hard it broke. As he said it, Cullinane turned around in the courtroom and revealed a forehead that appeared free of any recent injury. Cullinane insisted he had been cut badly that night and bled profusely but had healed since. Then again it was already two weeks since it had happened.

Cullinane continued saying Patrick Dempsey then threw a bottle which struck Burns and cut his face badly. Then stones rained down on them, Patrick Dempsey tried to free his brother and the crowd closed in on them. He ordered Burns to draw his sword and at the same time threatened to fire at the crowd if they didn't back off. According to him they didn't back off, the bottles and stones kept coming at them. He said to protect himself and his colleague he fired one shot of his revolver into the crowd.

RM Cronin asked "did you fire at random or into the crowd" and he answered, "I fired into the crowd". This he said cleared the crowd from the street and the shot was heard in the barrack. Sergeant McDermott and Constables Neill and Dwyer came to their assistance and Dempsey was taken to the barracks.

When he got his chance to cross examine, Shinkwin asked Cullinane what had he been doing all day before going on duty at nine that night. When pushed he admitted to being in one pub that day and having four drinks in total, two drinks in the pub two in the barrack. He swore to having no drink after nine while on duty but went into four pubs after ten in the course of his duties.

Shinkwin was on to something and kept pressing him "upon your oath were you drinking after nine o'clock in any public house here that night?" But Cullinane insisted "not that night or any other night". He did admit to something happening when he was in Kerry but wouldn't say. Shinkwin already knew everything about his past and dragged it out of him. Cullinane admitted to being drunk on duty in Kerry and also getting into trouble for disobeying orders. Shinkwin went back to the case in question and said to the witness "and now to crown all those offences you took away a man's life in Timoleague". All the constable could say was "yes I fired the shot". Shinkwin questioned the amount of force they used that night to apprehend Dempsey and how the sword was drawn. He denied that they went to strike Dempsey with their swords but instead struck each other.

Shinkwin continued with the questions:
How far was the crowd from you when you fired the shot? About fifteen yards, we were 40 yards from the barrack. The crowd was at the cross and the cross was fifty yards away.
And you fired into the crowd? Yes, I did.
With the intention to kill? Well no, I did not intend to kill but wanted them back from me.

What did you believed would be the result after you fired? I believed it would keep them back from us.

By shooting down those who were there? By firing the shot.

And shooting down? Yes (and this caused a sensation in the courtroom)

You didn't hesitate to shoot on the occasion? I did, I cautioned the people to keep back.

And that is what you call hesitating to shoot? I cautioned them to keep back.

Or else you would have given them cold lead? I didn't say that but I said I would fire.

How many people were there when you told them to keep back? I would say about fifty.

Upon your oath were there eight persons there? There were more.

You are improving on your evidence for you said in reply to Mr Wynne that there were about twenty persons there? I don't think I said that, I am only guessing."

At this point, the coroner went back over the records and sure enough, Shinkwin was right he had said twenty. Shinkwin then began questioning him about the so called riot that night. Cullinane reluctantly admitted that they were not struck by a bottle or any stone that night. Shinkwin also pointed out that not a window in the village was broken and despite being only forty yards from the barracks, the police there knew nothing of the trouble until the shot was fired.

Shinkwin ended his questions until the following morning having succeeded in showing that the police were exaggerating the trouble that night. As the proceedings were breaking up some of the jurors tried to get out of coming again the following day, saying they were too busy. They had not realised this had the potential to drag on for several days. Shinkwin chipped in saying that the jurors selected by the police were travelling several miles every day and had locals been picked they would have no such bother. The jurors were reminded of the severe punishment if they failed to show up.

The following day Shinkwin continued questioning Constable Cullinane. He asked was the crowd at the corner when he fired, the constable agreed but now said a few were much closer, within a few yards and closing in on them when he fired. He gave in and said Donoghue was fifteen yards away when he fired the shot.

Mr Wynne intervened and revealed that he saw Fr Murphy talking to one of the jurors. Gregg tried the same tactic saying he witnessed a juror talking to a reporter. It was a drastic attempt to destabilise the proceeding when it was not going their way. Gregg and Wynne were then seen passing notes to each other like school children and Shinkwin objected saying how it was so obvious what was going on.

Eventually, he began questioning the constable again about what was said when Donoghue gave his statement before he died. Cullinane was present but asked no question even though he was allowed.

Shinkwin then read out the deceased man's statement:

"Between ten and half past ten o'clock on last evening, I was standing about the middle of the street in Timoleague, opposite Tom White's public house. I was standing by myself at the time, while I was standing there I saw Constables Burns and Cullinane, they went towards the fountain. Burns spoke to Daniel Dempsey saying he assaulted a man. I did not catch the name, I saw the constables lay their hands on Daniel Dempsey. I then heard Burns say to the other constable to draw his sword. There were about a dozen people more or less on the street. The constable did draw his sword and they were dragging Dempsey towards the barrack. The next thing that attracted my attention, I heard like the breaking of glass. The next thing I heard was a shot fired, I saw the flash and I was struck and fell on the ground. I did not see who fired the shot, it came from the direction of the constables going to the barrack. They were between the dispensary and the post office. I did not see firearms but I heard the clash of their swords. I took no part in any obstruction of the constabulary that night nor did I see any given but it could be given without my knowing it. I think my sister Mary was the first to come to my assistance, I am at present attended by Dr Magner and Dr Garde".

Shinkwin turned to Cullinane and said why didn't he ask Donoghue any questions when the statement was given. The constable tried in vain to explain that was Donoghue's version and could be what he saw. Shinkwin persisted that both could not be true, had swords clashed that night, but Cullinane denied this. Wynne tried intervening when the constable became vexed.

The coroner remarked that days had passed yet they were still on the first witness. A juror said if the questions were answered promptly there might be some hope of finishing. Shinkwin then came to the police code and again had done his homework. He showed that Cullinane had acted in haste and not followed the police code which mentioned, only in extreme cases and as a last resort. Cullinane even admitted to always carrying a revolver but never practised firing it. When he got back to the barrack that night Sergeant McDermott told him to consider himself under arrest and he surrendered his sword.

Constable Thomas Burns gave a similar account to that of his colleague. He denied being drunk that night going on duty but admitted he had four drinks over the course of the day. Burns claimed their lives were in danger that night.

The jury was getting restless as they must have been under the impression the whole thing would be wrapped up a few hours. Yet after two days, only the two policemen had been heard. There were constant remarks and needling between Shinkwin and Wynne, to the point where even the jurors wanted to just get on with it.

On the third day, Dr Henry Garde was called to give medical evidence. He told of being awoken that night by the sound of the gunshot. The doctor got up, dressed and sent for Dr Magner fearing someone had been shot. The injured man was found in White's pub and Dr Magner joined him soon after. The gunshot wound in the stomach was easily found and they treated him as best they could before sending him home.

Dr Garde said he was then called to the barrack and treated Cullinane's injury. The constable had a small bruise on his forehead but it was bleeding quite a bit. The doctor said, "It looked bad, but it was not as bad as it looked".

He reckoned Burns had a worse wound on his face which he later dressed. He also attended to the Sergeant and the prisoner Dempsey that night. Dr Garde believed the constables were perfectly sober when he saw them.

It was Mr Gregg who enquired into the cause of Donoghue's death. The doctor called it peritonitis, an inflammation or infection in the abdomen. The doctor told how he tried to retrieve the bullet while Donoghue was alive but failed to find it. He and Dr Magner spent three hours trying but were afraid to go too far for fear of causing more harm.

During the post mortem, they discovered the bullet passed through the intestine but still failed to locate it. Several jurors and the coroner got involved asking the doctor where could it be gone to but he couldn't answer. Of course, Mr Gregg and Mr Wynne suggested that Donoghue was not hit by a bullet at all but the doctor swore nothing else could have caused such injuries.

When Shinkwin cross examined, the doctor described Cullinane's injuries as very slight. He freely admitted that Cullinane did not need to be in bed for four days with the injury he had sustained and could have been fit for duty.

When asked, Dr James Magner said he had not the slightest doubt that Donoghue had a bullet wound. He believed due to the great pain Donoghue suffered from it, that the bullet may have lodged in the pubic bone. He went into details of how he searched the body for the bullet during the post mortem but felt he would have mutilated it had they gone further. He was satisfied with the cause of death as peritonitis caused by a bullet wound that ruptured the intestines.

On the constable's injuries, he said they were no injury to life at all. The doctor believed that Constable Burns injury was done with a policeman's sword. He described the wound as straight and clean, therefore must have been caused by a straight weapon such as a sword and not a bottle.

By the fourth day in the courtroom, the jurors began to suggest cutting short the number of witnesses to bring the proceedings to an end.

Walter Henry Garde, (Dr Henry Garde's son) a first year medical student, gave an account of dressing Burns wound that night. He did not think Burns was drunk nor did he believe the wound was caused by a whole bottle or a sword.

Shinkwin asked for Constable Burns to be produced and held a sword to his face showing how it matched the wound. But Gregg objected asking how a man holding a revolver in one hand and a prisoner in the other could strike someone with a sword. Shinkwin said there was no evidence to show either constable had a revolver in their hand at that time. Even Wynne advised his counterpart, Mr Gregg, to let the point drop.

With the inquest nowhere near complete in early October, the Dempsey brothers were brought before the Petty Sessions. They were charged with assaulting and obstructing the police on the 3rd of September. It really showed the attitude of the police that they would try to secure a conviction and think the inquest would go in their favour. The charges were adjourned until after the verdict of the inquest.

For an inquest it was dragging on, nine days had been spent mostly with arguments between Shinkwin and Wynne. Dr Magner was recalled by Wynne who spent so long showing the doctor was political and no fan of the police.

The first of the witnesses on the street that night was Cornelius Reilly; he recalled meeting brothers Patrick and Daniel Dempsey by the courthouse on his way home. They were leaving for Tralee the following day and offered to buy him a drink in Leary's pub. He went with them and met Edward Hurley and Jeremiah Donovan.

He heard Donovan and Daniel Dempsey exchange a few words but saw no blows between them. It was then he said the police arrived and Donovan exclaimed "arrest that man" pointing to Daniel. Patrick protested that his brother had done nothing but the police began to shove him away and one pulled a sword. Reilly swore that nobody interfered with the police nor did he see stones or bottles thrown. What he did see was a flash of a gun, then the bang and heard a man cry out "I'm shot".

Before Wynne cross examined the witness he complained bitterly about the newspaper coverage of the inquest. According to him, it was only the Cork Constitution who published a true account, they called it the Timoleague Riot. The other papers such as the Cork Examiner did not agree with their version. If every argument Wynne had at the inquest was told here it would take up the whole book.

On the tenth day, the proceedings opened with Dr Magner telling of a threatening letter he had received. In it, the writer claimed that the police shot into the air and Donoghue was killed by the prong of a pitchfork. The doctor was referred to as being a disgrace to his profession and "mean, cowardly and vindictive". Everyone in court including Mr Wynne and Gregg could do nothing but condone it. Magner reminded them that others may have received similar and might now be afraid to give evidence. He was also sure enough that he could find the author of the letter himself despite it being posted in Dublin.

Eventually, the proceedings moved on and Daniel Leary, a driver from Bandon was called. He had been in White's public house on the night in question. He saw Donoghue being taken by the police and reckoned there were eight or ten people present at the time. Leary did not see stones or bottles thrown at the police that night. What he did witness was the gunshot, the flash of the gun and the man next to him screaming before falling to the ground.

Wynne tried everything to discredit the witness including asking him to guess how many were present in court and then counting them. Wynne's tactics of trying to drag out the proceedings were by now clear to everyone.

Local shopkeeper Daniel Harrington gave a similar testimony. He was standing in his hall when the shot was heard that night. Looking out onto the street he saw no crowd nor was there trouble with the police.

Wynne accused Harrington of being against the police and the witness admitted to being the treasurer of the local National Land League branch. Wynne then asked was it the National Land League who were paying for Shinkwin to go against the police.

At last Jeremiah Donovan was questioned; the man who the police said was assaulted. He admitted being with Ned Hurley at Leary's corner when they encountered Dempsey. According to him, it was Dempsey who challenged Hurley to a fight and the police appeared at the same time.

Donovan admitted that it was said at the time that he was assaulted but now cleared it up saying he was not. Still, he watched as Dempsey was arrested saying there was five there at the time, himself, Hurley, the two Dempsey's and Con Kiely. No one interfered with the police except Patrick Dempsey protesting his brother's innocence.

This time Wynne tried the same thing accusing Jeremiah of being the secretary of the Land League, but he announced it was Patrick Donovan. He then tried to make Jeremiah look like a troublemaker listing every misdemeanour he ever got caught for.

Witness Richard Collins recalled seeing Constable Burns drinking in Griffin's public house at twenty past nine on the 3rd of September. He even heard Burns say he should be on patrol at nine and knew it was twenty past because it was Burns who looked at his watch. He gave that age old Irish description that Burns was not drunk but under the influence that evening.

Another witness, Robert Travers, justice of the peace, had been present when Donoghue made his statement. Travers revealed he asked Donoghue did he know who shot him but he didn't. He also asked did he think the shot was fired intending to kill. Donoghue told him he believed it was fired with the intention of killing someone but not him.

Shinkwin asked Travers why he did not inspect the sword and gun of the police when he went to the barracks that night. Travers believed there was no need as the police admitted to firing a shot. He had seen Burns' sword the following day and there was still blood on it. Travers believed there was no doubt at all that Dempsey's cut on his forehead was caused by Burns' sword.

Mrs Ellen Stanton was called by Shinkwin and she detailed how she lived two doors from the barracks. On the 3rd of September about twenty past ten she heard a gunshot and ran to her front door. Outside only two yards away were two constables with their swords drawn standing over a prisoner who screeched out "for god's sake don't kill me". She clearly heard the clash of the swords but saw no other trouble or a crowd on the street at the time.

By now it was mid October and the inquest had sat for twelve days. The jury was now pressing the solicitors of both sides to refrain from bickering which was wasting so much time. There was also talk that the coroner was considering exhuming the body so that another search could be made for the bullet.

It had taken a long time but eventually, Daniel Dempsey who was arrested that night was called to give evidence. He admitted having six pints of porter and recalled being with his brother Patrick and Con Reilly. They tried for a drink in O'Leary's pub but it was too late and then they met Ned Hurley and Jerry Donovan.

Dempsey also admitted to saying something cross to Donovan but said there was no fight between them and the police arrived at that time. He didn't hear what Donovan said to them but Constable Burns drew his sword and caught hold of him. They accused him of assault which he denied and he was taken away with a struggle. The three of them fell near White's pub. Further on Burns got hit on the forehead with his sword which still bore a scar. Dempsey said this knocked him and while falling he grabbed Burns by the jacket as he was attempting to hit him once more. As he caught the constable a bottle fell from his breast pocket and it went to pieces on the ground. At the same moment, he saw Cullinane turn and fire a shot towards White's pub. The constable then drew his sword and while both police were trying to hit him they struck each other. Dempsey denied any resistance to the police that night and also said there was no big crowd gathered on the street.

When Wynne cross examined Dempsey, he admitted he was not sober and would have fought Jerry Donovan had the police not arrived. Wynne showed that he had been summonsed four times in the past. Once for assault of Donovan and being drunk and disorderly on the streets of Timoleague and Dempsey did not deny it.

When eventually all the witnesses had been called each side addressed the inquest at length. Wynne still maintained that Donoghue had not been shot at all and a riot of fifty people took place on the streets that night. Shinkwin argued it was a far more trivial arrest and that an innocent man's life was taken without any cause.

On the fourteenth day of the proceedings, the coroner, at last, charged the jury. It had been far more like a trial at an Assizes than an Inquest. Coroner Somerville in his address seemed to come down on the side of the police saying how they were assaulted in the course of their duty. He did admit there could be no doubt that Donoghue died from a gunshot but left it to the jury to decide.

The foreman returned after two and a half hours saying there was no chance they would agree to a verdict. Seven of the jurors were for justifiable homicide while the other seven were for wilful murder against Cullinane. The coroner had never presided over an inquest that failed to reach a verdict before and didn't know what he should do next. Meanwhile, Shinkwin asked that a new jury be found with twenty three jurors but this was rejected completely. All they could do was end the proceedings and the jurors must have been livid after spending fourteen days listening to it only to achieve nothing either way.

It was obvious from the very first day that the inquest would be farcical at best. It was up to the coroner really to ensure a fair impartial hearing of the evidence by an unbiased jury. Somerville failed at every turn and even had the crown and the police inspectors sitting on the bench with him. They might as well have stayed there throughout for what it was worth, as they were all on the same side. Coroner Richard Rice had heard similar cases in Youghal and Midleton in the years before; he had much more zeal in the face of the Crown and police. Twice Coroner Rice managed to return verdicts of wilful murder against the police and issued coroner's warrants for their arrest.

Within days Daniel and Patrick Dempsey were before the petty sessions again charged with assaulting the constables. Shinkwin who by now knew the case so well defended the Dempsey's and many of the same witnesses were called that day. Several people told of seeing Constable Burns in Griffin's pub until twenty past nine that night, where he had drank three pints.

Dr Magner again demonstrated how the cut on Burns' face was done with a police sword but Mr Sherlock who prosecuted asked why was the wound wider by the jaw. Magner explained in detail and even got Burns to hold the sword showing how he could inflict the injury on himself when drawing the sword back to strike with it.

Despite having not secured a verdict at the inquest Shinkwin now seemed to have the upper hand in court and used his knowledge of the case against the prosecution.

Sergeant McDermott still maintained the story that he saw forty people on the street after the shot was fired. He was also adamant that Burns and Cullinane were in the barrack at nine before going on duty that night.

It took five days in court hearing from the police constables and all the other witnesses before the magistrates made their decision. They felt it was utterly impossible that the constables inflicted wounds on themselves with their swords that night. Therefore they decided that an assault on the police must have taken place but no mention was made of how Donoghue lost his life. They said Patrick Dempsey put up the most resistance and was sentenced to three months for the assault of Burns and six weeks for Cullinane. Daniel Dempsey's involvement was far less serious and he only got two weeks imprisonment.

It's hard to believe there was no resistance given to the police that night, any man accused in the wrong would at least protest. But there certainly were not fifty people on the street and it certainly could not be called a riot. It demonstrates the attitude of the police at the time towards the ordinary man, they felt they were the law and could do as they pleased. You can't blame them for feeling that way when the law went so far to protect them. There were several such cases in Cork at the time and no matter what, the police were never going to be accountable for their actions. To prove their authority they secured convictions when they had carried out far worse crimes and gotten away with it.

Murder at the Old Head
Ballymackean Old Head of Kinsale 1895

Right down by the old head of Kinsale, a young servant boy Timmy Donovan was going about his duties looking after the cattle when he heard his name called from the house. At first, he took no notice of it but then he detected urgency in the voice. His master had gone to the fair in Kinsale that day with another servant and it had been quieter than usual.

The boy left what he was doing and returned to the house knowing it was a woman's voice calling. He went to the farmhouse door and lifted the latch but as he opened the door he stopped dead and went no further. In that split second he saw everything, there on the kitchen floor was Kate Manning covered in blood and her brother standing over her lashing her head with a weapon. Timmy ran from the house before David turned on him with whatever weapon he had in his hand.

All the young lad could do was run to the first person he could and get help. He found James Harnett and blurted out "Katty Manning is dead by her brother". Harnett told young Timmy to fetch a priest and the doctor. He went to the house but as he got there he saw David Manning coming out the door. Manning gave him a sideways glance but didn't stop going to the yard.

Inside Harnett found the same terrible scene but Kate was still alive. There was blood everywhere. Fr Cotter arrived from Ballinspittle.

Later that evening a doctor arrived from Ballinspittle but knew from the serious head injuries there was no chance of survival. He elevated her injuries and did what he could by way of bandaging them up.

About nine that night Sergeant Doherty arrived from Ballinspittle with two constables. David Manning was lying in bed upstairs fully dressed when the Sergeant found him. Doherty gave him the usual caution before arrest, but Manning denied it saying "I do not see her at all". The police searched for the weapon used before returning to the barracks with their prisoner. In the darkness it was impossible, and they vowed to return at first light in the morning.

The doctor returned later that night, early the following morning and later the following day but her condition did not improve, and she passed away on Thursday night.

The following day Friday the 23rd the inquest was held by Coroner Horgan. There was no doubt that she had been killed by her brother David, but the evidence had to be heard. County Inspector Bourchier was there with Head Constable Reddy of Bandon.

The jury was made up of all local men, Jeremiah Coleman foreman, from Ballymackean, were farmers John Dempsey, Daniel Dempsey and Patrick Donovan, labourer Michael Coughlan. From Lispatrick Upper were farmers, Humphrey Sullivan, Denis Dempsey, Lispatrick Lower Cornelius Keohane and labourer Patrick Connell. Also were farmers from Kilcolman, Cornelius Bohane, Jeremiah Galvin and Garrett Donovan and the final two were Timothy Dempsey and John Galvin.

The first witness was Charles Sullivan who identified himself as the owner of the house. The deceased was his sister in law and the accused, his brother in law. Charles told how on the day before he left home at 5.30 am to go to the fair in Kinsale with his wife and a servant. He left Catherine, David and baby John, who was only nine months old at home.

Long before he left the fair, news reached him in Kinsale that something terrible had occurred. It was 7 that night when he got home to a crowd gathered outside. The doctor had already left and inside all was quiet. Catherine or Kate as she was known was unconscious and remained that way until she died.

Head Constable Reddy asked
"Were you aware of any differences between the prisoner and his sister? There was a difference some time ago, I heard but I know nothing myself.
Was there anything peculiar about him? He was in the habit of getting fits."
Then the coroner asked:
"Did you speak to Manning when you came back? Yes he was lying on the bed with his boots and clothes on.
Had you ever a difference with him? Yes, a small difference some time ago.
Do you know of any ill feeling between the deceased and her brother? Well, that would be hard to say that.
I am only asking you? I don't."
It was later that night that he heard it was David who had inflicted the injuries on Kate.

The townland of Ballymackean close to the Old Head.

Charles then told about the police arriving early the morning after the killing and helped them find the weapon used. Hidden under cupboards in the kitchen, an iron bar was found. The bar was produced before the inquest and appeared to look a bit like a poker. Charles described that when the bar was found, it was covered in blood and hair that matched the deceased.

Young Timmy Donovan was sworn in. He told of the glimpse he saw as he opened the door on Wednesday. He recalled getting help, telling Patrick Collins and then sending James Dennis on a horse for the doctor and priest.

James Harnett described being informed by young Donovan and going to the house. When he saw Kate she was alive but even he knew then she was dying.

After leaving the house he also told James Dennis and then got his wife Ellen and Catherine Dennis. He said the women were afraid to go as David was still about but went to the house with him. The women moved Kate to a better position while he went for more help.

Dr Arthur O'Leary from Ballinspittle recalled arriving at the house about a quarter to five that day. He found Catherine Manning lying on a mattress and bleeding profusely from her head. There were several head wounds and the skull had been broken in places. Some wounds in the brain had been lacerated and visible, others the bits of the bone driven into the brain.

He concluded that death was caused by the laceration of the brain and the weapon produced would inflict the injuries he saw.

The jury found a verdict "that deceased died at Ballymackean on the 22nd of August of laceration of the brain caused by injuries inflicted on her by David Manning at Ballymackean on the 21st inst".

David Manning was forty years of age and had been born in Boston in 1855. The family returned from the states in the years afterwards and settled on a farm near to the point of the old head of Kinsale. His younger sisters had been born in Ireland.

He was only twelve when his father died in 1867 and it was his mother Ellen who inherited the farm. When she died in 1883 David did not get the farm and the situation was made worse a few years later when £75 was awarded to Hannah from her father's will. Maybe by the time his mother died, she knew a farm couldn't be entrusted to him.

David was the eldest son and excluded from all the wills. He was left with nothing. In 1890 he was jailed for assaulting his sister Ellen when he threatened to kill her, after several days in jail he was sent to the Lunatic Asylum for several months.

When he returned home he isolated himself even more from the family but seemed to be fond of Kate. Ellen married Jeremiah Coleman in 1892 and moved out of the family farm. The following year Hannah married Charles Sullivan and with the marriage, it was Sullivan who now owned the farm.

Back then a new house was rarely built for a newly married couple; everyone was expected to live in the same house. More labour was needed on a farm so the extra help in many cases became unpaid labourers.

David lived there but spoke to no one; he did little to no work on the farm and often spent his time in an outhouse. Catherine was also at home on the farm with the newly married couple.

On Saturday David Manning was produced before resident magistrate Pearse in Bandon. As he had no legal representation he was allowed to cross examine each witness.

Fifteen year old Timmy Donovan had already given a statement which was read out and it was similar to the account he gave at the inquest. He swore to it again and that it was correct.

Timmy then added that he had dinner in the house that day at two and all appeared to be normal. Before he heard his name called in the afternoon he heard activity in the house as if people were running about. He now believed there was a struggle in the house before he heard his name called.

The magistrate asked Manning had he any questions to ask but he had none. Pearse advised him not to say anything until he had legal representation but Manning said "I am not guilty of the like at all".

Then Sergeant William Doherty gave evidence of arresting Manning and finding what they now believed to be the murder weapon. He had examined Manning's clothes in the barracks and found fresh bloodstains on the trousers, boots and coat. The accused also had a cut on his right index finger.

James Dennis a fisherman recalled being fishing that morning but was home in the afternoon. He then recounted how as he left the house David went back in. He noticed a spot of blood on David's face and looking in the window saw him wiping blood from it.

Again Colonel Pearse asked Manning did he want to ask Dennis a question but he said "I didn't see him at all". Pearse who had not been encouraging Manning to ask anything suggested "do you wish to ask him if he did see you, he says he saw you". All Manning could do was repeat "I don't remember sir; I didn't see him at all".

Colonel Pearse had heard enough that day and told Manning he would be returned for trial at the Winter Assizes in the charge of murder. He asked Manning had he anything to say but reminded him again he did not have to say anything.

David wished to say little but did add "I don't want to make a statement, I never did this thing, I never witnessed the like".

Reports from the court described Manning as a medium height normal enough looking man with a forehead that usually indicated intelligence. His eyes however had a stare that showed a troubled mind.

In December when David Manning was charged with murder, by Justice O'Brien at the Munster Winter Assizes in Cork, he pleaded not guilty. Manning at least by now had legal representation, Mr Powell and a solicitor from Kinsale Mr O'Sullivan.

Mr Ronan opened the case for the prosecution and laid out the facts of the case. He described the scene and how in the house that day was

David Manning, his sister and the baby. The prosecution was in no doubt at all as Manning had been seen in the act and leaving the house after.

Ronan posed the question to the jury, was David Manning responsible for his actions that day? They would have to decide whether he was sane or not.

The crown called the same witnesses that had been heard before, Timmy Donovan, James Harnett, Dr Arthur O'Leary and Sergeant William Doherty. The doctor revealed that he thought Manning appeared deranged and described his appearance as "haggard, depressed and restless".

For the defence, Mr Powell called Charles Sullivan who said there had not been any quarrel between David and his sister. In fact, he said David seemed fonder of Kate than anyone else. This was someone who normally didn't even eat meals with the family.

When questioned Hannah gave a more detailed account of her brother's unusual activities. She told how it was seventeen years before when they first noticed he was behaving unusually. It was on harvest day when the corn was ripe and ready to be cut. She said David called his mother to look at the corn, she said it was ripe but he disagreed with her and then told her something was wrong with him. He went running about crying that his mother was dead and when he got a razor they had to get a man to get it from him.

Hannah told the court that from that day till this he was not right afterwards. He spent most of his time in an outhouse and would go down to the cliffs running about with only his trousers on. People had seen him running into the rocks hurting himself.

She then told how he had threatened to choke his sister Ellen a few years before and ended up in the asylum for seven months. Hannah said he never mixed with anyone, kept to himself and had not been to mass for eight years.

At this point, Justice O'Brien had heard enough. Instead of charging the jury, he said plainly that it was obvious that the accused was a madman. He suggested the jury would find that he committed the act but was insane at the time. When asked the jury duly obliged and found their verdict according to what the judge had asked. Justice O'Brien then sentenced Manning to be sent to Dundrum Lunatic Asylum and to be kept there at the pleasure of the Lord Lieutenant which meant he may never be released again.

Blueshirts and Beatings
Innishannon 1933

Just up the hill outside the village of Innishannon, at an ungodly hour in the morning, someone was knocking on a door. Mrs O'Reilly went to the door to see what was wrong and what did someone want at 5 in the morning. Without opening she asked who was there, the reply she got was "Broy Harriers, we want to search this house, open the door". No sooner was the door opened when four masked men burst in brandishing guns and weapons. One even had a sledgehammer on his shoulder. Mrs O'Reilly attempted to pull the mask from one and got a blow to the face. Her daughter Nora called them cowards for doing such a thing and she too got the same. The gunmen demanded her son Hugh. When Hugh emerged they announced "It is you we want" he barely had time to pull on his trousers when he was dragged from the house.

Hugh dragged himself back home sometime later, after getting a terrible beating from the masked men further up the road. Within a few minutes, Dr Eugene Callanan from Innishannon arrived and began to treat Hugh's numerous injuries. Sergeant P O'Keeffe from Innishannon was informed and he tried to trace the car that was heard speeding away after the beating.

Hugh's condition was so serious that later that day he was taken to Clancool Nursing home in Bandon. What the O'Reilly's didn't know then was that there was another attack in the locality, about three miles away an hour before. The house of Denis O'Leary was raided and he too was dragged out in a similar fashion. When O'Leary tried to make a run for it, he was shot several times in the legs before the masked men fled.

In Bandon, Dr Welply removed the bullet from O'Leary's leg and his condition improved steadily. Hugh's condition was critical but improved enough for him to go home in early December but this recovery didn't last. Two days later Hugh's condition was as critical as ever and he returned promptly to the Bandon nursing home, from then his condition became steadily worse.

Both Denis O'Leary and O'Reilly were prominent members of the National Guard better known as the Blueshirts, O'Leary was the treasurer of the local branch. At the time the country was politically volatile with clashes breaking out all over. Eoin O'Duffy had up until a few months before been the Garda Commissioner but was dismissed by De Valera when he came to power. He became the leader of the Blueshirts and within months the organisation was banned. Then several groups joined together to form Fine Gael.

The attacks were thought to be reprisals for an alleged assault on Denis O'Connor about a week before in Innishannon. O'Connor claimed he was ambushed and attacked when walking home on Tuesday night. He was marched up the road with a revolver pointed at him. Two more men tied him up and questioned him about the location of arms and ammunition. He was accused of being an informer and a spy for the IRA but denied it. They threatened to shoot him if he had not left the IRA within a week but he flatly denied their threat saying shoot me if you wish. O'Connor told that when he finally got home that night his house had been turned over and searched. It was strange that Denis O'Connor never informed the Gardaí and was only questioned after the other attacks.

A week or so before O'Reilly and O'Leary had been mentioned in the An Phoblacht in an article entitled "Imperialist Hooligans". It claimed Blueshirts paraded through Clonakilty with revolvers and assaulted a republican named Callanan. It also mentioned that O'Reilly and O'Leary were organising the Blueshirts in the Innishannon area and were constantly in the Garda Barracks.

Hugh O'Reilly was dragged up the road and beaten.

Within days General O'Duffy the leader of the Blueshirts gave a speech condemning the actions against his members. He claimed men were openly parading about the country brandishing guns and the government was either unwilling or afraid to take action. Speaking about his own members he said "individual members had been taken from their homes and beaten by armed cowards and many were now in hospital suffering from bullet wounds inflicted by people illegally in possession of arms". The parish priest in Bandon, Canon Murphy, also condemned the attacks calling them "cruel, diabolical and dastardly".

Coming up to Christmas, Hugh's condition which had been improving took a turn for the worst. On Saturday the 23rd, prominent blue shirt John O'Sullivan was released from prison and a rally was held in Innishannon. There were clashes between several republicans. There was also violence in Clonakilty the same night. The Blueshirts paraded through the towns. In Bandon, they went to visit Hugh O'Reilly who was still hospitalised almost two months after the attack on him. They found him in a critical condition and his condition deteriorated rapidly when they were there and he was once again in serious danger. Denis O'Leary had recovered sufficiently from his operation and had been discharged from the hospital about two weeks before.

By that time Hugh was back in the Bandon nursing home and his condition was very grave. Dr Welply did everything he could but an infection set in which complicated his condition. Hugh passed away on the 28th of December, he was only 34 years old.

The inquest was held on Friday by Deputy Coroner JJ Horgan in Clancool Nursing Home in Bandon. The jury was made up of local men from Bandon, Con Slattery foreman from Weir Street, publicans William Slattery, South Main Street and Thomas Kelly, Shannon Street, John Crowley a Leather merchant, South main Street, Roy A Lee, shopkeeper, Bridge Place, Daniel White, Corn merchant, New Road, John Murphy a grocer, Charles Coghlan and John Dineen.

State Solicitor Thomas Healy from Skibbereen was representing the state, James Neville, Bandon for the O'Reilly family. Mr Eamon O'Neill T.D for West Cork addressed the coroner saying how he was unsure of his role there but that he was a member of the same organisation as the deceased. The coroner told him that if he wished to ask a question he would have to do so through him and reminded him not to abuse this.

The O'Reilly's house just outside the village of Innishannon, with thanks to Irish Newspaper Archives and Irish Independent.

The remains were formally identified by John O'Reilly, father of the deceased. John was an ex RIC man and described his son as an ex British Army accountant who was unemployed. He recalled the 29th of October last when he awoke to tremendous knocking on his door. His wife went to the window and was told it was the Broy Harriers to search the house. They threatened to break in the door if it wasn't opened for them. Inside he asked them for their warrant and was told "oh you know the law alright". His daughter Nora had a candle but the masked men quickly quenched it. His wife Nora pulled the mask from one of them and received a baton in the face. None of the O'Reilly's recognised the unmasked man that morning in the darkness. When asked John reckoned that none of the men were local. When Hugh emerged at his bedroom door, it became obvious it was he the raiders were looking for. John said when he was dragged from the house his wife went after them but quickly returned. He went down towards Innishannon after them and heard a car running further up the road.

John said his son was gone for about fifteen minutes and returned covered in blood saying "they gave me a cruel beating". He then went to the barracks for Sergeant O'Keeffe and also got Dr Calanan who returned with him straightaway. Dr Calanan treated Hugh but advised to have him removed to the nursing home that day. Dr Welply arrived later.

The two women that were in the house that morning gave similar evidence. Nora recalled getting struck with a baton in the head when she called the men cowards for hitting her mother.

Sergeant O'Keeffe told the inquest of arriving at O'Reilly's to find the doctor there before him and Hugh in bed. Before leaving the barracks he had telephoned the details to Bandon Headquarters. He found Hugh covered in blood with several head injuries. Searching about the house as it got bright he discovered several large footprints. He also saw blood in the hall and followed a trail of blood about 300 yards up the old road to Bandon. There he found a large pool of blood about two feet wide and concluded that was the spot where O'Reilly was beaten. From there he traced fresh car wheel marks to Brinny and confirmed that a car had passed through Rockfort level crossing at 5:30 am.

Hugh O'Reilly, with thanks to Irish Newspaper Archives and the Cork Examiner.

O'Keeffe did reveal he had known already that morning that a similar attack had been made on O'Leary's near Bandon. He also confirmed from the wheel marks at O'Leary's that it was the same car that carried out both attacks.

The coroner commended the sergeant for the thorough investigation he had carried out.

Eamon O'Neill Fine Gael T.D was allowed to question the sergeant through the coroner. He asked was the sergeant aware of the article in the An Phoblacht that mentioned how O'Reilly visited the barracks and was friendly with the Gardaí. The sergeant answered that he was aware of it but did not comment further.

O'Neill's next question was disallowed by the coroner when he asked did he receive any further instructions from the authorities about the investigation. Coroner Horgan did comment that because of the mention of the Broy harriers and a baton being used that the local Gardaí should give a statement of any patrol detailed to visit the O'Reilly house that night.

The funeral leaving the church in Bandon, with thanks to Irish Newspaper Archives and Irish Independent.

Many will recall the name Ned Broy played by Stephen Rea. In the film *Michael Collins,* he smuggled the big fella into Dublin Castle. In real life, Broy joined the National Army during the Civil War and later the Gardaí. He was appointed the Garda Commissioner after O'Duffy was dismissed that year. By the summer of 1933 with O'Duffy organising rallies, Broy was unsure of the loyalty of the Gardaí to deal with O'Duffy so he oversaw the setting up of the Auxillary Special Branch. This armed special unit was made up of ex-IRA and Fianna Fáil men, it became known as the Broy Harriers and the nickname stuck.

The Funeral and O'Duffy giving his oration at the graveside, with thanks to Irish Newspaper Archives and Cork Examiner

Chief Superintendent Fitzgerald told the inquest that only 2 days before the attack, a special force was stationed in Bandon but had not yet performed any duty at that point. The ten members of that force were all in Bandon Barracks that night.

The funeral cortege leaving Bandon, with thanks to Irish Newspaper Archives and the Cork Examiner.

Dr Eugene Callanan described in detail the injuries he treated on Hugh that morning in October. He found Hugh O'Reilly in bed covered in blood, complaining of terrible pain and shivering with the cold. On the head were four big cut wounds which he believed had been done with a sort of club. Over the left eye was a triangular wound and the left arm was also bruised and very swollen. He stitched up the wounds and bandaged them but knew Hugh would need constant care and attention and recommended Dr Welply. The coroner asked the doctor "in your experience have you ever seen evidence of a more serious assault" and he replied "I have not".

Dr William Welply said when he arrived at O'Reilly's house the wounds had been stitched and bandaged and required no further attention. He found Hugh suffering from tremendous pain but in a very collapsed way and suffering from shock. He described extensive bruising to the back and particularly the left arm. In Bandon, he X-rayed the bruised area but found no fractures.

He said that on the third day in hospital Hugh developed cystitis or inflammation of the bladder which resulted in even more pain. One of the wounds had to be operated on and he stayed in Welply's care until going home on the 9th of December.

Dr Welply said that on the 11th he got a call that Hugh's condition had deteriorated again and he advised he be brought back to Bandon. The doctor treated him again for cystitis but another abscess had developed which led to complications. He was also treated for an infection in the abdominal wall but severe blood poisoning took hold. Dr Welply said that despite his best efforts to treat it, Hugh died on the 28th. Answering a question from Mr Neville he stated "I think if he had not been beaten up he would not have got cystitis or suffered from abscesses"

The cause of death he concluded was toxaemia or blood poisoning from an abscess and inflammation of the bladder as a direct result of the assault.

What followed was an exchange between Chief Superintendent Fitzgerald and Eamon O'Neill T.D. Fitzgerald suggested it was a reprisal for the attack on O'Connor days before but O'Neill denied it had occurred. The chief super, then read out a letter he had sent to O'Neill asking that his party not carry out further reprisals and keep the peace. It also said that whether O'Connor was attacked or not the IRA believed he had. O'Neill asked the chief super directly had he visited either O'Reilly or O'Leary while they were in Bandon, but Fitzgerald admitted he had not, instead Inspector Casey had.

Inspector Casey confirmed that he had taken a statement from Hugh on Christmas Eve but gleaned no information to help the investigation. Dr Welply told that he had discouraged visitors due to the patient's severe condition.

Superintendent Tom Keyes Bandon said that over 100 people some of whom were suspects had been interrogated about the attacks.

Mr Neville argued strongly to the jury to return a verdict of murder. Neville didn't want to go into the motive or the politics but mentioned that there was clearly a motive to it. The law he explained was that if a man died within a year and a day of an assault, that the perpetrator was guilty of murder. He said the attack was premeditated by well armed men who shot another man and if the jury did not find murder they were condoning such crimes.

Coroner Horgan summing up for the jury said "It is clear the action of the raiders was the origin of O'Reilly's death and that being so and this being a wilful and malicious act, those men are guilty of murder". He condemned political organisations that carried out such activities by saying "no organisation and no body of men outside the disciplined forces of the State has any right whatever to interfere with the life and liberty of anybody". The coroner admitted that he was not satisfied that Hugh was fit enough to make a statement on the 24th of December.

He explained the function of the inquest in detail and admitted that it might be the only court this case might ever appear in. It was a damning admission to make that he had no faith the Gardaí would find the men who had done it.

Finally, the coroner suggested a verdict that fell short of murder and the jury agreed to it.

The verdict was "that the deceased Hugh Thomas O'Reilly died from toxaemia, arising from perineal abscesses and cystitis, which conditions were predisposed to by the shock and exposure he received when assaulted wilfully and maliciously on the 29th October 1933 by persons unknown".

After the inquest that Friday evening Hugh O'Reilly's remains were brought to the church in Bandon. His coffin was draped with a blue flag as it was shouldered the half a mile to the church. A big crowd followed the coffin and many were young men dressed in their blue shirts.

Early the following morning Blueshirts poured into the town of Bandon by every means possible. Well before mass at eleven that Saturday morning there was 1200 men and 300 women in their Blue shirts and berets gathered at the church. Mass was said by the Bishop of Cork Most Rev Dr Daniel Cohalan. After mass, the bishop condemned the death of Hugh O'Reilly calling it a political attack. Quoting the commandment thou shalt not kill he told the congregation that this applied to political parties as well as individuals. He called for freedom of politics and reminded political parties that they should put the country first rather than the interests of their party.

After mass, a guard of honour lined the route towards Innishannon. A band made of the League of Youth led the cortege and the streets of Bandon were fully lined with sympathisers.

All the shops in Bandon were closed as a mark of respect. Behind the hearse was General O'Duffy in uniform with the O'Reilly family. Rows of Blueshirts marched four abreast for the four miles to Innishannon on a bitterly cold December day. The funeral cortege itself was about a mile long and up to 5000 people were said to have turned out.

Arriving in Innishannon a large crowd lined the route to the graveyard where the League of youth again formed a guard of honour. As the coffin was lowered the Blueshirts gave their salute while the band played The Last Post. O'Duffy addressed the crowd, he was known for rousing speeches but that day he mourned the death of his comrade. He called on De Valera to use his power to collect the illegal firearms that were being drilled and paraded nightly. O'Duffy also referred to the inquires made by the local Fine Gael branch into the attack. All information he said had been passed onto the Minister of Justice but no person had yet been arrested. He claimed that in the area the Gardaí were raiding the houses of law abiding people while others who boasted of having guns were not. He said, "Hugh O'Reilly is our first martyr, while we mourn his death struck down as he was in the prime of his manhood, we are strengthened by the example he set, let us try to emulate his noble qualities". O'Duffy offered his sympathy to the O'Reilly family saying Hugh gave his life for the country. He ended that day by saying "Hugh we will never lower the flag of blue, farewell till we meet again".

Hugh O'Reilly had no real connection to Innishannon and had only been there for a few years. His parents met when John was stationed at Kiskeam as a RIC constable and Nonie or Nora whose maiden name was O'Connor was working in Ballydesmond. John O'Reilly came from Co Longford but after marrying remained between Cork and Kerry. Their first child Nora was born in 1892, then Mary Ellen in 1895. The following year they were in Clonakilty when John William was born. The next year Hugh was born in December while his father was stationed in Dunmanway. In 1901 John was stationed in Goleen. A few years later John William died at the young age of eight of Tuberculosis when they lived in Millstreet. The 1911 census shows the family at Marine Terrace in Bantry. It was in the following years the family came to Innishannon. Hugh joined the Royal Munster Fusiliers during the war and was described as an army accountant.

John retired from the RIC around the time of the War of Independence, a local republican later claimed he had been in contact with John O'Reilly and advised him to retire. The family stayed in Innishannon and Mary Ellen married Thomas Kerrigan who joined the Royal Air Force. Thomas was stationed at Farnborough in Hampshire England where the couple was living. On Sunday in February 1930, she was tragically killed when struck by a car crossing the street after mass.

Nora married Michael Buckley, a cattle dealer from Innishannon in January of 1931 and the O'Reilly's built a house nearby on a site from their son-in-law.

Nobody knew better how the Gardaí operated than O'Duffy as he had spent over ten years as Garda Commissioner and shaped it into the organisation it had become. During that time he had become involved in several murder cases and was known for putting pressure on Superintendents to produce results and find a suspect. Now though O'Duffy had little faith that the Gardaí with a Fianna Fail government would find the killers.

It was claimed that it was not the first time O'Reilly or O'Leary had been intimidated or threatened. As a feud in the area, it could have continued tit for tat between the sides but it does not seem to have. Some people were truly shocked by the death but it wasn't going to change the political situation in the country any time soon.

When De Valera came to power in 1932 the Fianna Fail government was seen as friendly towards the IRA and republican prisoners were released. In parts of Ireland, the Gardaí were reluctant to deal with republicans. Over time De Valera's government was forced to change but it would be 1936 before he banned the IRA.

Once the funeral was over the mainstream media quickly forgot about the story. The investigation seemed to be going nowhere as no arrests had been made. It seemed like nothing was happening. It was only political papers such as United Ireland that proclaimed Hugh as a martyr. United Ireland went further telling how John O'Reilly while in the RIC had been sympathetic and helpful to the struggle for independence. Eamon O'Neill the Fine Gael T.D for Cork West asked in the Dáil was any progress made in the investigation. The Minister for Justice Patrick Ruttledge refused to comment.

Chief Superintendent Michael Fitzgerald led the Gardaí investigation and he suspected that Tom Barry was involved. He had heard through an informant that Barry had complained bitterly about the attack on Denis

O'Connor and promised vengeance for it. The chief Superintendent seemed reluctant to question Tom Barry saying it served no purpose and would endanger his informant.

The deputy commissioner at the time Eamonn Coogan who would go on to be a Fine Gael TD seemed keener to find the perpetrators. He appointed Chief Superintendent Stack from Cork city to lead the case and take more action. After a few weeks, Stack still suspected that Tom Barry was involved but believed the attack was carried out by Sean Mitchell, Denis Sisk, Charles McCarthy and Christopher Aherne who were all from Cork City.

It was April the 4th when all the suspects' homes were searched but no evidence to connect the men was found. In Tom Barry's house, they found a Thompson Machine Gun with 384 rounds of ammunition. When questioned Barry told the guards he was aware that they were reluctant to arrest him for some time, the IRA claimed Barry was unaware of the gun in his own house. Barry was convicted of possession of a gun and ammo as well as contempt of court by a military tribunal in May of that year. He was sentenced to twelve months in jail with the last three suspended. Nobody was ever arrested for the death of Hugh O'Reilly.

Hugh O'Reilly's death was commemorated for several years afterwards and O'Duffy returned several times to lead the ceremony and deliver a graveside oration. It was 1936 before De Valera banned the IRA and by then the Blueshirts had declined drastically and O'Duffy was preparing his crusade to fight in the Spanish Civil War.

For men that found themselves on very different sides politically, Hugh O'Reilly and Tom Barry had more in common. Both were sons of RIC men, although Barry's father had retired years before. Both men had enlisted during WW1, O'Reilly in the Munster Fusiliers, Barry in the Royal Field Artillery. After the war, both men had struggled initially to find their place in the world. Years later in the 1930s, each had found his cause to fight, on sides that had become so divided since the Civil War.

Glossary

Adze is a tool that dates back to the Stone Age, it is like an axe but the blade is turned at a right angle to the handle. It is mostly used to shape wood and is often used in boat building.

Allocutus is the statement a prisoner is allowed to give after being found guilty but before being sentenced.

Approver a person, who is suspected of a crime, confesses and then gives evidence against others.

Assizes periodic criminal courts held quarterly that heard the most serious cases before a jury.

Billhook large hooked blade fixed to a handle, used in farming since medieval times to cut shrubs and harvest crops.

Coulter part of a plough that cuts the soils ahead of the plough, is something like a long flat blade.

Coroner is a person who conducts an inquest into the cause of death, is normally a magistrate or solicitor.

Distrain to seize property normally in Ireland livestock in order to get rent money owed

Emergencymen employed by the landlord to guard a property after an eviction.

Flail two sticks joined by a short chain, used threshing corn and separating the grain from the husks.

Gibbets a gallows used to hang someone, gibbeting was the practice of hanging them in chains for display purposes.

Governor-General or Seneschal this role was created with the formation of the Free State in 1922. The role was to be the official representative of the sovereign in Ireland. The role was a controversial one as the sovereign was still the king. The duties included giving royal assent to legislation and dissolving the Dáil.

Graffawn or graffaun hand tool like a pickaxe but with a much wider blade used for digging or grubbing soil. Similarly shaped to an adze but the blade wouldn't be sharpened like an adze.

Grand Jury was normally made up of the largest local ratepayers or put another way were the landlords. They acted as a form of local government as well as sitting as jury on more serious criminal cases. Members of a Grand Jury could also sit as magistrates judging lesser cases.

Griffiths valuation land survey carried out in mid 19th century Ireland. The main reason was to value land and buildings to determine the tax liable.

Grub a heavy hoe used for digging soil and weeding.

Habeas Corpus is a writ to bring a person in custody before a judge and determine if their incarceration is legal or not.

Haggard is a small enclosed field or yard at the back of a farm cottage. Often used for storing winter supplies of hay, straw or fodder.

Indoor relief form of assistance given to the poor where they had to live in an institution.

Inquest is a judicial inquiry held in public into the cause of death. A jury is required when the death is suspicious or murder is suspected.

Nolle prosequi legal phrase used by the prosecutor to say the case is being dropped.

Martial Law usually a temporary measure where the military take over from the Government and impose the law.

Outdoor relief money given to the poor as relief without the need to live in an institution.

Penal Servitude or hard labour was introduced in the 1770s and could also include transportation to a distant colony. By the 1850s transportation had been abolished but hard labour remained the norm. Not all labour was productive some prisons used punitive exercise such as a treadmill. As a form of punishment penal servitude was abolished in Britain in the1950's but remained in Ireland until 1997 when the law was finally changed.

Petty Sessions local court of magistrates

Peritonitis is an inflammation in the abdomen as a result of infection, treated by antibiotics nowadays, little could be done medically years ago.

Prima facie in simple terms legally means there is enough evidence for there to be a case to answer.

Relieving Officer under the English system of Poor Law Union was the person who administered relief to the poor.

Riot Act a British law from 1714 which gave powers to local authorities. Any group of 12 persons or more could be declared unlawful and required to disperse. If the group did not go within an hour they were likely to face punishment.

Sapper is a soldier attached to the engineering regiments whose tasks are more engineering in nature such as bridge/road building or repairing.

Scullery small traditional room, used for washing dishes or laundering clothes, could now be referred to in some form as a utility room.

Settle a long wooden bench that normally has a high back, some could be settle beds, that could be converted into a bed.

Tithe a tax of a tenth of all farm produce, collected in Ireland by the English clergy.

Tithe proctor men whose job it was to value farm produce and set the tithe value and then collect it. Was not a popular job in rural Ireland and a dangerous occupation.

Turbary is an ancient right to cut turf from a particular patch of bog. Normally attached to the tenancy of a dwelling house and for domestic purposes only.

Under Secretary of Ireland up till 1922 was the head of the civil service.

Whiteboys secret organisation in rural Ireland, which used any means including violence threats and boycotts to obtain rights for tenants.

Bibliography

Newspapers:
Belfast newsletter
Cork Constitution
Cork Examiner
Evening Echo
Evening Herald
Freeman's Journal
Isle of Man Times
Irish Daily Independent
Irish Independent
Irish Press
Kerry Champion
Kerry Evening Star
Kerry Reporter 1924-35
Limerick Leader
Munster Express
Skibbereen Eagle
Southern Star
The Cork Southern Reporter
The Kerry Evening Post
United Ireland

Websites:
www.jstor.org
www.corkgen.org
www.landedestates.nuigalway.ie
www.irishgenealogy.ie
www.nli.ie
www.nationalarchives.ie
www.ancestry.co.uk
www.dippam.ac.uk
www.historicgraves.com
www.findagrave.com
www.askaboutireland/Griffiths-valuation

Publications

O'Flanagan's Munster Circuit 1880

Irish Wake Amusements by Seán Súilleabháin

Irish Murder Trials 1836-1914

Irish Topographical Dictionary of Ireland 1837 by Samuel Lewis

Griffiths Valuation

Police Reports from Dublin Castle Records,
Inspector General's and County

Inspector's monthly confidential reports

Guys Almanac

Convict Reference Files, National Archives

Church and Parish Records of the diocese of Cork, Cloyne and Ross by Rev J.H Cole.

Bandon Historical Journal no.6 1990 -
The Murder of Rev Charles Ferguson by Liam Ó Donnchadha

The killing of Michael Blanchfield by Fergal Browne

Tracton Newssheet October 2003
Recollections of a Village, Mrs Aine Ahern

Tracton Newssheet March 2004
Nohoval Post Office, Mrs Aine Ahern

Three Brass Balls, the story of the Irish Pawnshop by Jim Fitzpatrick

Other publications by the Author

About the Author

Peter O'Shea is a native of Ballycotton. This is Peter's fifth book. His first book 'Well, Here I am in Ballycotton' combines his appreciation for Ballycotton and its history, with his love of the sea and his passion for postcards. He received a lot of feedback about a local murder in his Ballycotton book, and from this the 'Murder Most Local' series of books was born. This South Cork book is the 4th in the series, following East Cork, North Cork and West Cork. While researching his East Cork edition, he found many other historical murders around Cork County.

Since January 2011 he has been the full time mechanic on Ballycotton Lifeboat, he joined the lifeboat as a volunteer when he was 18. During school and college Peter worked on local fishing boats and has always had a keen interest in all things maritime. Peter lives in Ballycotton with his partner Karen and their 3 sons, James, Edward and Henry.

More information: **www.facebook.com/ballycottonhistory**